J.C Macintosh

The Incarnation and Other Sermons

Gatherings from a Colonial Ministry

J.C Macintosh

The Incarnation and Other Sermons
Gatherings from a Colonial Ministry

ISBN/EAN: 9783337155216

Printed in Europe, USA, Canada, Australia, Japan

Cover: Foto ©ninafisch / pixelio.de

More available books at **www.hansebooks.com**

THE INCARNATION

AND OTHER

SERMONS,

BEING

GATHERINGS FROM A COLONIAL MINISTRY

BY

J. C. MACINTOSH,

CONGREGATIONAL MINISTER.

PORT ELIZABETH:
IMPEY, WALTON & Co., MARKET SQUARE.
LONDON:
ELLIOT STOCK, 62 PATERNOSTER ROW.

1887.

IMPEY, WALTON AND CO.,
PRINTERS, STATIONERS, AND BOOKBINDERS,
PORT ELIZABETH, SOUTH AFRICA.

ERRATA

Read ethereal for etherial, page 51, line 28.
,,   ,,   ,,   ,, 52, ,, 11.
,, the for this, page 138, line 26.
,, ? after "is" and not after "present," page 233, line 24.
,, : between "of" and "but," page 237, line 24.
,, . after "has" instead of "ever," page 262, line 6.

PREFACE.

―――:o:―――

"Every author," says a recent writer, "has, of course, a more or less sufficient reason for sending forth his book to the world."

To the reasons that I have already given in a circular, which the subscribers to this volume have seen—mainly the requests of friends and the shortness of my time now—whether sufficient or not, I shall not here add.

I there said that the sermons to be published would not be polemic, and any such utterances here are few and far between; but I have not omitted things that may seem so to some, which were really preached formerly, when the truth, as I see it, seemed to demand their retention.

My hearty thanks are due, and are hereby tendered, to all subscribers for a response to my proposal beyond my expectations; and I am specially thankful for many letters and short notes—all kind, some touchingly so—received from ministers and members of various religious communions, as well as my own. The general tone of these communications increases my serious fear lest the book, as it is, may disappoint many of the writers. I see many blemishes in it, and other and more impartial eyes will doubtless see more.

The fact of the sermons being written and preached at dates wide apart—for some are sermons of youth, and some of recent date—explains certain repetitions of ideas and expressions, which I have not tried to avoid, and also differences of style. For I have in every case re-written for the press, but in no case re-made, or seriously altered, the sermons as preached.

I may further say that about half the sermons in the volume are there by request. This precludes the sermons forming a series, or having much of a plan; but they are mostly about Jesus Christ our Lord. Sermons amounting to the whole number have been named and requested since my purpose of publishing became known; but these requests have come in at various dates, some of them after I had finished copying for the press; and the main reason why more of the sermons that have been asked for are not inserted, is the extra labour that putting these in the place of sermons already selected and copied would have needed.

"My design," I repeat, "is the promotion of true godliness, by asking my readers to look with me, in the quiet of their own homes, at some of the things which I have seen in God's Word."

That my readers may seize, prize, and profit by whatever of divine 'treasure' I, as 'earthen vessel,' may have been able to offer them here, is the desire and humble prayer of their brother in Christ,

J. C. M.

1, HAVELOCK SQUARE,
18th March, 1887.

CONTENTS.

---:o:---

I.
THE INCARNATION; OR, CHRIST'S VISIT.
FIRST SERMON.

Mat. i. 23. .. .. PAGE 1

II.
SECOND SERMON.

Mat. i. 23. 17

III.
GOD'S LOVE; OR, CHRIST'S ERRAND.
FIRST SERMON.

John iii. 16. 29

IV.
SECOND SERMON.

John iii. 16. 45

V.
THE GREAT BURDEN-BEARER.
FIRST SERMON.

Mat. xi. 28-30. 68

VI.

THE GREAT BURDEN-BEARER.
SECOND SERMON.

Mat. xi. 28-30. 90

VII.

THIRD SERMON.

Mat. xi. 28-30. 116

VIII.

FOURTH SERMON.

Mat. xi. 28-30. 132

IX.

LIVING UNION WITH CHRIST.

John xv. 4-8. 150

X.

ETERNAL LIFE IN CHRIST.

John vi. 47. 176

XI.

THE SUDDEN AND UNEXPECTED CALL.

Mat. xxiv. 44. 197

XII.

A LOOKING BACKWARD THAT PREPARES FOR GOING FORWARD.

Genesis xxxi. 13. 216

XIII.

THE LAWS OF SPIRITUAL PROGRESS.

Job xvii. 9. 239

XIV.

DIVINE TREASURE IN EARTHEN VESSELS.

2 Cor. iv. 7 276

XV.

THE PERFECT BOND.

Col. iii. 14. 306

I.

THE INCARNATION; OR, CHRIST'S VISIT.

FIRST SERMON.

"Immanuel: which is, being interpreted, God with us."—Mat. I., 23.

IN the sacred name of Him whom we meet to worship, and serve, I would say to each one of you this morning, my beloved hearers, "put off thy shoes from off thy feet," that we may together enter a holy shrine, reverently to worship God there. For I invite you, and would fain help you to contemplate for a little, with devout reverence and holy joy the incarnation of Christ, "the mystery of Godliness," to look on Him "who was manifested in the flesh." In one word, I ask you to behold, with me, Jesus our Lord, Him whom our text calls "Immanuel, which is God with us."

But before we turn our thoughts to the contemplation of God with us, and as preparatory to this attractive survey, let us try to meditate for a few moments on God, as he presents himself to us, his human family, otherwise than in Christ.

First let us try to grasp in our minds a correct conception of the invisible God in His own Nature and Attributes, as he is in Himself, apart from all manifestations, and expressions of Himself: and let us strive to worship Him, "in spirit and in truth," who was, and is, and is to come; "who only hath immortality, dwelling in light, unapproachable; whom no man hath seen, nor can see."

Yes, let us try with our keenest vision to see the invisible God, as He is seated on His Heavenly Throne, eternally self-existent, and the author of all existence, infinite in knowledge, power, wisdom, and goodness, infinitely just, and true, and holy—seeing all the past, the present, and the future. If we try so to look upon God, we see in a moment that we cannot fully realize what such descriptive terms as self-existent, eternal, and infinite mean. Nor can we grasp *Him* in our feeble thought, of whom alone the words are true: though it concerns us much to know Him the judge of our actions, and the God with whom we all have to do.

But in such an effort as I am describing, the mind painfully, but vainly, *labours* to draw near unto God. Some image of vast and vague sublimity rises before us, as we strain our exhausted powers in the vain attempt to hold immensity in our feeble grasp, and to pierce effectually with our short-sighted glance the gloom—from excess of glory—of the eternal God.

An emotion of awe overwhelms us in our efforts to see God, for we realize that he is; but no definite idea occupies the understanding, no distinct feeling touches the heart. And so it becomes evident to us that such a Being as the Infinite God is far removed from us alike in His nature and in His character. *We* are limited in every aspect of our being, while He is infinite. We are fallen and sinful, while He is the Holy One. And hence we cannot by native strength of intellect wing our way to His unknown seat, and see Him as He is. Nor, though we could enter His presence thus, is ours the eagle-eye that can gaze on this uncreated sun, undazzled and undimmed. Angels veil their faces with their wings in God's presence: and He Himself says: "Man shall not see me and live." And, if for relief from such ineffable brightness, we turn our eyes away from the direct effulgence of the divine glory to the reflections of it that are to be seen in the works of the divine hands, still "the eye is not satisfied with seeing, nor the ear filled with hearing." We consciously stand afar off from God. We cannot, by looking ever so intently on the face of nature, get nigh to God Himself.

We know that all nature as the product of God's hand proclaims aloud His power and His wisdom: but nature is not God Himself. And hence, even when we try to "rise through nature up to nature's God," the way is far to us, and the time needed for such a journey is long. God's great universe is far too vast for our little minds to traverse or to measure. We come back from our best search after God, throughout the wide creation, fatigued with our far and venturous flight, sighing and longing for a shorter and simpler revelation of God than the boundless creation presents. We feel our need of a revelation that comes more directly home to our hearts, and to our whole spiritual nature, than that does, and more fully meets and satisfies the natural and instinctive longings of our souls for God Himself.

Now the *Bible* yields us, and our *text* in particular gives us just that for which our hearts and minds alike crave, for it speaks of God, as not only being *every where present*, but as being specially *with us* men. It speaks of God as visible not only in all His great universe, but also, as more clearly visible in the *Man Christ Jesus*. Here is the revelation of God in a person, and in our own humanity!

O fact most wondrous, most glorious, and also most true and significant, " GOD WAS IN CHRIST reconciling the world unto Himself!" And to this much-needed and most welcome revelation of God, summed up in our text in one old Hebrew word, IMMANUEL, we now thankfully and gladly turn as the *best*, the *clearest*, the simplest, and the fullest revelation of Himself of all that God has given us. I shall invite your attention to the following points as included in the sublime and gladdening revelation of our text.

    I. God with us *in place*.
   II. God with us in *Nature*.
  III. God with us in *Love* and *Sympathy*.
  IV. God with us in *Work* and *Suffering*.
   V. God with us in our *Sin*.
  VI. God with us in *Dying*.
 VII. God with us both in *Grace* and in *Glory*.

And I.—I invite your attention, as specially appropriate to the season of the year, to the contemplation of Immanuel, God with us *in place*, to God dwelling with us upon the earth. It is indeed the unceasing and unsolved wonder of wonders that He, who cannot be limited to a place, but fills immensity with His glorious presence, should have been in a literal and peculiar sense, God with us in place.

Here is a true marvel, that though the Heaven of Heaven's cannot contain God, He should, in the person of His Son Jesus Christ, have submitted to the limiting conditions of an inhabitant of this world, and should in a human form, have visibly walked Judean streets and fields as a teacher revealing the highest truth to men. Is it no marvel that He should have climbed the hills, sailed the waters, and frequented the Synagogues of that fair land, and have at last hung on a cross of shame and pain, and that He the author of life, should have lain in a tomb among the silent dead? Yes, and have risen from the dead, and even walked the earth in His resurrection body?

God's thus coming to us in place, is itself a bright prophecy of coming good to man.

This cheering fact that God was with us in place, has made the whole earth a consecrated temple for redeemed men's worship of God. This has made the ordinary every-day walk of Christians a sacred pilgrimage from one consecrated spot to another, until they appear before the Lord in the Zion above, which is the place of Christ's rest, not, like the earth, merely the place of His sojourn.

Even Christ's temporary presence on the earth has removed from the ground and turned into a blessing the curse that followed man's sin. Manifestly " the earth is the Lord's," for He has visited it. Now, " the earth is full of the loving-kindness of the Lord."

Now we mortals, while we are here below, daily, in a literal sense, walk in Christ's footsteps. We now live in a God-visited, God-redeemed, God-blessed, and yet to be blessed world. For this is the birth-place and the burial-place of Jesus. This is also the hallowed scene of His glorious resurrection. Earth is holy, classic ground.

We all in some measure share the veneration that is felt by the wise and good for the birth-places, residences, and tombs of men of genius and worth. Such places become classic ground, and we delight to visit them on pilgrimages of affectionate admiration for their mighty dead. But this kind of hero-worship is for the most part the privilege of the few, and of the far-travelled. Few of us have either time or money for many such visits. There are many of earth's most famous spots which we have not seen, and shall never see in the body. But the fact of the text much concerns us all. It is now the glorious privilege of all to know that through Christ's presence with us on earth, the whole world has become classic ground.

The true glory of earth now is that Christ was here. The glory, not of Jerusalem and Judea, and Galilee and Samaria only, where Christ's feet literally trod—but the true glory of our whole world is that Christ Jesus was born into it, lived and walked on it, dwelt among us, and here on earth manifested His own, and His Father's glory. Heaven's best gift to earth was Immanuel, God with us *in place*. Do not then, I beseech you, think meanly of the world in which we live, for it is manifest that He, who made it, does not. It is only one of countless worlds all made by Him. It is but a small speck in the immensity of God's vast creation. And it is a fallen world too, and has had in many respects a dark and God-dishonouring history. But yet, *all* that has transpired upon the earth has not been dark, and all is not dark now. " The light is come into the world." " The darkness is passing away, and the true light already shineth " upon us. The annals of the earth record at least *one* fact, which makes all who know the worth of that fact exceeding glad. It is a fact that we should ever remember, and growingly prize; it is a fact that Heaven will not forget when eternal ages have run their ceaseless round. It is the fact of the text. For this shall be the everlasting song of both redeemed men and holy angels, that God *was* with us mankind upon the earth, that He Himself dwelt on it. And thus " we beheld His glory, glory as of the only begotten from the Father," veiled but not concealed; obscured, and yet exceeding bright.

And why was God here thus? I answer, and it is an answer sanctioned by the word of God: God was with us in place, God was here on earth, that we who believe on Jesus may yet be with *God* in place yonder in heaven where Jesus is : " which," scripture tells us, ' is far better " than here ! So that Jesus once descended to earth for a short time, that as the Captain of our Salvation He might lead us in our ascent to Heaven as our eternal home.

II.—Contemplate Jesus as IMMANUEL, *God with us in nature :* God in our human nature.

It is much to us in many ways, as we have already seen, that God was literally here with us in place. Such a celestial visit made to us is proof sufficient that God has not forgotten man : and that He is not indifferent to man's well being. But it is far more to us, and far better that God was also with us, and is yet with us in nature. Holy Angels have been with us in place. They are doubtless with us often, as protectors and benefactors, when we know not of their presence. "Are they not all ministering spirits, sent forth to do service for the sake of them that shall inherit salvation." We often owe these ministering spirits much. We owe them far more than we shall ever know in this world. For they are as yet unseen, unknown benefactors, with whom we cannot at present establish personal friendships We can on good grounds rejoice that there are in the universe of God such holy servants of His, and willing benefactors of ours as the Holy Angels are. But still they and we are strangers at present, dwelling far apart from each other in place and nature: and we feel the chilling effect of being at this great distance from them. We do not see the angels, nor do we know them, when they see, know, and are near us. Moreover, those of our race who, here on earth, have seen Angels have not been filled with joy and strength at the sight, but with fear and weakness. We mortals cannot at present know the Angels personally and love them one by one.

We occupy much the same position towards angelic benefactors that the mass of the ignorant heathen do towards the unknown contributors in distant lands who combine to send them the Gospel. Those of them who are taught from above to value the Gospel, will feel grateful to their benefactors who send it, even though they are unknown. But those who really represent Christendom to the heathen, those who beget their confidence, and draw forth their love, are not so much the distant and unseen givers of money, as the Missionaries who are present and visible, who come to live and labour among them, and speak to them the word of life. And so is it with us and the unseen angels whom we cannot at present know and love individually. For it is not angelic visitants to earth, on offices of love to man, however beneficent, who really touch our hearts: But it is the SON OF GOD, who is *with us in our own* nature as the Son of Man, who forms the *One and only* appropriate Mediator between God and man, and wins back the alienated heart of man to his Father God. For though the Holy Angels are strangers to us, not so is Jesus the Son of God: and through him who is "the way, and the truth, and the life," God the Father is no stranger, to man, but is revealed. God is not now "the unknown God" to us who know Jesus, for He, the only begotten Son of God, and the revealer of the Father, is our great elder brother, *one* with us in nature, while He is also one with God, who in Him has thus come very nigh to us. For Jesus is truly "bone of our bone and flesh of our flesh." He had a human body that became hungry, and thirsty, so that he ate and drank: that became weary and drowsy, so that He rested and slept like as we do. He had a human heart like ours, and felt as we feel joy and sorrow, pleasure and pain, hope and fear, love and anger. And yet, He was and is very God, and could say without robbery, "I and the Father are one." And He proved it by turning in a moment by His own will water into wine: calming the stormy sea with his mighty word, and walking on it, as on the solid earth : healing any sick in a moment, and without means : raising the dead to life whenever he pleased : knowing and answering the unspoken thought of men : knowing also the mind of God : Lord alike of matter and of mind, and yet truly and really a man, with us in nature! There is a mystery here which we cannot fully solve : but the Incarnation is not all obscure. Nay, the mystery of Christ's person is delightfully illuminated by an inner light and glory. The fact involved in these mighty deeds which is *God with us*, is well fitted to fill our whole soul with holy wonder, solemn awe, and unending joy. The meaning of this fact Christ with us in nature, must be good. For He who is with us in nature is very God : and thus He is *able* to help us. And He is also *very* man : and thus He can feel for us : and we can know Him, trust Him, and love Him. Thus he is able and willing, he is fit and forward to save us! Man's case demands both divine and human help : and Jesus Christ gives us both. For he is Immanuel God with us in nature.

Do you wonderingly ask : And why is God with us in nature? The answer is simple and joyful. God is with us in nature, that we may be with God in His moral nature, in the possession of His own holy image. With God, not in possessing divine attributes. That is impossible to us. But that we may be with God, yea, that we may be one with God in having the divine image vividly impressed upon a regenerated, holy human nature. And therefore, my fellow man, and fellow Christian, do not, I entreat you, degrade our human nature by willingly yielding it up to the ignoble service of sin and Satan. For it is Christ's nature that we are wearing, as well as our own nature, and "he is not ashamed to call us brethren." No, Christ is never ashamed, and he is nowhere ashamed of our nature; he is only ashamed of our sin.

Nay, so great is God's love for mankind that *He*, "the high and lofty one that inhabiteth eternity, whose name is Holy," kindly courts a lowly alliance with our fallen family in order to break up our degrading fellowship with sin and Satan, and to raise us permanently to more than our prestine glory and honour.

And Christ's community of nature with us is something permanent. It is not, like Christ's humiliation and sufferings, which were only temporary, and are now left behind Him for ever. For Jesus not only *was* a man, but He *is* a man. Jesus not only *had* a community of nature with us when He was on earth, but He retains it still. He has carried human nature to the throne of the universe, and still wears it in his state of glory. The Apostle John saw Jesus in apocalyptic vision, amid the splendours of Heaven, not like an Angel or an Archangel, but still like to what he was on earth, still "ONE LIKE UNTO A SON OF MAN." And He is the same to-day. He is still clothed in a glorified humanity. He is still God with us in nature.

III.—Consider Jesus Christ as Immanuel, God with us in *love* and sympathy; God with us in giving us his tenderest love and sympathy. And this you will see is more still than to be with us in *place*, and even to be with us in *nature*. For *all* who are with us in place, and with us in nature even, are not, as they ought to be, with us in love and sympathy. The divine doctrine of the universal brotherhood of mankind, as the children of the one Father, is not very generally believed and practised, is it? Nay men, though "made of one blood," may be widely alienated from each other. There may be no brother's heart binding them together. There is in truth but little love to one another among fallen men till the God of love changes and renews their sinful hearts into His own holy image. Nay, there often is in human hearts hatred in place of that love, which, as containing the germ of all duty, is the fulfilling of the law.

Yes, mutual hatred well nigh overspreads the world. Men being alienated from God are hateful, and hate one another. Look at only one illustration of unrealized human brotherhood, war, and at two late seats of war, America and France; and you will see that it is *not* the same to be one in nature and one in sympathy. What a terrible spectacle was it to see in America brother men, lately one people, and happily again one people, mangling and killing each other, and sometimes by thousands in a day, and for years!

And yet war is not worse, and hardly more terrible than some other outrages on human brotherhood, as slavery, oppression, extortion, and the vanity, pride, ambition, and lust of territory, that often bring on wars, and of which war is both the fruit and the punishment. In America the crime of slavery prepared for the destructive curse of war as its punishment, and its cure. For,

"Remember Heaven has an avenging rod;
To smite the poor is treason against God."

And, moreover,

> "There is a time, and justice marks the date,
> For long, forbearing clemency to wait ;
> That hour elapsed, the incurable revolt
> Is punished, and down comes the thunderbolt."

And much in the conduct of man to man, provokes the descent of divine thunderbolts. How often must the Christian still say,

> " My ear is pain'd, my soul is sick, with every day's report
> Of wrong and outrage with which earth is filled ;
> There is no flesh in man's obdurate heart ;
> It does not feel for man : the natural bond
> Of brotherhood is severed as the flax,
> That falls asunder at the touch of fire."

But in striking contrast to the sad failure of our common humanity in the manifestation of human brotherhood, is the attitude of Jesus Christ, who is God *with us in nature*. For He is also in the fullest sense *God* with us in love and sympathy. And in order to acquire and manifest this sympathy, Jesus became not only a man, but a servant. He came quite down to the humblest of us, and was made in a low condition. Nor was Christ's choice of a lowly career of slight meaning and of slight utility. His low condition formed a real part of His manifold fitness to be the world's Redeemer. For it is all but impossible for a great man in the world's sense, whose residence is in courts and camps, and whose employments relate to the affairs of nations and of dynasties, fully to sympathise with the interests and feelings of common men. Great national schemes of war and policy, by which the few become renowned and great, seldom take much account of the real interests of the many. A great and famous victory, or a successful campaign, by which a new province is added to an empire, by whatever means, and at whatever cost, may make one man famous and one home bright with honours and rewards; but may destroy many other men just as worthy, and darken and desolate many other homes, with hearts just as loving and as precious as the conqueror's. But not such as these were the career and the conquests of Jesus Christ. His victories *were* not won, and *are* not now won, with "the armed men in the tumult, and the garments rolled in blood." Jesus was with us on earth, not as a great actor in courts and camps, skilfully diplomatising away, or trampling down by the brute force of war, the most precious of human rights, instincts, and interests. For not only may an ambitious warrior unrighteously deluge his own or his neighbour's country with blood, but even a war that is on the whole just and beneficent entails the shedding of much innocent blood. Jesus did not defend even the *rights* of men by such rough means. But Jesus *was*, and *is*, with us *all* in manifesting the profoundest sympathy with all the interests of all men. The meek and lowly Jesus knows—the great throbbing, suffering heart of common humanity—for such a human heart throbbed in his own breast. Thus Jesus was, and is, God with us in feeling for us the fullest sympathy. His love passeth knowledge. What but love made him, who is the invisible God, become God with us? And He who was so truly *with us* in love and sympathy, that He "spared not his own Son, but delivered Him up for us all, how shall He not also with Him freely give us all things?"

Jesus, as an expression of his sympathy with us in our varied human relationships, and also to set us an example of the loving discharge of the duties therein involved, which form so large a part of the sum of our human life, Himself assumed the relations of son, brother, preacher, teacher, friend, pastor, host, and guest. And in all He was the perfect pattern of all human duty and of all brotherly sympathy. Jesus revealed to us as had never been done before, both God and man. "No man hath seen God at any time; the only begotten Son, which is in the bosom of the Father, he hath declared him." And Christ declares, as the sum of all His teaching, that God is love, and He, the sent of the Father, abundantly proves this by word and deed. And as no man hath seen God aright, but as He has seen Him in Christ, so no man hath seen God's ideal of our humanity; but as he has seen that also in Christ, God's living law. This law is lovelier, more persuasive, and more perfect than that law which was written by the finger of Jehovah on the tables of stone on Mount Sinai. So that Jesus was *with us* to reveal in his own person both God and man to us.

And *why* did Jesus manifest Himself as so truly one with us in sympathy, but to make us one with God in sympathy? Jesus knows that it is our ruin and misery not to love God, and that it is our very life to do it, and so He who first loves us makes us feel that it is so, and thus draws out our love to God. And the love of Jesus, as shown to us, is further meant to restore us to the fullest sympathy with our fellow men. Hear His own words: "This is my commandment: that ye love one another, even as I have loved you." So that the manifested love and sympathy of Jesus bless us not only directly, but as showed to us and felt by us, they do more than anything else to beget in us a like love to each other. And thus Christ's love brings to us in large measure the double benefit of knowing that we are loved by God, and of awakening our love for our fellow men.

II.

THE INCARNATION; OR, CHRIST'S VISIT.

SECOND SERMON.

"Immanuel: which is, being interpreted, God with us."—MAT. I., 23.

IN the morning I showed that not the invisible God, not God in nature, but God in Christ; God with us in place, God with us in nature, God with us in love and sympathy was the revelation of God that we most need.

Now, IV.—I invite you to contemplate yet again Jesus Christ, of whom my text speaks, as Immanuel, God with us in *work* and *suffering*.

This is another idea, and one of no small practical moment, for we live in a world of toil. Most men, and many women, must work hard during all their days on earth. Work, not play, is the common lot of man. "All things are full of weariness," or labour; "man cannot utter it." And Jesus Christ as one proof of both his love and sympathy was with us here, in our heavy toil, to share and to lighten it. "The Son of Man came not to be ministered unto, but to minister." His life was a life of unceasing and laborious activity for others. "He went about continually doing good" to the souls and to the bodies of men.

His avowed motto was, "I must work the works of Him that sent me while it is day: the night cometh when no man can work." And in Him execution kept pace with aim. Such was the pressure of life's work on Jesus Christ that sometimes "He had no leisure so much as to eat." "The zeal of God's house ate him up." In any act of humble, active good doing which we perform for man, we are not innovating on the master. For we can claim Him who is Immanuel as having been *with* us, and *before* us in doing it when he was on the earth.

And even the veritable working man, who has most of his waking hours filled up with some engrossing—it may be hard—secular toil of his hands, may yet remember for his great ennoblement Jesus, the carpenter of Nazareth. Yes, the carpenter for far more years probably than He was the public teacher and preacher. And he, the man of work, may thus see his own humble and hard toil ennobled by a real companionship in labour with the God-man Jesus, who has gone before him even in that. For He who could say "My Father worketh even until now, and I work," did not exclude from His own consecrated activities such works as any of yours may be.

And not in toil only was Jesus with us. For Jesus is Immanuel, God with us in *sufferings* also. And we much need Him, too, in this fiery furnace. There are some who would willingly work with us at life's lighter and pleasanter tasks, who would yet fain flee the yoke of fellow-suffering if they could, and would selfishly leave us alone in those dark hours when we most need sympathisers, friends, and helpers. Not so did Jesus. He was not only a real man, a real human brother, but He was a fellow-sufferer with us as a Man of Sorrows.

Jesus was *one* with us in heart, and gloriously evidenced this great love by suffering with us, and for us. And this fellow-suffering is much to man. There is a special strength and a special sweetness in the bonds that unite well-deserving fellow-sufferers. The furnace of fellow-suffering cements and strengthens all holy ties, all proper bonds Sorrow and suffering weld a family more firmly into one. Husband and wife, parent and child, brother and sister, become doubly united when they have suffered and sorrowed together, and after mutual help rendered in the furnace of affliction, they, having been brought out of it, are led to rejoice together in the Lord's deliverances. Still it is very difficult, if not quite impossible, for any two human beings so to blend in heart and experience as to be fellow-sufferers fully. Even husband and wife, parent and child, brother and sister, cannot be so in all things.

Every man, every human, must bear his own, or her own burden. A fellow-man not only often will not do it when he can, but quite as often he cannot do it when he would. Jesus alone can, and has borne the burden of all men.

Jesus was really with us, among us, of us, as our fellow-sufferer. Only remember this aright, fellow-Christian, and it will help you much to bear all *your* sufferings well. For as Jesus was made perfect through sufferings, so are we, too, made perfect. No human character becomes perfect in strength, gentleness and beauty, without the discipline of suffering.

But Christ's sufferings were far more than *with* us; they were all *for* us. He had none of His own apart from us. He was the ever blessed God. He dwelt in celestial glory. "He covered Himself with light as with a garment." But what a change! When the prophet, condensing His history in a brief prophecy, says of Him: "Surely He hath borne our griefs and carried our sorrows. * * * He was wounded for our transgressions, he was bruised for our iniquities; the chastisement of our peace was upon Him, and with His stripes we are healed." Yes, that was fulfilled which was spoken by Isaiah the prophet, saying: "Himself took our infirmities and bare our diseases."

And why was Jesus thus with us in work and in suffering? The answer is a real gospel to man. For Jesus was with us in work and suffering, that we with Him, and by Him, may enter into final and glorious rest, and have all tears wiped away from all our eyes.

Do then, and suffer all God's holy and righteous will, afflicted Christian brother, leaning lovingly on the bosom of Jesus, who was for us the greatest of all sufferers. For "if so be that we suffer with Him," it is "that we may be also glorified with Him." For "if we endure, we shall also reign with Him." Weeping may tarry for the night, but joy cometh in the morning." And the joyful morning of the true Christian will soon dawn, and become an unending day.

V.—I invite you to contemplate Jesus Christ as Immanuel, God with us *in our sin*. Yes, my hearers, God's Christ was with us in our sin. For "the Lord hath laid on Him the iniquity of us all." He was with us, *not* in the guilt of our sin, for He was "holy, guileless, undefiled, and separated from sinners." But He was with us in its penalty. Jesus was with us, not in sinning; but He was with us in enduring sin's consequences.

This is the strangest, grandest fact of all Christ's strange, lowly, sublime career.

This is the most Christ-like thing in Christ, and for us the most blessed and the best. This is the thing without which all else that Christ has done would avail us little. This voluntarily assumed relation to our sin was Christ's great errand to earth. "For the Son of Man came to seek and to save that which was lost."

Jesus became the Son of Man to give Him a brother's right to interfere on man's behalf, who by his sin is lost indeed. Jesus is thus the brother born for adversity. He is the friend of sinners. "For all" other men "have sinned, and fall short of the glory of God." "All we, like sheep, have gone astray." Jesus offered himself to bring the wanderers back to God. He came into the world for this very thing. "Now once at the end of the ages hath He been manifested to put away sin by the sacrifice of Himself." And such is the worth of Christ's sacrifice that the law of God asks no more. "It pleased the Lord for His righteousness sake, to magnify the law and make it honourable." The righteous judge justifies the ungodly for Jesus' sake. "There is therefore now no condemnation to them that are in Christ Jesus." In truth, the law of God is more magnified and honoured by Christ's willing obedience to its demands, and by Christ's eager suffering of its penalty, than it would have been if all the sinful race of Adam had unwillingly suffered its just penalty both here and hereafter. And God, because He is rich in mercy, accepts His own provision, His son's person and work, as the sinner's surety. He acknowledges the worth of Christ's atonement. He proclaims pardon on the ground of it to every one who believeth on Jesus, and He bestows it, too, as a present blessing. This many living men everywhere can gratefully testify; and that not a few here can do so, I gladly believe.

I have already said *why* the Holy Jesus was with us in our sin. He came to put it away. He came to deliver us from its power and curse. He was with us in our sin, "that we might become the righteousness of God in Him" now, and that He might at last "set us before the presence of His glory without blemish in exceeding joy," "not having spot or wrinkle or any such thing, but holy and without blemish."

VI.—I invite your attention to the contemplation of Jesus Christ as Immanuel, God with us *at death*, and in dying. For He himself died with us and for us sinners. "And apart from shedding of blood there is no remission" of sin.

The ever living God could not die; but Jesus, who is the only begotten son of God, died. And the atoning efficacy, the meritorious worth, the saving power of Christ's death come from His super-human person and nature.

"None * * can by any means redeem his brother" from this death of sin. "For the redemption of their soul is costly." But this more than man can and does redeem *his* brothers from death eternal. It is by His death that we live; it is by His stripes that we are healed. And the death of Jesus has a twofold aspect to the believer as a believer after he has been made alive by Jesus.

First, the death of Jesus takes out the sting from the believer's own death. So that he can say, "O death where is thy victory? O death where is thy sting? The sting of death is sin." And that tormenting sting Christ takes away from the believer's death. For sin has no more dominion over him. "But thanks be to God which giveth us the victory," over death also as well as over sin, "through our Lord Jesus Christ." Yes, "precious in the sight of the Lord is the death of His saints."

And then, *secondly*, as to the influence of Christ's death on ours. The believer on Jesus gets from his Lord companionship in dying. The godly man need not fear to die; and he does not greatly fear to die, since he is not alone even in dying.

Jesus has gone before him. Jesus waits for him, and is with him even in dying. And the Christian need not fear, and he does not—in so far as he walks by faith—fear to follow Jesus whither-so-ever he goeth, even when the path of Jesus leads direct to the tomb. For He, our Saviour, hath "abolished death, and brought life and incorruption to light through the gospel."

VII.—And, finally, out of all this companionship with **Jesus** comes this blessed truth more, to which I now invite your attention, that Jesus Christ is Immanuel, God with us *both in the state of grace on earth* and in the state of *glory in heaven.*

Jesus is with us in both worlds. He is with us here on earth, and He is with us yonder in Heaven.

The Incarnation of Christ is the fullest answer which we have ever gotten, or will ever get, to the momentous question. " But will God in very deed dwell with men on the earth?" For in Christ He has already done it. Christ's body was God's truest temple on the earth. And God does in His spiritual presence, God does by His Holy Spirit, still dwell with men upon the earth. God's presence is to the godly a quickening, transforming reality. And He says to His Church: "And lo, I am with you alway, even unto the end of the world." We read of Christ being *in* believers the hope of glory. He is called the life—our life. And again we read : " Your life is hid with Christ in God." The Apostle Paul says of himself, " I live ; yet not I, but Christ liveth in me."

And again we read of the believer being *in* Christ, and abiding in Christ. Each such expression denotes, and all such expressions taken together strongly denote a real, close, abiding union between Christ and believing souls— a blending of their life with the life of Jesus.

Bible words teach that *His* life is not apart from theirs, nor is their life apart from His ; but the Bible shows both to be more and more mingling and blending into one. Yes, the life of Christ, and the life of the believer is one, as the springing fountain and its running stream are one. They are one, as the dropping cloud and the falling rain are one. They are one as sources, and their issues are ever one. They are one as the head and the body are one. Thus are Christ and His people one, by a living and abiding union. And in and through Christ all real Christians are one with God. God dwells with them, and in them, and they dwell in God. They are the temples of the Holy Ghost. A blessed state it is to have Christ *with us* thus now on earth. For through Him we may and do even now walk with God.

And yet this is not all that we shall be. We are heirs of glory, and Jesus is Immanuel, God with us *in* glory. He is with us there, not because we are men, not as we are mere men, but it is as redeemed men that Christ is with us in *a state of glory*.

The Lord Jesus Christ is now in Heaven, and Heaven is the home of the redeemed of the Lord. Hence Jesus is most truly with us of the redeemed who are there. And there where Jesus now is, all the redeemed from among men already are, unless the few by comparison who are at any one time still upon the earth.

You know that there are, at the best of times, only a *few* of the redeemed here on earth, and there are a great many of them yonder in Heaven. For "we are compassed about with a great cloud of witnesses." It would not be very difficult to number all the godly people in the world, if we had any sure mark to know them by. Many we hope and trust they are, and ever increasing. Still, if we knew who they are, we could count them soon, and easily. But the redeemed myriads, ever increasing, who are in Heaven, are spoken of as "a great multitude which no man could number." So that when we speak in the name of the whole redeemed family, the words "Immanuel, God with us," will now mean, and will growingly mean, Christ in Heaven, rather than Christ on earth; Christ as being with the many, rather than Christ as being with the few. Just as "the British people" must be taken to mean the many residents of the mother country, rather than the comparatively few residents of this Colony.

The Lord Jesus Christ was, and still is, as we have seen throughout both these sermons, in a most important sense with us, who are pilgrims for Heaven, but are yet on the earth. But now I pass on to urge upon your best attention the glorious truth that Jesus, in a fuller, truer sense than even when he was on earth, is with those of us, with those of the redeemed family, who have already got to Heaven. "For the throne of God and of the Lamb is therein, and His servants do Him service; and they see His face, and His name is on their foreheads."

But those celestials are of us; and we are of them. For "from the Father every family in Heaven and on earth is named," "One family we dwell in Him."

And Christ the great elder brother of the human family has carried human nature to the throne of the universe. He is still a man; and where He is, that is our true final home to which we are journeying. And soon *where* He is, there shall we be also: *with* Him yonder, who is now with us here.

And now, *in conclusion*, let us retrace our steps, and glance backward for a few moments over the most prominent ideas that have claimed our notice.

Let it be carefully noted, and daily joyed in, how widely the advent of Jesus has changed man's condition and prospects for the better. "The old things are passed away" with us. "Behold all things have become new." We have seen that the earth itself is a different place to live on since God, its maker and ours, was with us upon it to bless it and us. We mortals even now inhabit a royal residence of the King of Glory, prepared for Him and for us.

And then we have seen that human nature is different now since Christ shared it. The possibilities and the prospects of our humanity are different as night and day, since Jesus rent the skies, descended to earth, and declared the Father's love to man. The spiritual atmosphere of earth, once dark, and chill, and cheerless, has now more of the light and joy, and love, and sympathy of Heaven in it than it ever had before.

And we have also seen that earnest human work is now a nobler and more bracing discipline of the whole man, mind, and body than before, and leads to nobler issues as "we work out our own salvation with fear and trembling; for it is God which worketh in us both to will and to work for His good pleasure."

And human suffering is a more ennobling and purifying furnace since Jesus shared our work and suffering, and sanctified them, and showed what man may become amid, and under, and by them.

And even that thing of dread and horror, human sin, is no longer, as a matter of course, a hopeless curse and an endless misery. That cruel tyrant sin shall not have dominion over *us*, who come to Jesus for help and deliverance. For he is mighty to save. In Him the sin-sick soul ever finds sovereign balm, and an almighty physician.

And moreover human life on earth is not the same empty, disappointing, grovelling thing since Jesus became the perfect pattern, and fair copy of all human worth and duty as it once was. Any human life may now be a life of grace below, growing into a life of endless glory above. Nor is our last enemy, pale and ghastly death, the same dreadful and dreaded enemy now since Jesus died, as it was once.

> "There is no death! What seems so is transition;
> This life of mortal breath
> Is but a suburb of the life elysian,
> Whose portal we call death."

We now see that death may and does lead and open into endless glory. "I heard a voice from Heaven saying, write, blessed are the dead which die in the Lord from henceforth."

Yes, brethren, let us look and we shall see that all the present is greatly changed to us, and all the future is changed still more by the birth, and life, and labours, and death, and resurrection, and reign of Him who bears the name Immanuel.

All our darkness becomes light in the Lord by means of this one fact, long promised, and now also, blessed be the Lord, long fulfilled, that "the light of the world," God Himself, was visibly with us on the earth for a time, in order that we may be with Him in Heaven for evermore. Amen, and amen. Thus may it be with us all, and with ours, and the glory shall be His through endless ages. And that it may be so, let us more and more look unto Jesus. Yes, let us all continue "ever looking unto Jesus," who is at once the perfect, *ideal man* and *God* manifest in the flesh.

III.

GOD'S LOVE—CHRIST'S ERRAND.

FIRST SERMON.

"For God so loved the world, that He gave His only begotten son, that whosoever believeth on Him should not perish, but have eternal life."—JOHN III., 16.

THE common places of life are many. There are plenty of common place things, common place thoughts, and common place people in the world, but the great is ever rare. Yes, so rare, that all our important interests for time and for eternity form a unity. "But one thing is needful." That attended to, and we have not remaining over really a great mistake to make in life; but that neglected to a dying hour, and we have made the grand mistake of life, which cannot possibly be remedied, and "it had been good for us that we had never been born."

That "one thing needful" is religion, is the securing of our soul's salvation.

But as all our important interests centre in this infinitely important one thing of personal religion, so do all our relationships, though they are many and multiform, centre also in one, even our relation to God, who is the object of that religion.

And this, like all the really great things that belong to us, is true of all men equally. This supreme relation oversteps age, rank, and all other circumstances. This relation belongs to our common humanity, and it reminds us of our common immortality. For widely as we may, and do, differ in many things, our relationship to God is common ground. We are all equally God's creatures, and he is our common Creator. Nor is there any other relationship in which we can possibly stand that deserves a moment's consideration in comparison with this our relationship to the most high God. This rises above all other relationships, and stands alone, as does the infinite God above all His creatures.

And this our supremacy of interest in the things of God arises from what God is in Himself, and from what He is to us. Since God is the most powerful of all beings, with Him for our friend none can make us afraid; with Him for our enemy none can secure our safety. With Him for our friend, infinite power, infinite resources are with us, and though all the universe beside were ranged in opposition to us, finite power, finite resources only would be against us, and victory must be ours.

While with God for our enemy we are miserable as despair, and impotent as infancy. For on Him alone both our existence and our happiness depend. In His hand our breath is, and our happiness is entirely in His power. By a mere volition, He, the Almighty, is able to crush us into hopeless misery.

And God is not only all-powerful, but He is all-seeing, and everywhere present. With Him for our enemy escape and concealment are alike impossible; for we are ever in His presence, and ever in His power. Yes, whether we remember or forget it, God is ever near us. "For in Him we live, and move, and have our being." So constantly present with us is God that He leaves us not alone for a single moment.

Would any of you, my friends, desire to have a solitude where the eye of God shall not break in upon you? Well, this cannot be for even a single moment. You have not had this solitude from the first moment of your existence, and you cannot get it throughout eternity. That all-seeing glance which God cast upon each of us when He breathed into our nostrils the breath of life, and made us rational souls, has never been withdrawn from us, and never shall be while eternal ages run their unceasing circles. Forget, therefore, if you will, a thousand objects of lesser interest; but oh! remember, as you would be happy for ever, the eye that never either slumbers or sleeps, and ever sees us. Forget, if you will, all earthly relationships, and your crime and punishment will be small by comparison, for they are but short-lived, and are travelling to the land of forgetfulness. We shall soon leave all our friends, even the most valued and the best loved, or they shall soon leave us; but here or yonder God and we shall never part company; therefore let us never forget Him. This, my hearers, is for us the question of questions. Do we all believe in this great unseen, but everywhere present, and all-powerful God, who knows all that we are, whose gaze is ever on us, whose eye penetrates to our inmost thoughts, and even detects their very formation before they have assumed a definite shape to our own consciousness?

Then, if that be our faith, whatever our worldly circumstances may be, or our connections in life, there are no other questions half so important to us personally as these: "What does God, who knows my heart and life, think of me? How do my character and conduct please Him?" "If I should cease to oppose Him, and should give myself wholly up to Him and His purposes, will it be for my advantage or for my injury? Will He prove my friend or my enemy?"

"What are God's intentions with the race to which I belong? Does He intend our destruction, or desire our good? With what feelings does God regard us? What are His aims and purposes with man?"

Now, when we look within, and ask these questions at our own guilty conscience, it gives a dark answer, and says: That we deserve, and must endure the wrath and curse of the holy God for our sin.

And when we look abroad upon a guilty world, we get in substance the same dark answer. We cannot but think, when we are left to ourselves, that the holy God must hate a wicked world like this.

And men too often look within them and around them for answers to these questions: "What is God, and how does He look upon man?" But brighter, better, and truer answers to these momentous questions may be got in the Bible than from man himself. For this book is given to explain God's mind, and to reveal God's heart to us. And in this very passage of sacred writ we get the affirmation of the Son, who came to declare the Father's character and will, as to what God's feelings towards us really are.

This text, then, brings before us the most momentous theme in the Bible, namely, the love of God to man. For that God does love man, not hate him, is what Christ here affirms. Let us then, by the aid of the Holy Spirit's teaching, aim to see and realize the delightful meaning and moment of this cheering affirmation "God is love." That so we may be prepared to reciprocate the divine love of which our text speaks.

The doctrine of the text is and must be a true saying, as it is a glad saying. For it is one of the greatest utterances of God's great Apostle to the world, Christ Jesus.

And it is as glorious as it is true. Hear again Christ's own gracious words, "For God so loved the world, that He gave His only begotten Son, that whosoever believeth on Him should not perish, but have eternal life." Look with me, then, at the following points contained in the text:

I.—The state of mind that is here affirmed of God. Jesus says that God "loved the world."

II.—The practical manifestation into which God's love shaped itself. Namely, into the gift of His Son.

III.—The gracious purpose or end that God had in view by the bestowment of His unspeakable gift. "That whosoever believeth on His Son, Jesus, should not perish, but have eternal life."

I.—And, first, the state of mind which is here affirmed of God on the highest authority is deeply interesting to us. For Jesus says that "God loved the world."

Our first inquiry is: What is the extent of the term "world" which is here used? How extended as to its objects was the love which God felt for man? I reply, that when Christ speaks of "the world" he means "the world." And He here speaks of the world in the most general sense. For the Greek word which is here used for world is one of the widest import It is not the word which is employed in Luke's gospel when we read: that "there went out a decree from Cæsar Augustus that all the world should be enrolled." This is a word which is often used in a restricted sense. It is so in this case. It probably means Palestine and the adjacent countries, or, at the widest, the Roman Empire.

But the word for "world" that is used in our text is the word which is used in John's gospel, where Christ says: "For I came not to judge the world, but to save the world." There it means the inhabitants of the world generally, mankind. And it is the word which Jesus uses when he says of Mary's anointing, as recorded in Matthew's gospel: "Verily I say unto you, wheresoever this gospel shall be preached in the *whole world*, that also which this woman hath done shall be spoken of for a memorial of her." There it means the globe in its whole extent. It is in truth a word which is generally used in the widest and most unlimited sense. And in our text the word needs no restriction. Nay, we have scripture authority for taking the word world here in its ordinary sense Since this passage does not stand alone in assigning to the love of God, and to the work of Christ a reference to the world in its widest extent. For the apostle John, addressing

Christians, says of Jesus Christ: "And He is the propitiation for our sins; and not for ours only, but also for the whole world."

And when we are told that God loves man, we are in this fact assured of God's doing man all needed good. God loves man; he is therefore man's friend, not his enemy. For love is the one essential, indispensable element in friendship

Without love friendship is a mere pretence; while he who loves us is, in virtue of that relation to us, our friend. We can have no better security for anyone proving a kind and faithful friend than to have obtained a firm hold on his best affections. "For the whole law is fulfilled in one word, even in this: Thou shalt love thy neighbour as thyself." And again, "For he that loveth his neighbour hath fulfilled the law." And the explanation of these strong statements is found in such words as these: "And if there be any other commandment, it is summed up in this word, namely, Thou shalt love thy neighbour as thyself. Love worketh no ill to his neighbour; love therefore is the fulfilment of the law."

That is, love is the fulfilment of the law, not actually in standing for every detailed act of duty, but it is the living germ which naturally produces all the services that we owe to the loved ones. For to love our neighbours as ourselves is to be prepared to treat them in every way as we ought. It is thus that love acts between man and man; and it is thus that love acts between God and man.

And strange as it seems to us, and grandly strange as it is, "God loved the world." He loved the undeserving world, the wide world of sinners, who had defied His lawful authority, trampled upon His righteous laws, and even hated His glorious person, His holy character, and His just government.

Let us rejoice, and give thanks to God, that His love was not circumscribed, and is not, within the limits of man's desert. For God loved, and God still loves the perishing, self-destroyed, and ill-deserving world of sinners. "We love, because He first loved us." And if God had not loved us before we possessed any good desert, He would never have loved us at all. To Him, therefore, and not to ourselves, let us ascribe all the glory of our salvation from first to last.

This text, my Christian brethren, speaks powerfully to us. It prompts us to say: 'Since God loves the world shall we not be like Him; and prove that we are His by cherishing a growing love and pity for a world that is perishing in its rebellion against its Creator and Lord? And shall we not give those practical manifestations of our love to our fellow-men, which God by word and deed has so earnestly enjoined upon us?'

Let us all ever strive to realize and remember, Christian brethren, that we are in God's hand the instrumental saviours of this lost world in which we live.

And as God has loved the world with His infinite love, and in the exercise of that great love has stretched out His infinitely powerful arm to raise degraded men, in that highest sense which God only can do, so let us, His people, cherish such a love for our fellow-men, and feel so deep a sympathy with their spiritual ruin, as shall lead us stedfastly to aim, under God, and within our measure, to be the instruments of bringing eternal well-being to as many of them as we may, in raising them from sin, and bringing them back to God. As we so do, we are thus co-workers with God.

But what does Jesus Christ mean to teach us by these words, " God loved the word, " as to His Heavenly Father's state of mind and feeling towards sinners?

Not, surely, that God felt complacency in the persons, or was pleased with the conduct of those who were setting at nought His lawful authority, trampling upon His righteous laws, and hating His perfectly holy character.

No, no; that be far from God. Such complacency with evil is impossible to God. We dare not think of this moral indifference in connection with Him Not so did God love the world. It would introduce complete confusion into our ideas of right and wrong to believe that the Holy God loves sinful man approvingly. This involves the false idea that God is pleased with all His creatures, because they are His creatures, whether they glorify Him and serve the end that He made them for or not. And that God's love has therefore no visible and close connection with the moral character of those who are its objects. In this case there would be no moral discrimination in God's love. To have it would be no longer the reward of goodness, and of likeness to Himself.

God's love would be a mere passion, or feeling, regulated by no principle, having no visible connection with worth, and therefore leaving no well-defined path in which it could be confidently sought and surely found. All God's rational creatures would have His love, as a matter of course, and all would have it alike, which is not the case. God does not love sinners, while sinners, approvingly.

And yet love is so far different from approval, and so much deeper and wider in all noble natures than approval, that the Holy God does love sinners.

But once again, it is impossible that the Holy God should entertain towards beings of opposite moral characters the same feelings, either of approval or disapproval. And God does, by a moral necessity of His nature, love holy unfallen creatures, who remain what He made them, and He does view with entire complacency His own moral image as seen in them. So that He cannot in the very nature of things love, in the same sense, creatures who are the very opposite in moral character, in whom that holy moral image is defaced and obliterated, and in whom that resemblance to Himself in goodness is awanting.

And this is so by an inevitable moral law. For no being, neither man nor angel, nor God himself, can love approvingly, moral opposites. Of the moral opposites, holiness and sin, good and evil, the one of them, in whomsoever found, must always have been pleasing to God's moral nature, and the other must always have been revolting to it.

Good beings or evil, the one class or the other, must ever have been the objects of God's complacent love, and not them both. And so it was, for the love which is spoken of in our text is not the love of complacency, but the love of pity. It is not that love of complacency and approval which God feels to those in whom He sees His own holy image reflected, and who compose the members of His own redeemed family. God's love, spoken of in the text, is that general love of pity, benevolence, and good-will which God cherishes towards all men as His rational creatures, as His human sons. A love, or good-will this, which forms the stable foundation upon which all God's manifested kindness to man rests—the perennial fountain from which all God's positive gifts to man flow forth. "God is Love." And our text affirms "the universal and eternal existence of that love which God Himself is." It says that God loves the world.

God did not, and could not approve of what man, the sinner, was, and had done. But though God did not approve of man's evil conduct, He pitied his lost condition. Though He did not delight in man, the sinner, as he was, He felt deep compassion for him, and desired with ardour his highest happiness.

Let me illustrate this love of the Holy God for erring men by what exists in men to men, and in particular by a mother's love.

I know that human feelings and human relationships are very imperfect aids when we try to rise, by means of them, up to what exists in the Divine Being. And yet "the things of a man" are real aids, and God-given aids to our conceptions of "the things of God." We have no better. Human relationships are all Jacob's ladders. They are "set up on the earth," but "the top of" them reaches to Heaven. They begin in lowly places, but they end on high; and they are used in the word of God and in our text as means of our rising to what is divine. For we can best understand what "Son of God" and "love of God" mean by looking at human sonship and human love as interpreters of them. And we find in the love of a pious mother for her profligate son such a real God-given aid to the right understanding of what God's love for the world was and is. For she, like God, often loves the persons of her very own, without approving of their character and career. Can anyone suppose that a God-fearing, bible-reading, prayer-loving mother also loves the God-hating, the bible-despising, the prayer-neglecting, the sabbath-breaking, the profanity, and the immorality of her godless and abandoned son, because she still loves her son himself? It is not so. Nay, she sympathizes in her whole mind and soul with God's violated and down-trodden authority, and powerfully pleads His righteous cause with that erring son. She is deeply grieved and shocked with his crimes, and loathes and hates them heartily. This godly mother cannot hear the Holy Name that she reverences above every other name, and which alone she adores, profaned by her godless son, and approve. She cannot listen while the truths which are the light of her mind and the rejoicing of her heart become food for his mirth, and ridicule, and scorn. She cannot see in him the traces of his intemperance and impurity without displeasure, and distress, and sometimes even agony of mind. But her entire disapproval of his profligate conduct, and profane language has not, and never will extinguish her great love for him. No, she, his mother, loves him still, and she will never cease to love him, even when he is most degraded in character, and most deeply depressed in circumstances. That he is still her son, and that she is still his mother, she never forgets. She cannot, and for love's sake she would not forget. And should her son be laid on a bed of sickness or death— even should his condition of health be clearly traceable directly to his own vices—she will yet tend him, on his sick bed, with all the loving care and tenderness with which she watched over his helpless, but innocent and hope-inspiring infancy. She will shed over him, in his lowest degradation, uncounted tears of love and sympathy, and will lavish upon him, in his deepest misery, even though deserved, all the rich, untold treasures of affection that are divinely lodged in the depths of a mother's nature. Nor does she desire his life to be spared and his recovery to health less because, being lost to all sense of duty, gratitude, and even shame, he may have heaped upon her venerable head a thousand indignities, and dishonours, and cruel neglects, in place of that deep reverence and warm affection which are a mother's righteous due. And in any circumstances, in sickness or in health, he is interesting and even lovely in her eyes long after others have come to shun him with indifference or contempt. Nay, he cannot sink so low that she, with her eyes of love, does not see redeeming, and even hopeful features in his character.

And so is it with God's love for the world. It also extends to the undeserving. Yes, the great Father of all feels for, pities, and loves the sinner, notwithstanding and despite of all his crimes. For it was not the deserving only, but, our Lord says: It was the world that God loved.

And as the son's wretchedness, even though self-inflicted and deserved, hardens not, but only pierces and softens the mother's heart: so our Father God's bowels of compassion are moved on behalf of foolish, blinded, miserable men, who are ruining themselves by sinning against Him. And He is heard crying in mingled pity, grief, and love: "How shall I give thee up, Ephraim?" Or in the tenderly melting words of Christ: "O Jerusalem, Jerusalem, which killeth the prophets, and stoneth them that are sent unto her! How often would I have gathered thy children together, even as a hen gathereth her chickens under her wings, and ye would not?"

It was thus that God loved the world! His was a love of pure compassion. His was a love that sorrowed over man's wretchedness, and longed to put an end to it. His was a love that pitied man's degradation, and longed to raise him from it. God, though he had been deeply dishonoured by the rebel and sinner, man, looked down upon him, not with the severely just eye of a condemning judge, but with the pitying eye of a sorrowing Father. Yet there was on God's part no conniving at man's sin. There was no overlooking of man's guilt. There was no winking at man's rebellion. There was no relaxing of God's law to meet man's relaxed morality. God's pity for the sinner did not dim his clear discernment of the enormity of man's sin. God's love to man did not blind him to the moral wrong which man had done. God, who loved man, hated man's sin with a perfect hatred. God's love, with far more depth and tenderness in it than any human love, has yet nothing of that human weakness that often makes a wrong done by one whom we love, to one with whom we stand in no special relation, seem to us less of a wrong than it would seem if it were done by one in whom we felt little interest, to one in whom we felt much. For in God's love there is nothing of the weak partiality and sin-excusing spirit which human parents so often entertain towards the sins and crimes of their own children.

Yet with more than all the purity from evil, and the impartiality of a just and righteous judge, there is combined in our Creator God the large and tender heart of a loving Father. So that He looked down upon a world of rebel sinners, not with hate and scorn and wrath. For pity, and compassion, and love reigned supreme in his Fatherly bosom.

And all of this love and pity that we see upon the earth comes from above.

Thus felt the Heavenly Parent towards His unworthy children of the human family, or else earthly parents would never have known and shown such compassion as they do for their erring offspring.

It was the God of love, the Father of us all, who formed the parent's heart, and implanted in it its deep compassion for an erring child. And His own large heart of love, yearning for the happiness of the rational intelligent creatures, whom He has made, is the glorious original design from which the earthly parent's heart was drawn, and of which the parent's heart is but a faint copy, and yet a copy so far real and true. For earthly parents are so pitiful and long-suffering to their erring children only because God was, and is, so pitiful to His erring children. God made parents in this respect after His own image and in His likeness. And the love of parents to their children, is one of the few traces of that largely lost image which they retain the least obliterated. But earthly parents do not surpass our Father God in love and pity and long-suffering! More than all a father's and a mother's loving tenderness joined in one towards erring children is His tenderness!

God only implanted in human parents a little of that love of which He has much. But how much, none but He Himself can measure and know. The large-heartedness of God our Heavenly Father, no one has a heart to perceive as it is, or a tongue to tell! The ocean of God's love none can map out and fathom; none can explore and describe. The sounding line that easily measures the deepest fountain of human affection, and soon reaches its bottom, when it is let into the ocean of divine love, finds at its utmost stretch no bottom, and the keenest, clearest eye of man can discern no shore.

In that boundless, bottomless, shoreless ocean of divine love all God's unfallen and redeemed creatures may bathe themselves eternally, and leave depths never stirred: for God is infinite, and God is love. So that in order to fathom the love of God, we must fathom God Himself; and in order to fathom God, we must fathom measureless infinity.

Thus you see that we cannot measure the love of God, though we may know that its length, and breadth, and height and depth are boundless.

IV.

GOD'S LOVE—CHRIST'S ERRAND.

SECOND SERMON.

"For God so loved the world, that He gave His only begotten son, that whosoever believeth on Him should not perish, but have eternal life."—John iii., 16.

WE have considered in the first discourse the state of mind that our text affirms of God.

But it may be asked: How do we know that God so loved the world that all human affection seems, and is in the comparison, contracted, cold, and selfish? The answer is: that we know this from the words of Jesus in the text, but we also know it from His own and His Father's acts. For consider,

II.—The practical manifestation into which God's love shaped itself: the gift of his son. "For God so loved the world that" for its salvation He gave His only begotten son. Herein is the love of God to us, manifested. And this practical test is ever the true test and crucible of love. What can it do, and suffer, and give up for the sake of its object?

This tests love's quality and measures love's power. For love, in virtue of its very nature, ever seeks out-going and manifestation. Love, wherever found, bears its own appropriate fruits. This is true of the love of *complacency* and of the love of *pity* both. The love of complacency is fruitful. The love of complacency in God is so. For His approving love diffuses its fragrance throughout the celestial mansions, and fills all Heaven with bliss.

God loves all the inhabitants of Heaven approvingly, and His love makes all happy.

And the love of complacency in the creature towards God makes suitable and admiring returns.

Unfallen angels and redeemed men around the throne of God on high, because they are perfect in love, are free. There is no place so free as Heaven. There are no fetters forged to bind the inhabitants of Heaven to God's throne, and to keep them in allegiance to it. Those blessed ones may go wherever they please, and may become whatever they choose. There is no external constraint put upon them. It is love, and love alone that binds the inhabitants of Heaven to God's throne. But drawn by divine love, they are secured to the service of God by the strongest of all ties. There is perfect freedom in Heaven, and may safely be where there is perfect love. For it is love that binds the moral universe together. And the love of complacency in holy beings towards each other is fruitful. Love in Heaven is perfect, and therefore bliss knows no alloy.

In like manner the love of *pity* is also fruitful. In fallen man even it is so. It is the love of pity that feeds the hungry, that clothes the naked, that houses the homeless, that instructs the ignorant, that elevates the degraded.

It was the love of pity that raised the infant Moses from the Nile. For when the young and helpless Hebrew babe wept, Pharaoh's daughter, with a kind and womanly heart, had compassion on him, and drew him out of the water. So David loved and pitied his son, but was far from approving of his conduct, at the time when he exclaimed in an agony of grief: "O my son Absalom, my son, my son Absalom! would God I had died for thee; O Absalom my son, my son."

But far more fruitful is God's love of pity than man's. Mark how this love was displayed in Christ's human nature. He, the Son of Man, felt for all human woe; His human sympathies brought sighs from His bosom and tears from His eyes at the grave of His "friend" Lazarus. Here Jesus wept with them that were weeping. And He wept tears of pity as well as spoke words of pity over guilty and judgment-doomed Jerusalem.

But I dwell not on any other instances of God's love of pity than the one which our text brings before us, namely, the gift of His Son. This proof of God's self-sacrificing love rises up, and stands quite alone in single Alpine grandeur. Let us apply our practical test already spoken of to the love which is here displayed, and ask: "How did God love the world? Up to what practical manifestation did He love it? What could His love do, and give up, and suffer for the world?" And we find upon examination that God's love nobly stands every test. For the triumphant answer to our question is: "God so loved the world that he gave His only begotten Son" to die for its salvation. We know that parental affection is almost unfailing. We know that it is the most uniformly strong, and the most largely instinctive of all love by what parents in general can do, and suffer, and give up for their children.

And our Heavenly Father God, who is the best of Fathers, to help us to see and know in some degree the strength of His love for man, tells us that He, a Father, gave up His Son, His only begotten Son for man.

God not only gave up something dear to Him, some one dear to Him; but He gave up for man that one object for whom the parents would give up all other objects. He gave up even His Son, the dearest object of His affection. "God so loved the world that He gave" up for its salvation what He had most valuable to give. For the son is the Father's most valued possession.

And less the terms here employed cannot be meant to teach us than this: That when the omniscient eye of the omnipresent God embraced all space, which is bounded only in Himself, and scanned that eternity, past and future, which is His own life time: and when it comprehended in its view all existence, past, present, and future, it did not rest upon another object so valued by God, so dear to Him as this one, His son Christ Jesus. All this is meant by the words of the text. For care is taken to mark Jesus out as God's only begotten son, to show that the universe does not contain another being whom God puts upon an equality with Christ.

And this is much to say. For none can number all God's creatures or estimate their worth, but He who made them all.

But because this is no created being whom God gives up for man, therefore no creature can compare with him. "For God put all things in subjection under His feet." Nay, we read, "Christ * * who is over all, God blessed for ever." He, and He alone, is in the highest sense the Son of God. As Creator, God the universal Father has many sons and daughters; but he has only one son of equal nature. In this sense Jesus Christ is God's only begotten Son.

If you would behold the love of God to man think of the worth of that Son whom God so freely gave up for man! Christ's worth and dignity, and rank stood so high that when the Father "bringeth in the first born into the world He saith: And let all the angels of God worship Him." And again He saith, "Thy throne, O God, is for ever and ever. And the sceptre of uprightness is the sceptre of Thy kingdom."

Now, God is not only a God of righteousness, and can do no wrong to any, but He greatly delights to honour and reward worth in all. And we may well ask, 'What honour, what favour, what dignity, what reward did Christ not deserve from God and man?' Rejection, shame, suffering, and death were not the due rewards of such noble deeds as His. Even a condemned malefactor could clearly see this, and say to his guilty companion in crime, of their own condemnation and of Christ's: "And we indeed justly, for we receive the due reward of our deeds; but this man hath done nothing amiss."

How, then, did the just God give His Son Jesus up to so great shame and suffering? "God so loved the world that He" did it. Jesus thus suffered, brethren, only because God's love to the world could not find another fit object whose willing sufferings could effect its benevolent purpose. But why God would rather give up His own Son to all that He suffered for man than abandon this, His great purpose of love, I cannot explain. Jesus does not try to explain this mystery of divine goodness, but only affirms the fact. The reason of this self-sacrifice lies deep down in the heart of God. "God so loved the world that He" did it, and love is its own reason. And it is noblest in the noblest. We cannot get beyond love for an explanation of love to anything lying deeper. It is just the nature of love to be self-sacrificing. That is all that we can say of this divine thing. It will not be further questioned, and give reasons lying outside itself, for its self-sacrifice. And thus love can only be understood by a kindred spirit. Only love interprets love. Hence, "he that loveth not, knoweth not God; for God is love."

Behold the love of God to man, yet again, as you think of the *great love* that must have subsisted, and does subsist, between the Father and the Son! Jesus was, and is, God's beloved Son in whom He is well pleased. This means much. For none can inter-penetrate and unfold their pure and holy inter-communings together. None can enter fully into such sacred sympathies as theirs. None can conceive how hallowed, and holy their intercourse—as the Son lay in the bosom of the Father from eternity—must have been! How weak and imperfect are our strongest attachments compared with the love of this Father and Son! How selfish, suspicious, and distant are our closest unions in comparison with this holiest of holy affections! The bonds of which I speak were so close, and the union was so strong, that Christ says: "I and the Father are one." They are two persons, but only one God, and in sympathy as in nature, one.

How, then, I ask once more, could God the Father give up to suffering and death a Son so beloved? Only God's great love to man can explain the wondrous fact. The great dignity of man's nature, admitted to its fullest extent, cannot half explain why Jesus the Son of God died for us. The full reason of this unspeakable gift is to be found alone in God Himself, who is love. "God so loved the world, that He gave" up His Son for its salvation. If it had not been for this, God's so great love to man, He would, He must have spared His own Son. But God's love for man was too strong for any reserve in its flowing forth to save him. The ocean of God's love—now when the fulness of the times had come—no ancient tide-mark could restrain. That love swept away every barrier which kept it from joining together in abiding union, Heaven and Earth. God's Son, even His only begotten Son, was not spared, but freely given up for sinners.

And to what did God give His Son up, let us ask? First God gave Christ up to the ordinary weaknesses and sinless infirmities of our humanity. God gave Him up to become a man, a real man. "For indeed we that are in this tabernacle do groan, being burdened." Yet we have had no experience of a higher, and more etherial state of existence. If we had once known a higher and happier state, doubtless we should now groan more heavily, and feel our burden of clay to be yet more burdensome. How much harder in some respects would it be for Moses, and Job, and Daniel, and Paul, and all the martyrs of all ages, to descend from the bliss of Heaven to the sorrows of Earth, and to suffer now again what they suffered once before? Do we not say, through our tears and in our loneliness, and rightly say: 'That we would not, even if the power were given us, bring our loved ones back from glory to repeat the sufferings of earth?' 'We would go to them rather than bring them back to us.' And yet Heaven, that higher and more etherial state of existence, was Christ's native home.

All its joys and honours were His by nature and by right. And still God gave Him up to share our weak and suffering humanity. God gave Him up to what is, at its best, but an imperfect and burdened condition, from which the renewed spirit often longs to be free, and earnestly desires " to be clothed upon with our habitation which is from Heaven," " a building from God, a house not made with hands eternal in the Heavens."

Think of Jesus Christ, the mighty God, enduring childhood's feebleness, just as we have all done. Think of Him, the wisdom of God, condescending to be subject to the sometimes wise, sometimes foolish, commands of Joseph and Mary. Think of Him, the maker of the world, working with His human hands as a carpenter!

Think of Him " that sitteth upon the circle of the earth," and before whom " the inhabitants thereof are as grasshoppers—that stretcheth out the Heavens as a curtain, and spreadeth them out as a tent to dwell in "—wandering over the land of Palestine, weary and footsore, as an itinerant teacher and preacher! Think of Him, who is the Bread of Life, and upholdeth "all things by the word of His power," hungering and thirsting, and being wearied! Think of Him who has gone to Heaven to prepare mansions of glory for all His people, oftentimes on earth not having "where to lay His head!" Well, God the Father gave His well-beloved Son up to all this for man. But still further, Christ's lot was not the ordinary lot of humanity. It was not even the ordinary lot of the labouring poor; but one of special suffering and reproach. Christ's life was no average human career. He was "a Man of sorrows, and acquainted with grief." He says: "I gave my back to the smiters, and my cheeks to them that plucked off the hair: I hid not my face from shame and spitting." "He was despised and rejected of men." Wherever He went His real followers were but few, and His open or secret enemies were many. But these were not all, or the worst of Christ's many sorrows. He had come to do the Father's will, not man's; and the rejection and persecution of men He could lightly esteem.

But Jesus bore on earth heavier sorrows than man's hand laid on him. For to deepen his sorrows far more than any hand of man could do, the heavy hand of the righteous law-giver and judge of the universe was laid upon him, the sacrifice for the sin of man. Penetrate and solve, if you can, the deep mystery of that dread conflict which Jesus endured in the Garden of Gethsemane. See the Son of God with no hand of man laid upon him, suffering no disease of body, in the prime of life, and feeling no remorse within, and yet He says, "My soul is exceeding sorrowful even unto death." Whence comes His great sorrow? He is in a great agony, and as it deepens He prays the more earnestly to His Father, asking 'that if it be possible the cup may pass from Him.' And that agony of soul becomes so intense, that, though it is now the cool of night, and Jesus is in the open air, His temples are suffused with a profuse perspiration, and the great drops are seen falling down to the ground. But when we draw nearer, and look more narrowly on the sacred sufferer, the greatness of His agony becomes yet more manifest.

For the moisture that oozes through His hair, dies His throbbing temples, and falls to the ground in large drops, is sweat, mingled with His own most precious blood. History records a very few instances only, of human agony having risen to this intensity of sweating blood as Jesus did. Yet God freely gave up His only begotten and well-beloved Son to such agony on our account. "God so loved the world."

But, again, God gave up His Son to a propitiatory death. Jesus left the garden of His agony only for the mockery of a judicial trial, and for the cross. Our world was then, to an uncommon degree, reeling in crime, and groaning in blood. It much needed a saviour. Every man from Adam, all down the ages to Christ, had been a sinner. But a break in the wearisome succession has taken place.

Jesus, the first immaculate child, had at length been born into the world, had grown up a sinless man, and had lived a sinless life. But the privileged nation in which God had long placed His own word, the nation which God had put in training for ages, to know and receive His own Messiah at His coming, now rose up, and leagued itself with God's avowed enemies, both with militant heathendom and with hell, to banish incarnate goodness from the earth. And hence, by the joint efforts of men and of devils, the only spotlessly pure and sinless man, upon whom the sun had shone for four thousand years, was now condemned to death, and crucified in the sacred names of law and justice! "O justice, what terrible crimes have been done in thy sacred name?" And this is the worst of all such crimes before or since. Jesus condemned by men, and left in their power by God, was led forth to crucifixion, and nailed upon the cross between two robbers. He said to His enemies, "This is your hour and the power of darkness." But a still deeper draught of sorrow must be drunk before Jesus could say in triumph, "It is finished." For upon Him, although God calls him "my Shepherd" and "my Fellow," awoke the sword of the eternal Father. And this extorted from the hitherto uncomplaining and silent sufferer the melancholy and agonized cry, "My God, my God, why hast thou forsaken me?" As if Jesus had said: "I have been all through my life on earth despised and rejected of men. And now in the hour of my greatest trial, even my few hitherto steady and loving disciples have all forsaken me, and fled. One has betrayed me, and another has denied me. At all this I wonder not. For all this I am prepared." But, "My God, my God, why hast Thou forsaken me?" It was that hiding of His Father's face from Him that was the source and essence of Christ's extremest agony.

See, my hearers, God's only begotten and well-beloved Son a spectacle, and a sufferer upon the Cross of Calvary, that would make any father and mother here shudder to think of seeing any child of theirs become.

See the Holy Jesus dying a criminal's death at the hand of law, like one not worthy to live! What does this mean? Our text explains the unparalleled fact. "God so loved the world," that He made Christ's pure and spotless soul an offering for sin, though He had done "no sin, neither was guile found in His mouth."

And now, my fellow sinner, what think you of this love of God, and of the gift which is its richest fruit? I would fain fire your soul with a glowing admiration of God's great love, and fill it with holy gratitude for the priceless gift of His Son. I gladly confess, and solemnly protest to you, that I have found nothing anywhere so wonderful and so noteworthy as this fact—that Jesus died to save sinners; and that though I had years in which to address you instead of this one hour, I have nothing else to relate of equal importance or of equal interest either to myself, or you, as this wonderful Story of the Cross.

The love of God displayed in the gift of His Son is the gospel which I both rejoice to believe and to preach. The only begotten Son of God dying for sinners, for love's sake, seems to me the most wonderful and the most glorious fact of which it is possible to know or conceive.

Ask human history for another fact like this, and equal to this; and history, looking abashed, meekly owns "It is not in me." Ask the inventive human mind for a fiction to match this fact; and the fertile brain also confesses: Such an imagination "is not in me."

The Cross of Christ stands quite alone on the horizon of humanity, a matchless celestial phenomenon, towering in glorious, solitary grandeur above fact and fiction both. "And, without controversy, great is the mystery of godliness; He who was manifested in the flesh, justified in the spirit, seen of angels, preached among the nations, believed on in the world, received up in glory." Well, this manifested one, "suffered for sins once, the righteous for the unrighteous, that He might bring us to God." "The breadth and length, and height and depth," of the divine love that is here displayed pass knowledge. Holy angels and redeemed men ever desire to look more and more deeply into this love. But it will require the unending length of an eternal day, and the perfect light of the divine presence in Heaven, after "this corruptible shall have put on incorrution, and this mortal shall have put on immortality," fully to master this study of studies, and theme of themes.

But do you ask 'what worthy end this unparalleled gift of God serves?' And the question is a reasonable one. Well, our third head of discourse treats of this, the why and the wherefore of the gift.

III.—The gracious purpose or end that God had in view by His bestowment of this unspeakable gift on man, Jesus tells us, was "that whosoever believeth on Him should not perish, but have eternal life." This is a glorious, as well as a gracious purpose. Facts, the doing of God, so unparalleled as the incarnation and the death of Christ, must have had some worthy end in view; and these had.

For we learn here that fallen man's state by nature is a state of condemnation; is a state in which, if he remain, he must perish. "The soul that sinneth, it shall die." "And so death passed unto all men, for that all sinned." "Cursed is every one which continueth not in all things that are written in the Book of the Law to do them." And that curse rests on mankind. So that if God had not sent His Son into the world to die for sinners, we, and all mankind, must have perished, because we have not continued perfectly in anything, much less in all things that are written in the book of the law to do them.

We have all deserved to perish as breakers of God's holy law. Have we ever seriously thought, and all of us, what this means? What is it for a sinner to perish? This cannot be fully conceived of by us, and I will not attempt to describe so much even as I can conceive. To perish, however, may not mean to cease to exist, but to be deprived of eternal life. To perish may be for one to exist, and yet feel existence to be his greatest curse. In the Bible, goodness, in union with happiness, often means life; and sinfulness, in union with misery, often means death. To perish may not be the being annihilated, but the enduring of great misery. And that misery flows in upon the lost in a twofold stream whose one origin is sin. The sinner's misery arises first from his own character, from what he is in himself. Being bad, he must be miserable, and the worse that he grows, the more unhappy he becomes. And, secondly, his misery also arises from God's treatment of him. We must glance at both these elements of misery in the lost.

To perish, is first for the fever of unholy desire and passion to grow up to the madness of entire God-hating; and that state, when reached, is of itself misery and torture unutterable. For sin loved and cherished in the soul naturally tends to putrify and destroy its every source of enjoyment. And the presence of sin, loved and unrepented of, also banishes the vivifying, purifying presence of God, leaving the sinner to perish hour by hour of the misery of his own moral loathsomeness. And with God ever awanting to the soul there must be growing misery. "For lo, they that are far from Him shall perish." Alienation and separation from God are the death of the soul. For He is its life, and light, and joy. Oh, the untold and unsupportable pain and weariness of a whole existence of dreary ungodliness in that region where no smile of God shall ever come! How shall the sensitive soul of man, made to live in God's love, sustain this? Such an existence must be to the soul, ever thirsting for wells of joy, an infinite desert of parched, leafless, burning sand. For the unholy soul, unblessed of God, will be a hell to itself. There "their worm dieth not, and the fire is not quenched."

But all the lost sinner's misery will not be from within. Heaven and Hell are places as well as states. They are respectively the palace and the prison of the moral universe. And need you wonder that the monarch of all worlds has not fitted up and prepared the prison that He has made for the wilful and persistent enemies of

His throne and government, in the same manner as He has prepared and adorned the endless home of His own beloved family, both angelic and human?

No, brethren, both places have been prepared for their respective inhabitants. The one place has been prepared to show the riches of God's glorious grace, the munificence of His unspeakable love towards them that believe on Jesus. And the other is a place that has been "prepared for the devil and his angels," to show the power of God's wrath towards His wilful enemies, the dreadfulness of His injured goodness, "the wrath of the Lamb!" These abodes have been prepared, the one to manifest how wise and safe and right it is to fear God and serve Him. And the other to show how unspeakably foolish and wrong it is to reject Christ, to live in sin, and to have God and our own consciences for our enemies.

Where this glorious Heaven is, I cannot tell you. But this I can safely say: That the place in the universe of God which is best fitted to promote the well-being and enjoyment of its residents, and is most richly stored with proofs of the divine wisdom, love, and goodness: that place, wherever found, must be Heaven. And that region which is least of all blessed with tokens of God's goodness and benevolence, and most of all darkened with manifestations of his just displeasure: that place, wherever found, must be Hell.

Now, it was to raise sinful men from that fathomless gulf into which they were sinking by their sin, and to elevate them to that unspeakable glory amid which God dwells, that Christ came into the world.

And we have here set before us the present state of all gospel hearers as produced by the incarnation and atonement of Christ. It is not now what men's state would have been but for Christ, one in which they must have perished. Nor is it, as a matter of course, a saved state. But Christ's completed atonement puts sinners into a salvable state. For the work of Christ is not a special remedy made for persons, but a general remedy provided for man. The work of Christ itself does not define who shall be saved, but it opens up the way for the return of all who are willing to come unto God by Him. It is not the work of Christ, but it is the work of the Holy Spirit which is special and seals believers unto the day of redemption.

But Christ's work has been long finished, and yet many have heard of it, and of its being a finished work, and, after all, have perished; and we may. That you and I shall never perish, my hearers, is not an infallible sequence, from the glorious fact that Christ has died to save sinners. But the condition is, that whosoever believeth on Jesus shall be saved. Actual personal benefit from the great general remedy comes to each one to whom it is offered only through a personal reception of the saving truth of Christ, which act of faith is our own act. Christ's work has left for us all an open way of return to God; but along that way we must each personally walk, under the guidance of the Holy Spirit, in order to obtain the provided salvation of God.

Do you ask, 'how sinners pass from an unsaved but salvable state into a saved state; or, in other words, how sinners pass from a state of nature into a state of grace?' By faith, I answer, by soul sympathy, or trust in Christ. For Christ died that whosoever believes—*i.e.*, whosoever puts himself into the divinely appointed position of mind towards God's Son—the divinely provided remedy—should not perish, but have eternal life. He that believes on Jesus receives the unspeakable boon, salvation, eternal life. All believers on Jesus are saved, and all unbelievers perish. Thus you see that the soul-act, the mind-act of faith on Jesus, is the turning-point in our personal salvation. And faith, as we have seen, is in its actual exercise our own act; but in its moral prerequisites faith is the gift of God, and to be had for the asking. It is a fruit of the Spirit.

But you ask again, "What is the saving truth of Christ that is revealed to our faith, and in what way does it become saving to us?"

The saving truth that is offered to our faith in the text, and in all scripture, is Christ; is "the Lamb of God which taketh away the sin of the world;" is "that Christ Jesus came into the world to save sinners;" is that God so loved the world as to send Him for this purpose of grace.

And the way by which this message of God's love becomes saving truth to the individual sinner is, as we have seen, through faith. It is His own faith that forms the meeting-point, the act of saving contact between the believing sinner and the reconciled, forgiving God.

There is no wrath on God's part to remove by something that we can do. He is reconciled to sinners. He is the sinner's friend. His gift of Christ proves this. And the work of Christ on earth completed the salvation of man in so far as that salvation is without, not within, the sinner. But our personal salvation is also the renovation of our moral nature by the action of God's love as seen in Christ. And that salvation cannot begin within a man until his mind lays hold of the glorious facts without him relating to Christ, that become his salvation. The saving object held up to our faith is "God in Christ reconciling the world unto Himself." Not something for us to do for salvation, but something for us to believe and accept, and rest on as done, Christ's own finished and God-accepted work. For the man who takes God at His own word in this matter, who honestly and cordially believes that God speaks the truth when He says that He "was in Christ reconciling the world unto Himself," and that the man addressed is the sinner who needs the blood of reconciliation, that man shall not perish. And the reason is a good reason. For if any man really believes that God means such a free salvation for him, and that he needs this very salvation, he must, he surely will, entreat God on his bended knees for it. It never fails to be so. Every such man asks. And if he ask salvation for Christ's sake, the word of God is pledged that he shall receive it. Nay, a present salvation is a Christ-offered, Christ-urged blessing, that the sinner has only to put out his hand and take. For Jesus says: "Come unto me all ye that labour and are heavy laden, and I will give you rest." "Him that cometh unto me I will in nowise cast out. "Take my yoke upon you, and learn of me....and ye shall find rest unto your souls."

So that those who believe on the Son of God shall not perish, because they lay hold of the divine appointment that has been made for their salvation. They obtain the Lord Jesus Christ as their mediator and representative. And thus they are dealt with by God, not as they sinners deserve, but as Christ, the righteous one, deserves. He was no sinner, although He was treated in many ways as if He had been one while He stood in the room of sinners. And sinners, too, when they are "found in Him," are not counted to be sinners in the eye of the law. And not being counted sinners, there is no cause why they should perish.

Nor is this present exemption from condemnation all the salvation that believers on Christ obtain. For He, their representative and head, raised " far above all rule, and authority, and power, and dominion, and every name that is named, not only in this world, but also in that which is to come," now lives in Heaven, renowned and honoured, and glorified. And believers on Him being still treated not as they themselves deserve, but as He, the Holy one of God, deserves, shall also, like Him, and with Him, live for ever renowned, and honoured, and glorified. God's favour on earth, and a seat among the redeemed in Heaven, and the sunshine of His gracious countenance for ever, are theirs because they are Christ's. For the Father who loves the Son because He lays down His life for us, deems the bestowal of such a reward on Christ's redeemed people as Heaven with all its blessings, as only a fitting expression of His own approbation of His Son's person and work. This is the eternal life of which our text speaks: to be like Christ now and to be with Him anon.

Come, then. to Christ all of you who have not already come. For there is here in Him provision for the necessities of sinners plenty and to spare. Many have already come to Jesus, and still there is room; and room for you my fellow sinner. Yes! there is room in the love of God, there is room in the work of Christ, there is room in the offers of mercy, and there is room in the mansions of glory for you, and for us all, my fellow sinners. "The blood of Jesus, God's Son, cleanseth us from all sin."

Why should any one delay in coming to Jesus? What more would you have from God, my fellow sinners, in order to win you back to Him? Would you have a greater gift than Christ? That is impossible. Heaven could not have furnished that; Heaven cannot now furnish that. The God of all grace has not a greater gift to give us than Christ. God has already given His best and greatest gift for man, and to man.

Know then, my fellow sinner, that if this gift of God, offered us in the text, do not win you back to Him, even the rich treasury of Heaven is too poor to purchase your allegiance. For God when He gave Christ for man, gave His unspeakable gift, His best, His richest gift.

What more, then, would you have, fellow sinner? Do you ask a greater display of love to man by God? That also is impossible. I challenge you to conceive of, and to name anything that would have been, or would now be, a stronger proof that God loves men than what He has done! For " greater love hath no man than this: that a man lay

E

down his life for his friends." But "God commendeth His own love toward us, in that while we were yet sinners Christ died for us." And now "there remaineth no more a sacrifice for sins." God's provision is made and offered us. Christ's work is finished and ready for our acceptance.

Why, then, oh why should any here trifle with and neglect this great salvation? Why should any remain unmoved by this matchless display of God's love? We shall not, my hearers, and cannot always remain so. Not one of us. Only for a little time shall any of us remain uninterested in the salvation of Christ the Saviour. Look with the eye of the mind at yonder Cross, that was once erected upon Calvary. Behold the suffering Son of God dying upon that Cross for sinners.

You have often read and heard of that Cross of pain, and shame, and glory. It has pictured itself upon your mind. And you can not only call it up when you please, but you cannot always forget it even if you should wish to do so. For we can never efface a thing from our memory by a mere act of will. That crucified Saviour will remain with you throughout eternity, ever in your view. In bliss, as the main source of your bliss, or in woe to agonize your spirit. For no redeemed spirit forgets the Cross of Christ. No other theme so moves and interests Heaven as that. Its myriad hosts ever praise the Lamb which was slain for us. And no gospel despiser, now lost, can forget that he has ruined himself by trifling with the crucified one and His work. None of us can forget, or feel uninterested in the Cross, therefore, so soon as we have burst the thin veil of time and entered eternity. How deeply important to us, then, is the truth of Christ that raises the believer to Heaven! How momentous is the present choice that we are making! If wrong it may sink us to endless, helpless, hopeless ruin. While the present choice of Christ as our Saviour will one day leave us redeemed spirits around the throne of God. Just as the rejection of Christ now will one day sink us to be companions of all the lost and miserable. "For he that believeth and is baptized shall be saved; but he that disbelieveth shall be condemned."

V.

THE GREAT BURDEN-BEARER.

FIRST SERMON.

"Come unto Me, all ye that labour and are heavy laden, and I will give you rest. Take my yoke upon you, and learn of me ; for I am meek and lowly in heart : and ye shall find rest unto your souls. For my yoke is easy, and my burden is light."—MAT. XI., 28-30.

"NEVER man so spake," was the touching and truthful reply of the wondering Officers of the Sanhedrim, who had been sent to take Jesus, to the reproachful inquiry of their superiors, "Why did ye not bring Him?"

This was surely a strange answer from the men who returned it. And it forms a clear testimony in favour of Christ's own claims, as those that could be made by no other man. This is a testimony to Jesus, emanating from an unlikely quarter in unlikely circumstances. For, if ignorant and hardened inferior officers of justice, who were sent by their superiors with the plain order to seize and secure this man as a criminal, dared to *not* do it, but felt a strange spell about the words of wisdom, purity, grace, and truth that fell from His lips, surely no honest, earnest truth-seeker required to have been at any loss to discover in Jesus of Nazareth " the Christ, the Son of the living God," " of a truth the prophet that cometh into the world."

"Never man so spake," most true! Because never man besides Christ was anything else, or anything more than man: and mere men have ever spoken and acted like mere men. The greatest developments of human wisdom, power, and goodness which the world ever saw have borne so distinctly the stamp of a human origin and measure, that though men may wonder at the things done and taught, and learn much from them, they at once recognize their origin to be human, and find themselves able, not only to learn the lesson taught, and to master the discovery made, but very soon to improve and perfect them.

The world makes advancement in knowledge and in its applications, by the scholar learning all that the master knew, and then making further discoveries for himself.

Some men, it is true, have taken a giant's stride before their kind, and have left all other men a generation or two behind them; but all the difference between them and others has been that a longer interval was required, or a very remarkable man was needed, before anyone else was able to advance beyond them. Still, sooner or later, that time comes, that man arises, and that advance takes place.

No human inventor has discovered all that could be known even about his own invention. No human author has composed a book to serve the world for ever upon the subject of it; so that men should never require another upon the same subject. But our Lord Jesus Christ has produced a completed discovery. He is the author of salvation. He is the discoverer of a perfect remedy for man's spiritual ruin. For the gospel proclaims a perfect and complete plan; yes, a most divine invention for bringing rebel man back to God, and one that cannot be improved upon by the united wisdom of the world. The gospel tells us of a glorious plan of salvation that has come from the hand and from the heart of its great maker, with the clear stamp of the divine workmanship upon it. It is a plan whose divine simplicity has never been amended, but always marred and disfigured by human emendations. We serve it best by seeking to see it, and to set it forth as it is. And as of the gospel message, so of the whole Bible. For God has also composed a book to serve the world for ever on its subject. For it is He who, in the highest sense, is the author of the Bible. A book commencing in so remote an antiquity that the voracious devourer, time, has entombed all man's mental productions of a like date with its remoter records; while Holy Scripture has come down to us unchanged and unimproved. Nay, in so far as what was the very writing of inspired men has been changed at all, it has only been defaced by human mistakes; though we have many reasons for believing that they, happily, are few and far between. But, though the Bible that came from the thoughts and hands of inspired men be unchanged and unimproved; yet it clearly proves itself to be the Book of God, by continuing to 'give light to every age, and borrowing from none.' And the Bible is now as suitable for man as ever it was. It is alike fitted for the meridian both of civilization and of barbarism. For no human intelligence rises above the need of the Bible, and no ignorance sinks below its all-embracing and uplifting grasp.

The teacher who in this sacred book, and in this gracious passage, condescends to instruct us, has been superseded by no pupil. And this is so, because He is the Son of Man and the Son of God in one person; and His sayings are the joint product of the wonderful connection between divinity and humanity. And such sayings, coming from Christ, can only be explained by admitting His divinity as well as His humanity. For if Christ had been only a great human prophet—no matter how great—His personal claims and assumptions would have been most derogatory to the claims of God, the divine Father. Such as when he says: "I and the Father are one." "The Father loveth the Son, and hath given all things into His hand." "For as the Father raiseth the dead and quickeneth them, even so the Son also quickeneth whom He will." "The Father is in Me, and I in the Father." And as in our context where Jesus says: "Neither doth any know the Father save the Son, and He to whomsoever the Son willeth to reveal Him."

If in truth, after saying all this, Christ was only a mere human prophet, no true prophet was ever so unfaithful to the God who commissioned and sent him as was the prophet of Nazareth! For, He said of Himself: "The Son of Man hath power upon earth to forgive sins." And, again, "He that hath seen Me hath seen the Father."

And that Christ's personal claims, though they were the

greatest that He could make, were not viewed by God as unwarranted and blasphemous assumptions, every single miracle wrought by Him attests. For of each of them we may say, what the magicians of Egypt owned of one of the miracles wrought by Moses: "This is the Finger of God."

How much more does the unbroken chain of miracles that was interwoven into Christ's whole life and history, beginning with His conception, which was miraculous, and ending with his ascent into Heaven, which was also miraculous, form God's own direct testimony to Christ and to His claims. Each single miracle wrought by Jesus in His own name, and by His own power, forming a God-given, guiding star to lead the sincere seeker of Him, who was born King of the Jews, to find Him, the world's deliverer, and the King of Men, as the Star of Bethlehem did the " wise men from the East," in Jesus of Nazareth, the speaker of our text.

As both God and man, Jesus speaks in this verse. And so viewed, the text is one of the largest and most encouraging promises contained in the Word of God. In truth this is a promise that would not be over-estimated, but only rightly understood and appreciated, did the face become habitually bright, and the heart lastingly glad, of every one whose eye has scanned the New Testament page, and seen this utterance; or upon whose ear the sweet sound of this rich gospel-promise has fallen.

Yet mild and alluring as the invitation and the promise of our text are, in the mouth of the God-man mediator, Christ Jesus, the words would form in the mouth of any mere man only a grossly ignorant, or else a presumptuously arrogant boast, and would thus be a cruel mockery of, instead of a strong consolation to human misery.

In order to see the truth of this more fully, mark how much the words of the text promise! The gracious words, "Come unto Me, all ye that labour and are heavy laden," addressed to fallen, burdened, weak and suffering humanity, on whose toil and travail, misery and trouble, vanity and vexation of spirit, the orb of day completes his daily revolution, nor shines on a land that is exempted from such toil and trouble, and hardly on an exempted family, or heart; with the sublimely audacious addition put to the words, "and I will give you rest"—could only have been so uttered as a cheering reality by Him who, having all fulness and all healing virtue residing in Himself, had measured man's deep necessities and was competent to supply them, had probed man's deadly wound, and knew its cure to be in Himself, the sent of the Father.

A human mouth, it is true, spoke the boldly gracious words of our text; but in the case of Christ a human form veiled glory ineffable, purity immaculate, and power infinite.

So that though these words, "Come unto Me, all ye that labour and are heavy laden, and I will give you rest," be not fitting for the mouth of a mere man to utter, they well become the actual speaker, "He that hath the key of David," "the child born unto us, the Son given, who has the government upon His shoulder, His name Wonderful Counsellor, Mighty God, Everlasting Father, Prince of Peace." For He is "Immanuel, God with us." He is "The Lamb of God which taketh away the sin of the world;" "a Lamb without blemish and without spot;" "the Lamb that hath been slain from the foundation of the world,"

But clear as were the proofs of the Messiahship of Jesus, the Jews generally remained unimpressed and unconvinced by them, and by Him. And in the chapter containing our text Christ exposes their insincerity, and the culpability of that state of heart which produced their unbelief. The proof of that insincerity which is here urged Christ finds in their alike bad treatment of both His forerunner, John the Baptist, and Himself. John's Heaven-taught nonconformity, and Christ's condescending conformity to their ordinary habits and modes of life, as to food and clothing, and familiar intercourse, though opposite courses were both, in the Jewish nomenclature of the day, offences against God.

John's Elijah-like devotedness, self-denial, significant singularity, and asceticism, formed the shallow stocks on which they ingrafted their base insinuations of demoniacal possession. John, Nazarite-like, came "eating no bread nor drinking wine;" and they said, "He hath a devil." He is dangerous; he eats too little and he thinks too much. Shakespeare makes Julius Cæsar say to Antony of Cassius in something of the same spirit of fear and hate:

> "Let me have men about me that are fat;
> Sleek-headed men, and such as sleep o' nights:
> Yond' Cassius has a lean and hungry look;
> He thinks too much: such men are dangerous."

So the chiefs of the Jews feared and stigmatised John's abstemious, unworldly habits of life.

But they used our Lord no better, though He acted very differently. For Christ's familiar, and not singular habits of life, in eating and drinking, and mixing freely with common, and even with sinful men, formed the ill-laid foundation for their base inuendo that he was guilty of excess in eating and drinking, and that he associated with corrupt and vicious society, for the purpose of the better indulging in those appetites. "The Son of Man came eating and drinking, and they say: Behold a gluttonous man, and a wine-bibber, a friend of publicans and sinners." And again, "And the Pharisees and the Scribes murmured, saying: This man receiveth sinners, and eateth with them."

That is: "See who His associates are; the man must be like his company." But they did not understand, or they forgot that for the Physician of Souls to be found among the sin-sick, no more proves a personal preference for bad people than does the physician's passing by, in his daily rounds, the doors of the healthy and happy, and entering the doors of the sick and suffering, prove his personal preference for the company of the sick over the well, and the disease-laden chamber over the healthy home. The Physician's glorious battle field, where He the professionally-armed enemy of disease wins His victories over it, is the sick-room: and so is the sinner's side and the sinner's heart the Saviour's field of glorious victory. Christ in our context adores the Father's procedure in concealing from those wise and understanding ones, those insincere cavillers at God's revelations, the all-important discoveries which He has revealed to babes, to the meek and teachable, thereby "destroying the wisdom of the wise, and rejecting the prudence of the prudent," "that no flesh should glory before God." From which Christ is led to speak of the opposite spirit from that which is entertained by the wise and understanding, a meek and lowly spirit, as being that to which alone God gives grace. And He introduces Himself as being the matchless and perfect development of this lowly spirit, and thus as being He who alone can teach us how to approach God acceptably. To this spirit alone God will bow, and in it alone can the Kingdom of Heaven be entered. To have this spirit is to find favour of the Lord; to know Christ is to learn it; and from Him alone it can be learnt. How suitable, then, and how practically important, is the invitation of Christ, "Come unto Me!" "I am your way unto the Father. I will remove your heavy burden of sin and trouble, and give you rest. Not by giving you no burden to bear, but by giving you a delightful exchange. Lay down your heavy burden of sin, and guilt, and sorrow, and take up my light and easy yoke of love and obedience, and learn of me." But do it now. There must be no lapse of time between closing the old service of sin, and opening the new service of Christ. For man can never be independent. He must always have a master. And he cannot serve two masters. The text naturally divides itself into the following topics, only the first of which I shall treat this morning :

    I.—The *state* of those who are here addressed by our Lord.

    II.—The *invitation* which is given them by Christ.

III.—The *promise* which He makes to those who come to Him, especially in so far as it finds its fulfilment now!

IV.—The *contrasted yokes* and *burdens* of which our text speaks.

V.—The *qualifications* of Him who invites and promises, for the fulfilment of what He undertakes.

VI.—The *companionship* that may be enjoyed by Christians in all their labours.

You see that we have here before us an almost inexhaustible text, which I cannot see any good reason for attempting to hurry over in a single discourse.

I.—Notice first, then, the state or condition of those who are here addressed by our Lord. And to this one point I confine our attention now. He speaks to them in these terms: "Come unto Me, all ye that labour and are heavy laden." He to whom all things have been delivered, here addresses and calls to Him, not those that are "at ease in Sion," but the toil-worn and heavy laden. Not the well-off and full, but them that hunger and thirst. Not the rich and increased with goods, who have need of nothing, but the wretched and miserable, and poor, and blind, and naked. Christ addresses and invites more especially all who know themselves to be what they are, weary and heavy laden sinners. For we have in these words man's real state by nature described. But the class more especially denoted by those "that labour and are heavy laden" are the consciously exhausted and spent, those who are sensibly pressed down by their various burdens, and can bear them no longer.

And all men as sinners, and in some degree sufferers from the effects of sin, are to a greater or lesser extent actually weary and heavy laden. All men are more or less labouring and dejected under the yoke of sin and vanity, of waste and death. And so far, the invitation of our text is to all; but, as I have said, it is especially addressed to those who know and feel their state to be such.

Those who are here addressed are sinners in their unconverted state; and the burden of which our text speaks is threefold.

The first part of the burden was somewhat peculiar to those whom our Lord here directly and immediately addressed. It was the burden of the moral and ceremonial law; that yoke and burden of which Peter, speaking to his Jewish brethren, says, " A yoke.... which neither our fathers nor we were able to bear." Even the law which God imposed on Israel, just as He imposed it, and meant it to be observed, was, with all its wearisome and hard observances of worship and service, a heavy burden. "So that the law hath been our tutor to bring us unto Christ." And the law was so hard a task-master as to make all earnest souls who really tried to keep it, often long and sigh for the coming of Him who was 'to bring in a better hope.'

And this yoke, which God had Himself imposed, was made much heavier by the additions and perversions of the Scribes and Pharisees. For Christ said of these men: " Yea, they bind heavy burdens, and grievous to be borne, and lay them on men's shoulders." *They*, not God, did this. And to all who were crushed and bowed down under this daily load of ceremonialism, Christ in our text addresses Himself and offers relief. And to many a pious Jew, oh! how welcome must Christ and His salvation, with their spiritual inwardness, have been in place of the manifold rites and ceremonies of the actual Judaism of Christ's day. And to all here who have no better religion than a round of wearisome, because heartless forms, Christ addresses Himself still, and offers real relief, true rest for the soul.

Man's great burden, however, is sin, as we shall immediately see. But in the meantime, and as the second part of the burden here meant, Christ in these words by no means excludes those who are burdened and miserable through physical disorders, and all other kinds of earthly unhappiness. Nothing human is foreign to the sympathy and aid of Christ. So that our text does not speak of the burden of sin alone, though it speaks of that mainly; but it speaks also of all sin's indirect effects. It speaks of all the things that, by reason of the entrance of sin into the world, make this life toilsome, and burdensome, and sorrowful to mankind. Such as bodily disease, both personal and relative, poverty, overwork, disappointments of all kinds, family trials, the separation of friends by death, or otherwise, and trials and afflictions in general. And in brief all that large class of evils that has followed the entrance of sin into the world, and that makes us in this tabernacle to groan, being burdened. Christ feels for all sorrow, and can help all. In a word, Christ here addresses all the sorrowful in heart. And though He does not in every case remove these burdens entirely in this life, He invites all such to come to Him, and He causes even the weary on these accounts to enter into immediate and comparative rest, as we shall see. For the rest in the soul, which Christ bestows on all who come to Him makes all yokes easy, and all burdens light, even now, and here; and it grows into final and eternal rest. But Christ mainly addresses those who are burdened with the yoke of sin. For the dominion of sin, and its direct consequences, form the great elements of the burden of which our text speaks. The real burden of humanity, my hearers, is sin. It is the disquietude of an evil conscience, awaked by sin, and not yet calmed by the atonement of Christ.

In ten thousand ways, in all men everywhere, does this burden make itself not only felt but grievous. Yes, the most of the heavy burden under which the natural man labours is sin. And the burden of sin consists of two main parts: the sense of guilt on the conscience, and also the reigning power of sin in the heart. Or, in other words, the sinner's burden consists in the present effects of the moral plague, sin, in shutting him out of God's presence, a felt alienation from God that leaves him wretched. And his burden consists also in the process of moral defilement, decay, and degradation that is ever going on within the unrenewed. Or, to use different phraseology still, the burden of sin consists in the weight of a holy law broken and demanding vengeance, crushing the sinner down with an overwhelming fear, as its first part. And the second part of the burden of sin is gratified evil propensities, "crying like the two daughters of the horse-leach, give,

give;" and asking ever the more vehemently the oftener that they are gratified.

This is the sinner's burden; and all by nature have it. And what is more pressingly to our present purpose, all of us here present, from whom Christ has not already removed the burden of guilt and reigning sin, still bear the grievous load.

This universal necessity existing in man's whole nature and circumstances for a redemption from spiritual bondage and misery, is to be seen developing itself in the whole history of the race. Unconverted men in all ages, and amid every variety of circumstances, have been ill at ease in their higher relations, consciously "sowing the wind and reaping the whirlwind." What discontent has there been in the world! A discontent too deep for anything earthly to remove. What revolutions have there been! What wars! What struggles of ambition! What excessive straining after wealth, and honour, and pleasure, and peace, and friendship, and love, or some other unfound good that was to heal all the world's woes, and remove all men's burdens. But men of the world have never agreed on what this unfound good is, much less have they found it. "Many there be that say: Who will show us any good?" This is still the eager cry of the world. For men, as men have been, and still are, burdened and toil-worn. And are often ready to cry out: "Vanity of vanities, all is vanity. What profit hath a man of all his labour, wherein he laboureth under the sun?"

Scripture testimony is explicit to the same effect as general history. The alienated from God are not happy.

"The wicked are like the troubled sea, for it cannot rest." "There is no peace, saith My God, to the wicked." "Man is born unto trouble, as the sparks fly upward." "Man that is born of a woman is of few days, and full of trouble." "The wicked travaileth with pain all his days."

Having thus spoken of the testimony of history and of Scripture as sources of evidence of man's burdened condition, I would direct your attention to another source of evidence, our own consciousness, that I may, if possible, rivet your attention the more closely upon the investigation, and that we may each for ourselves conduct it the more personally.

Have you, my hearers, not discovered anything in yourselves to confirm the testimony of history and of Scripture, that you are burdened and heavy laden sinners?

If you have no humbling conviction of alienation from God as your sin, as something that you ought to be sorry for: yet do you meet with none of its effects as a curse and plague, and a destruction of your peace of mind? If you plead innocence of the crime of rebellion against God, whence come its effects? Whence comes the brand of unhappiness with which you are stamped? How has the God-given fountain of joy, with which He always accompanies existence, become dried up within you?

If you are not sinners, how are you sufferers? If you are not sufferers, then you must be like all the other creatures of God, completely happy. Look around you, and even downward upon the inferior animals, and you will perceive every creature to be all that it wishes to be, and enjoying itself to its utmost desire, unless when the cruelty of man, or of some fellow, mars its enjoyments.

And where is the natural man who can honestly and truthfully say this of himself?

You, my unconverted hearers, are not satisfied to the full with your enjoyments. Is it not so? Hence your strange unsettledness of mind, your endless craving after something which you have never yet found. Something which change of place, and of circumstances, and of pursuits has often promised you: but the promise you found to be a mockery, and the pursuit only vanity. There is a deep-seated disease within the soul of man for which no clime of earth grows a cure. Its only balm is in the celestial Gilead, and its sole physician of value, is there in the Canaan above. We all need the rest and healing of my text; the rest and healing of the soul that come only from Christ.

What say you to man's state? How are we thus by nature? Has God made us, the crown of this lower creation, to be miserable, and all His other creatures to be happy? We dare not entertain the ungenerous thought. God made all His creatures happy, and fitted for remaining so.

Does it follow, from our high elevation above the brute creation, that we must be miserable? Is it no precious gift, but rather a curse, to be endowed with the high prerogatives of conscience, reason, and immortality?

Such suppositions would be greatly derogatory to the character and power of God. For they would contain the assumption that He, the great Creator, in making man, had made a being with necessities for his happiness greater than the power and bounty of God could supply; and who is miserable, therefore, not from himself, but because God is too poor to fill him with real joy. No! this thought is monstrous, and degrading to God. The real explanation of man's condition cannot be found in such a view of his relations to God. For God is infinite in power and in goodness. And since He is so, "in His presence is fulness of joy; in His right hand there are pleasures for evermore." Every creature that remains as God made it is not only "very good," but happy. It is so throughout creation, from the insects that sport their short day in the sun, to the mighty, everlasting arch-angels before God's throne, "His ministers that do His pleasure."

In truth, the cause of our misery is in ourselves, not in God. We have fallen from our first estate. We are sinners, and therefore burdened with a load of guilt on the conscience. For God has linked sin and suffering together in eternal and indissoluble union. This is why man is burdened and heavy laden.

The moral laws of God are immutable, and their penalties cannot be avoided.

Is not this your experience, unpardoned sinner, if I speak to one? Does not your sin bring with it suffering? Why can you not enjoy yourself as fully in the ways of the world and of sin as you could wish, and at the same time feel and realize the claims of the divine law which you have broken, and meet the all-seeing gaze of the holy, and sin-hating God, whom you have justly offended?

The world with all its delights is now before you. You may " walk in the ways of thine heart, and in the sight of thine eyes." The ordinary rule of God's procedure with men upon the earth, is that " sentence against an evil work is not executed speedily."

The hand of God is not now laid upon you to punish your sin, as it will soon be laid upon all the persistent workers of iniquity. Why are you not more happy, ye who love the world and live for it? What hinders your full enjoyment of the ways of sin? And yet you know that you do not, and cannot, reap real bliss from these wicked ways.

What is the inevitable inference from your past and present experience? It is, without doubt, that you are in a course that permits no true enjoyment, because of what that course is in itself, and also permits none to you because of what you are. A course of sin will not yield you joy, because you carry with you a deep consciousness that you are wrong, and that the end of these things is death. You have a consciousness of being wrong, and of doing wrong, that itself becomes an open confession to God.

Since for anything to be is to be known to Him. For anything to have an existence is to lie fully disclosed in the light of His countenance. There is no pretence avails in the presence of God. What only seems to be, or pretends to be, is nothing to Him. But He sees every reality in the life and soul of man, as in the whole universe. He reads the unexpressed language of the heart, before it has been formed into words.

This whispering of the sinner's conscience, that all will not be well in the end if he go on, forms a large part of his burden.

Are some of you, my hearers, not sometimes afraid that all is not well with you for eternity, when you reflect on the actual past of your life, and think of the possible future?

Well, God can read and interpret that incipient dread. For there is no need for fear unless you are in a wrong way. It is unmanly and weak to be afraid unless there be a sufficient cause for fear. But in this case there is: and you know it. To be afraid of the future is to confess to God that there is a reality and an importance in religion, which your ordinary conduct in the world denies to it. A time will come when the secrets of all hearts shall be made manifest; when all the secret convictions of the present shall be the open evidence of the future. And it will then be seen that at present you are not conscientious in the ways of sin, but are foolish enough to go on, knowing, or suspecting, all the time that you are wrong. If conscience now makes you afraid when you think of your sins, what will you do at death, and in the day of judgment, unless you now obtain forgiveness through Christ? "If Thou hast run with the footmen, and they have wearied thee, then how canst thou contend with horses? And though in a land of peace thou art secure, yet how wilt thou do in the pride of Jordan?"

But I have already referred to man's burden as also in part consisting of the fruits of sin in the life.

When unfallen beings, of whatever order, follow the

promptings of their pure and perfect natures, and gratify the desires which God has implanted in them, they find and fulfil the high end of their being, they reach all that God made them for; since that sinless nature which they thus gratify ever gravitates towards infinite goodness as its centre of attraction. But with man, on earth, it is far otherwise. In him there is a moral disorder and disorganization, so strange, that as a rule he rises in moral excellence, not as he indulges and gratifies his own nature; but as he sacrifices and denies himself.

If we, my hearers, would rise from sin to holiness, we must often oppose and struggle against ourselves. We must "put away....the old man which waxeth corrupt after the lusts of deceit," and * * * be renewed in the spirit of our mind, and put on the new man, which, after God, hath been created in righteousness and holiness of truth."

For we must remember that there is no lasting peace without purity. "First pure, then peaceable." Every holy desire, in so far as it is gratified, gives peace and satisfaction. But what proves that man was never made to gratify sinful desires, appetites, and passions, is that the more they are gratified and indulged, the farther from peace and happiness the sinner has gone. For to gratify a sinful desire is only to apply a stimulant to an inflammatory disease.

And now we may well ask: "What shall a world of sinners in so sad a state by nature and practice do?" "And what shall the individual sinner do to be rid of this

his so great a burden?" "Come unto Me," says Jesus Christ." "This do, and thou shalt live."

The sense of suffering in man, while he remains beneath the yoke of sin, largely emanates from the remnants of what is divine, that are yet found dwelling in our humanity. The utterly ungodly, though they really bear about with them the burden of unforgiven sin, often feel it but little. But he who feels the burden of sin to be really painful is in a measure prepared to welcome deliverance. For "they that are whole have no need of a physician, but they that are sick."

When the law, and the world, and the flesh, and sin, have so long and so grievously burdened the soul that the man on whom the burden rests is brought to confess and mourn over his state, and to despair of deliverance in his own strength, then Christ's gracious invitation, "Come unto Me," becomes truly welcome.

We find an example of the consciously burdened sinner in the words: "I have surely heard Ephraim bemoaning himself thus: Thou hast chastised me, and I was chastised, as a calf unaccustomed to the yoke; turn thou me, and I shall be turned; for thou art the Lord my God." And also in the prodigal son, when he came to himself, and said: "How many hired servants of my father's have bread enough and to spare, and I perish here with hunger!" And in the publican, who "standing afar off, would not lift up so much as his eyes unto Heaven, but smote his breast, saying, 'God, be merciful to me, a sinner.'"

And in Peter's hearers at Pentecost, who "were pricked in their hearts, and said unto Peter and the rest of the Apostles, 'Brethren, what shall we do?'" And in the case of the Philippian jailor, when he said, "Sirs, what must I do to be saved?"

And to those who feel thus is our Lord's invitation specially addressed; and to that invitation I shall direct your attention in the next discourse.

VI.

THE GREAT BURDEN-BEARER.

SECOND SERMON.

> "Come unto Me, all ye that labour and are heavy laden, and I will give you rest. Take my yoke upon you, and learn of me; for I am meek and lowly in heart: and ye shall find rest unto your souls. For my yoke is easy, and my burden is light."—MAT. XI., 28-30.

IN last discourse I brought before you some introductory remarks on the speaker and the context; and, firstly, I showed the state of those who are here addressed. And now,

II.—Secondly, the gracious invitation which is given by Christ to all who are in the sad state already described, next claims our attention. Jesus says to all such, "Come unto Me," which means the same thing as "Believe on Me." For we can only come to God, and to Christ, by faith. "And without faith it is impossible to be well-pleasing unto Him: for he that cometh to God must believe that He is, and that He is a rewarder of them that seek after Him."

Nor is the gracious and inviting "come" of our text a single, or an uncommon expression. For we read: "Ho, every one that thirsteth, come ye to the waters, and he that hath no money; come ye, buy, and eat; yea come, buy wine and milk without money and without price." And so does this kind of language in substance and spirit pervade the Bible, and is ever in the mouth of God's servants. As, "We are journeying unto the place of which the Lord said: I will give it you; come thou with us, and we will do thee good: for the Lord hath spoken good concerning Israel." And in the Book of Revelation, "the spirit and the bride say, come." And here in our text the Lamb Himself says, "come," and leaves the loving word on the page of divine revelation as a standing invitation from age to age, to us and to all.

"Come unto Me," says Jesus; cast away all your fancied worth, wisdom, and prudence, and confess your sin and folly: confess that sin has mastered you, and without a Saviour from its guilt and power, will ruin you. Come you thus, my hearers, and be free. For Christ requires nothing as the condition of all His divine gifts; absolutely nothing but coming to Him, and taking them from His hand. He says to the Jews, " come," ' wait no longer for another Messiah. You wait in vain.' He says to the Gentile sinner: " Come," ' come from slavery to freedom, from misery to happiness, from the service of satan to my service, from all other objects to me, as the portion of your souls, as the bearer of your burdens.'

On this invitation, " Come unto Me," I will notice more in detail.

First, its condescension. Christ assumed human nature mainly that He, the Saviour of Sinners, might have the materials of a sacrifice for sin. Yet, not for that purpose only, but also to show what human nature ought to be, and to place before the genuine aspirant after holiness one real life free from all the taints and weaknesses that had in every case marred human virtue in her holiest sons.

Nor did our Lord give a cold and distant patronage to human nature when he appeared on earth; but, on the contrary, He came quite down to humanity, and clothed Himself completely in it. Nor did the divine in Christ repress the development of the human in all its sinless completeness. He was a complete man; and He felt and acted as a real man among other men. He went among them. He saw with His own eyes their individual cases of need, and administered cures, both to soul and body, in person.

There was in Him dignity unequalled. He could with a word and a look awe the mightiest of those proud questioners, who came to entrap Him in His speech, so that the most boastful and imperious "durst ask him no more questions." But there was in Him so great condescension withal, not only in humbling Himself to become man, but as a man among other men while on earth—that the illiterate, the humble, the lowly, the timid, and the sorrowful were not awed into distance by Him. The humblest found Him easy of access as a benefactor and friend, and easily understood as a teacher of religion. In His private intercourse He received sinners; and in His public ministrations the common people heard Him gladly.

There is great condescension shown by Jesus Christ in using the very terms here employed. For the language is that of easy, friendly familiarity.

He who here speaks to us, says: " Come unto Me; " and this, the condescension of Christ, is to be imitated as well as admired. For it is part of the mind of Christ that ought to dwell also in His people. Too many of man's gifts to man are given with the tongs, and too few with the hand; too many with the hand only, and too few with the heart. It is kindly intercourse, and friendly familiarity among men, that interest them in each other, and bind them together in the bonds of a genuine brotherhood. Man's best gift to man is unaffected sympathy, expressed in needed help. He who should say to us, we being in need and distress, " go, and I will think of your circumstances," would deserve our grateful thanks; but He who, showing a personal interest in us, says: " Come to me, and I will hold a personal interview with you concerning them," deserves to gain our heart. And so Christ here speaks. What infinite condescension in Him to us!

Secondly, notice again the compassionateness of the invitation as seen in the class invited, as well as in the words spoken, and in the blessings offered.

" Come ye that labour, and are heavy laden," says Jesus. Yes, come all. Come all ye who are sinful, sad, and suffering. How grandly strange is this utterance! Men in general shun the miserable, because they are selfish, and do not like their own enjoyments to be broken in upon by the sorrows of others. But this is not all. For many others often shun misery and sorrow because they are weak and helpless in its presence. A human arm is short, and powerless. " For each man shall bear his own burden." And even an unselfish man would oftentimes fain escape from the view of a misery which he cannot remove, and yet feels for. But neither of those obstacles interposes itself between Christ and the wretched. In Christ, in place of human selfishness, there is divine benevolence; in place of man's weakness there is God's power. And thus, instead of shunning the miserable, or keeping them at a distance from Him, He, unlike all besides, would draw all such around Him, of all classes, and characters, and circumstances, with all their woes and burdens. And He, the great burden-bearer of humanity, unappalled by the awful weight of that solemn concentration of guilt and misery that is sinking a world, and world's hopes to the gloom of eternal night, promises to stop this dreadful descent of the perishing, and to lift off all their burdens, that they may stand erect in liberty, and be raised on the wings of hope. Christ, the divine Redeemer, promises all who come to Him that He will change their groans of misery into songs of praise; promises "to appoint unto them that mourn in Zion * * * a garland for ashes, the oil of joy for mourning, the garment of praise for the spirit of heaviness."

This invitation of Christ to come to Him is further compassionate, because He is Himself our only way unto the Father. "And in none other is there salvation; for neither is there any other name under Heaven that is given among men, wherein we must be saved."

There is no other spot in the universe where God, the law-giver, and man, the sinner, can meet together without the sinner's just condemnation following, but at the Cross of Christ: "Whom God set forth to be a propitiation * * to show His righteousness * * that He might Himself be just, and the justifier of him who hath faith in Jesus." Christ and His cross are our true refuge. At a distance from Christ there is no hope for sinners. To ask us to come to Himself is to ask us into the ark of safety, where alone we can meet the Holy God, and be, not condemned, but justified. For Christ to ask us to Himself is indeed compassionate; for He is the "only mediator between God and man." He is the "daysman betwixt us," that lays "His hand upon us both," and makes lasting peace between God, the law-giver, and man, the law breaker. And He has done it, fellow sinner; and because He has done it, He graciously says, "Come unto Me."

And what can be more compassionate than this invitation, since man cannot lift off his own burden; since no fellow man can do it; since Christ Himself alone can do this?

Our Lord displays the same spirit here as we find already recorded in the words: "But when He saw the multitudes, He was moved with compassion for them, because they were distressed and scattered, as sheep not having a shepherd." And in this spirit of compassion He says: "Come unto Me."

Thirdly, notice again the comprehensiveness, the universality, of the invitation. It is, "Come unto Me all ye that labour and are heavy laden." Come not a few, or many, but all. For all men do by nature, knowingly or unknowingly, labour under the grievous load of sin, and its effects, as we saw in the former sermon. And the invitation of Christ here given goes, not on the lower principle of man's mistaken perceptions of his own state and circumstances, but on the higher principle of Christ's perfect knowledge of them. It is therefore an invitation to all men; since all, whether they know it or not, do labour under the disease of sin, and really require the divine remedy that is offered by the great Physician of Souls.

And the comprehensiveness of the invitation is seen, not only in the persons invited, but also in the burdens removed. There is not a single exception made to any kind of burden, more than person. Come to Christ with all that weighs you down, my friends, no matter what it is. He invites you, and offers you rest from it.

Christ does not say even to the proud and self-satisfied: "Remain you at a distance from Me, and perish." But they do remain away, because they are proud and self-satisfied. For though Jesus calls all men to Him, yet His call is heard and responded to only by those who feel their burden to be heavy, and would fain be freed from it.

The invitation is to all. For the need belongs to all. But only those who feel their burden, and their need of rest, accept the invitation, and come to Christ. How is it with us? Have you all come to Christ, my dear hearers? He invites us all; and an awful responsibility rests upon us in this matter. For He who now, to all of us, mercifully and graciously says, "Come unto Me," will one day utter the awful words, "Depart from me," to all who have not come while He continued to invite them.

Take care lest any of you turn the gracious "Come" of Christ, unto an awful and final "Depart." For we must accept the gracious invitation, "Come," or we must hear the awful summons, "Depart." Which shall it be to us? We are settling that now.

III.—Thirdly: And now we shall notice the promise which is here given by Christ to those who do come to Him, especially in so far as it finds its fulfilment immediately, or even in this world. He says, "Come, and I will give you rest."

Notice first, the manner of the great promise of our text. On the manner of the promise first notice its standing, where its very opposite might have been expected. When we think of our own deserts, being, as we are, sinners against the Holy God, we see that not only might Christ have justly come into the world to judge and condemn the world; but we the more wonder, the more that we reflect upon the subject, at the display of infinite wisdom that made Christ's coming into the world possible, for any other purpose than to condemn.

And we wonder not less at the love and grace that prompted God to the execution of what His wisdom saw to be possible, even the sending of Christ " to seek and to save that which was lost."

If the soul-cheering truth that Christ, the Son of Man, has come to save us, had come from man, we must have rejected the testimony. For it was so unlikely, in view of God's character, so far as known to us, out of Christ—He who is so holy and just—and in view of man's evil deserts: that less trustworthy testimony than the word of God Himself, who cannot lie, for so astounding a fact would not, and could not, have satisfied us.

Condemnation is what the sinner, while a rebel, not only

justly deserves, but naturally expects. For this tendency of the unrenewed mind to gloomy foreboding and despair of God's mercy, a distorted gospel infusing too much of Sinai, and too little of Calvary, too much of law, and too little of love, into the character of God has often been blamed. And such one-sided teaching has been, and has no doubt had an influence in producing this unholy dread of God in some minds. But we are easily taught what is ingrained; and we are hard to teach what is against nature. No such special and occasional influence as the teaching of a too gloomy theology is sufficient to account for the effect which is general, while the alleged cause is but occasional. We see the feeling working in Cain, who lived before Calvin!

There is a deeper and more creative cause for our dark forebodings than a one-sided theology, something firmly fixed in our own nature as sinners. It is that we have a conscience. As sinners we are self-condemned by the tribunal of conscience; and therefore we antedate and dread the sentence of the Judge who sits upon a higher tribunal.

So long as we sinners have not submitted ourselves to God's righteousness, but are still looking in some way or other to ourselves for salvation, to be void of all dread of God, would not bespeak a true knowledge of the divine character, but gross ignorance. Since such a false confidence could only arise from our non-realization of the solemn fact that God, even now, holds a higher and holier, and more condemnatory tribunal on our character and conduct than our own consciences do.

This supposed self-confident indifference in God's presence would bespeak on our part, not a clearer light as to the character of God than distrustful fear would do, but a denser darkness. To mistake God's character, so far as to think of Him, and to dread Him as our enemy, is a great error. But to lose the realization of God as great, and holy, and just, and terrible to the workers of iniquity; and to feel and act in His presence as if there were no God, or else that He were the least to be heeded of all beings, is surely the greatest of all errors.

To dread God as our enemy is to disbelieve His whole character and gospel summed up in His own declaration: "As I live, saith the Lord God, I have no pleasure in the death of the wicked; but that the wicked turn from His way and live." But neither to dread nor to love God is, in fact, to disbelieve His existence altogether, and to become practical Atheists. And it is the fool who "hath said in his heart, 'There is no God.'"

Secondly: But again on the manner of the promise. We have here, you will still further observe, a free promise given unclogged with conditions. We must come to Christ, it is true; but that is a natural necessity of the case. And such necessities are different, and must be distinguished from meritorious conditions being introduced which act as barriers to keep us away from the possession of salvation. And there are none such. There is no more merit in our coming to Christ, as perishing sinners, for salvation, than there is merit in the pauper's coming abroad to seek his food from door to door, or in his putting out his hand to receive the alms that the hand of benevolence holds out to him.

Here in our text there are no exactions made, and no rigorous securities demanded. But Christ's first word is an invitation, and His next word is a promise. And with Jesus Christ words and acts ever go together. Here is rest for the soul first promised, and then bestowed on all who come and receive it from Christ.

Passing from the manner,

Notice the matter of the promise, or the promise itself, especially in so far as it finds its fulfilment in this world. The promise is rest. "Come unto Me * * and I will give you rest." 'Ye shall find rest to your souls in Me; ye who so much need the boon.'

All the toil-worn both need rest, and enjoy it, whether toil-worn in body or in soul. For "the sleep of a labouring man is sweet, whether he eat little or much," says the preacher. It is so with the wearied body. It needs and enjoys rest.

And if the heavily-burdened in soul feel their burden, and feel their need of rest, then shall they, on coming to Jesus, find in Him the needed rest for their souls. For His words, His acts, His spirit, all bring peace and rest to the troubled soul. He says to His disciples: "These things have I spoken unto you, that in Me ye may have peace." "Yes, and His blood is peace-speaking, as well as His word. Rest to the soul is promised again, to those that walk in the good way of the Lord. "Thus saith the Lord: Stand ye in the ways and see, and ask for the old paths, where is the good way, and walk therein, and ye shall find rest for your souls." And He, who in our text invites sinners to Himself, says: "I am the way, and the truth, and the life." To be found in Him, is to be found in the good way, and is thus to find rest to the soul.

And remember, my fellow-sinner, that this rest to the soul is the grand and crowning blessing of existence. It is the great need of humanity. And here in Christ it may be obtained. They who come to Jesus, seeking for rest to their souls, will assuredly find that rest in Him if they seek it truly and perseveringly.

But though all men are seeking rest to the soul in some of many ways, yet none find, elsewhere than in Christ, the rest that they need.

Those who seek the soul's rest apart from Christ, find instead of rest an ever-increasing burden of disquietude settling down upon them.

Nor can the sinner who comes not to Jesus ever find rest in any true and high sense. The most toil-worn body, that groans under the curse of excessive and exhausting toil, may look with certainty for the arrival of the evening. Even for him comes the night's repose. *He* finds rest. But not so fares the sin-burdened soul that comes not to Christ.

And, again, should the usual slumbers of the night be too short, time after time, to renew a man's exhausted energies, yet the most toil-worn son of Adam may look with assured confidence to the grave as an undisturbed place of rest for the body. Even the poor toil-worn slave at length finds rest for his body in the grave. "There the wicked cease from troubling, and there the weary be at rest. There the prisoners are at ease together; they hear not the voice of the task-master. The small and great are there; and the servant is free from his master." So is it with men, and all merely worldly burdens. Not so is it, however, with the soul that is burdened with the load of sin. From this load even the grave brings no rest. Souls lie not there. The unsaved soul ever sinks deeper and deeper under its accumulating burden of sin and guilt. The night of death will come to the soul to separate it, for a time, from the body; but not to bring to the unsaved the rest and repose of spiritual health. Only to bring the painful night of the fever-smitten patient, with its perpetual unrest, its wearisome thirst, its horrid dreams, and burning pain. And that restless night to be suddenly broken in upon by the painful and startling light of the judgement morn. And in order to escape all this present and endless unrest, the sinner absolutely needs the rest that Christ has to bestow, given him now as the growing germ of an eternal rest.

The rest that Christ gives to His people corresponds to the sinner's burden, and is threefold. First, it is the rest that comes at once by believing on Jesus. Next, it is the rest that comes growingly by taking up Christ's easy yoke, and learning of him. And it is at last the final and complete rest of Heaven.

The first instalment of Christ's promised rest is spoken of in the words: "Being therefore justified by faith, let us have peace with God through our Lord Jesus Christ." That is an immediate rest, and comes from without us.

The second element in this rest is described thus: "But the fruit of the spirit is love, joy, peace, long-suffering, kindness, goodness, faithfulness, meekness, temperance." As such holy dispositions rule the heart and life, there is an ennobling rest springs up within the heart and fills the life. And the last constituent of this rest is spoken of thus: "There remaineth, therefore, a Sabbath rest for the people of God," namely, the rest of Heaven.

And in further speaking of the *matter* of the promise, which is in one word, rest, I would speak of it as including the three elements already mentioned.

First, the immediate removal of guilt from the conscience: that is, rest. We have already spoken of this felt sense of guilt as forming a large part of the unforgiven sinner's burden. The sentence of condemnation has been passed upon him as a transgressor of the divine law. " The soul that sinneth, it shall die," is the sentence.

And so long as a clean thing cannot be brought out of an unclean, so long the sinner can never make himself deserving of a better sentence from the lips of law. And so long as desert in himself, or from another, is awanting, so long will the just sentence of his condemnation stand unrevoked. For God " is in one mind, and who can turn Him?" And His law expresses His mind about sin. The sentence of "eternal destruction from the face of the Lord" hangs over every unbelieving sinner, and its execution only waits the individual sinner's brief span of life.

But on the sinner's coming to Christ, who has 'magnified the law and made it honourable,' the sentence of condemnation is removed; or rather, the sinner so coming to

Jesus, now ceases to be an implicated party in the sentence. The sentence of condemnation stands unrevoked as before against all whom it may concern; but "there is therefore now no condemnation to them that are in Christ Jesus."

And the believer being in Christ Jesus, has peace with God, because threatenings addressed to unbelieving sinners do not refer to him in his new relation to God, and to His law.

In the eye of God, he who has come to Jesus is not now a law-breaker, but he is part of the body of Christ the great observer and vindicator of law. The new relation that I have just spoken of is the transference of the complacency which God has in Christ, the sinner's surety, to the believing sinner himself; and thus begins peace with God, " the peace of God that passeth all understanding," the rest promised in our text. This new relationship to God commences with each one when the sinner takes home God's charge against him: "Thou art the man," who hast sinned against Me, and art perishing; and when he, stripped of every creature refuge, and of every creature hope, commits himself to the gospel to stand or fall with the truth of God's promise of pardon through Christ. It is then that He enters into rest. The man who, believing himself to be the sinner that God says he is, at the same time gives a real credence to God's true testimony, that His Son Christ Jesus has made a full atonement for sin, and that God Himself, the law-giver and judge, is satisfied with and honoured in that atonement, so that he the believing sinner may go free, enters into rest. The man who believes this has an immediate and blessed rest from the alarms of conscious guilt. But such rest is found nowhere else. For it is Christ alone that gives rest to the soul.

Secondly: But the promise of Christ also includes, as I have already said, deliverance from the power of sin. That is rest, too. The seat of the sinner's disease is in the heart, and there the cure is applied. To change his position in the eye of the law, though a great step towards what follows, would of itself be but a small matter. The promise of Christ is rest. But to the wicked there is no rest, there is no peace within. Rest must not alone come from without man, the sinner, but must also be wrought within him.

Man could not have been saved from sin, without a great salvation being wrought without him. But he cannot even now be saved, without a great salvation being wrought within him. For it is within that the root of the sinner's misery is. It is there that wild confusion and anarchy reign. It is there that treason against the King of Heaven is nursed. And it is there, too, that the gospel, whose effects are "righteousness, and peace, and joy in the Holy Ghost," begins to operate. And it is there that the work continues to progress. It is in the heart, so far as the origin of anything good is human, that all the graces are moulded, coined, and stamped, that adorn the Christian character, and prove its vitality.

Religion, where the heart is awanting, is but an empty and hollow form, that can fill the place of a real living heart-religion no better than a dead body can fill the place and perform the duties of a living man. And thus true rest to man is found in his soul, not in his circumstances.

The spiritual change which is wrought in the believing sinner, does not consist of mere negatives. There was in some natural men positive hatred entertained towards God formerly, and now there is positive love; in others there was distrust: now admiration and gratitude rule. The believing sinner has become, in the fullest sense, a son of God; and the relationship produces its own appropriate feelings. To be a son of God, and an heir of glory, is not merely a new state into which the sinner has come in the eye of the law—although it is also that—but it includes a new character and life. For the very thought that he, the forgiven one, occupies such an honourable, but undeserved, position, becomes a purifying furnace in the soul of the man, that begins to consume the dross of sin as soon as it has an existence in the mind.

All this change of heart and life is wrought by faith in Jesus. Faith purifieth the heart, and overcometh the world. Nor do we find in this connection between faith in Christ and holiness of heart and life any insoluble mystery.

There is here in faith no arbitrary, nor hidden, nor mysterious principle at work. So that we cannot understand nor see, in a measure, how such effects should flow from it. Faith is a simple act of the mind. There is no unusual mystery about it. Not in the act of faith, but in the wonderful object of gospel faith, our Lord Himself, does the mighty transforming power of the gospel reside. For gospel faith lays hold on Christ crucified, and there-is in Him "lifted up," the proper object of faith, transforming cause sufficient to account for all the change that any human character ever underwent.

To avoid technical, theological terms, and to employ the language of the home, and the heart: When fear, and hate, and suspicion of God have been removed from the heart, and we begin to breathe the air of liberty, of love, and of trust; it is impossible but that the influence of the new state should be to repress and crush all the fiercer and baser qualities of humanity, and to strengthen and develop all the finer and gentler, purer and nobler principles and affections of man's whole nature. A reconciliation between loving friends who have differed, and been separated, but are again united, when it is genuine and complete, has a most joy-diffusing, healthful, and mellowing influence on the character. How much more 'peace and reconciliation with God, through our Lord Jesus Christ.'

The understanding of the pardoned sinner finds rest in the knowledge of God; his affections find rest in God's love; and his whole being finds its rest in looking upon God in Christ with admiring complacency.

I spoke formerly of the sinner as oftentimes labouring under the burden of an oppressive ceremonialism, engaging in religious services which he yet feels to be no joy, but a burden, to him. But faith in Jesus sets us free from a burdensome ceremonialism, and makes all the services of religion sweet and pleasant. By the believer on Jesus, these services are no longer looked upon as the means of wringing from an unloved but dreaded being a future salvation; but they are the willing expressions of his gratitude and love towards a loving Father who has already saved him. They who come to Jesus feel like the Indian devotee, with his self-inflicted tortures. For when he heard the missionary under a tree proclaiming that 'the blood of Jesus cleanseth from all sin,' he at once felt, and said: "That is what I need." He ceased his penances, and found rest in Christ. And so do all who come to Him.

But Christ gives rest from the manifold burdens of life already spoken of, which are all the effects of sin, such as disease, loss, disappointment, and all that causes sorrow. Although it is not the main design of Christ's coming into the world to remove these secondary burdens from men, yet He does lighten all kinds of burdens to those who come to Him, and He removes many burdens altogether. For true religion goes to mitigate, or to remove, all the ills of life.

As an example, much human suffering arises from the conduct of man to man; from the ignorance, and selfishness, and cruelty, and want of love existing among men.

And as Christ and Christianity are ever warring against all these evils in human character, so, just as Christ comes to bear a wider and fuller sway over men, do the same men come to lighten the burdens that they impose on their fellow-men. And thus it is Christ, who does really what those who are influenced and inspired by His spirit do.

Again, as the Christian sees all his burdens to be ordered for him by a God of love, and believes them all to be working for his good, he feels them to be light.

And this spirit in relation to God's dealings, Christ teaches. The man of the world knows it not.

And, again, the Christian's burdens become light as He obtains the aid of the Almighty in bearing them, and also as He sees them by faith to be but "light afflictions, and for a moment." Forget not, my hearers, the quarter from which the promise of our text emanates. It is Christ who says: "I will give you rest." This rest is the result of His redemptive work. It comes through His peace-speaking blood. "He is the one mediator between God and man." And he may well so speak, when God's entire satisfaction in His character and work found, among many other striking manifestations, audible expression for itself by a voice from the excellent glory: "This is my beloved Son, in whom I am well pleased." When the divine Redeemer gives rest to the soul of man, there is no object in existence that can produce unrest and fear. And that rest Jesus here promises to all who come to Him.

"God is not a man, that He should lie; neither the Son of Man that He should repent. Hath he said, and shall He not do it? Or hath He spoken, and shall He not make it good?"

Thirdly: But the promise of our text, as already said, includes not only a present rest from the guilt and power of sin, but also a prospective and complete rest in Heaven.

The sinner who comes to Christ is at once united to Him, as the living branches are united to the vine: and thus he becomes conformed to Christ in his sufferings, in his death, and in his glory.

We see even now the Christian's conformity to Christ in his sufferings, and we know that because He lives they shall live also. We know that those who take up the Cross and follow Christ shall, without fail, obtain the crown.

Notice in few words the complete fulfilment of the promise of our text in the final and perfect rest of Heaven.

The yoke of humanity is sin, and also sorrow, which is the fruit of sin.

In Heaven there is no sin, and there is no sorrow.

Nay, there is the very opposite. There is perfect holiness and an ever-growing excellence. And hence there is joy, positive and perfect joy. 'There is fulness of joy, and there are pleasures for evermore.' Who of us, then, will be so foolish as not to listen to Christ's invitation; as not to come to Christ?

Let no one fail to come to Him. Come all, come now; come daily. And final perfect eternal rest is sure to us.

The promise of Christ must include this prospective and perfect rest in Heaven.

First, because of the imperfection of the rest which even the true Christian now enjoys. The history of Christ's Church has been generally a record of visible struggle and suffering, poverty, and privation; it has been rarely a record of external peace and outward prosperity. And in such circumstances Christians have felt and said: "If in this life only we have hoped in Christ, we are of all men most pitiable." And yet Christ has never taken His people by surprise in this matter. This state of earthly suffering they ought not to look upon as a "strange thing." For it is what He gives them all to expect in measure. Here are the terms of our enlistment into Christ's service. "These things have I spoken unto you, that in Me ye may have peace. In the world ye have tribulation; but be of good cheer, I have overcome the world."

These words point us "unto an inheritance incorruptible and undefiled, and that fadeth not away, reserved in Heaven for us," and not to earth, nor earthly circumstances, as fully exhausting the promise of Christ: "I will give you rest."

But when we embrace the future life as included in the promise of our text, this fully makes good the consistency of this absolute promise of rest with the present imperfection of its fulfilment. There is in Christ, when we come to Him, rest even in this life, compared with the former slavery of sin. For within the unconverted heart the fever of sin rages uncontrolled. But within the renewed heart, only its dying fires smoulder.

Within the unrenewed heart spiritual darkness reigns; but within the renewed heart light and darkness, holiness and sin, struggle together. Purity, even in the pure, is not complete, and cannot yield perfect peace, which is its proper and natural result. And still more true is it that sin is not the master principle of the renewed soul, and cannot bring forth death as it does in the unrenewed.

The moral opposites, holiness and sin, so counter-work each other in the average Christian man, that neither has an unfettered development. So much is this the case, that where the divine life has begun, man's heart is sometimes the seat of a struggle between holiness and sin, between light and darkness, that is a real miniature of the greater struggle that divides the moral universe; the struggle between holiness in its author, and sin in its author, between light in its origin, and darkness in its origin, between the righteous government of the almighty and eternal God, and the unrighteous rebellion of that proud arch-angel, Lucifer, Son of the Morning, who daringly seized upon the sceptre of the Ancient of Days, and strove with angelic power to wrest it from His almighty grasp; but strove for this in vain. For he, having been driven from Heaven by the matchless arm of Omnipotence, has made earth the disputed borderland of his kingdom, and has transferred the seat of the combat against God and goodness from Heaven to earth: and now struggles with only a partial, and yet a too great success to wrest this earth from the rightful rule of Heaven, and add it to that dark domain of which he is the actual lord.

But as surely as the divine arm shall finally quell all rebellion in the universe, so surely shall final and perfect peace be the lot of every child of God. And it is so in part now.

But the Christian, while imperfect in holiness, expects not, and even wishes not, perfection in happiness. It were—did we understand its full meaning—an impious and unholy wish to desire to feel complete satisfaction with a state of imperfection and sin. The Christian does not wish to be perfectly happy until he shall have become perfectly holy. He does not wish to be pleased with a state in which there is anything offensive to God's pure and holy eyes. "The wisdom that is from above is first pure, then peaceable."

But the causes of this continued imperfection in the Christian's happiness are not only in him but also around him. The world is too full of sin and misery of all kinds, for him to be as happy a man as he could and would be in himself, were all like himself.

Men are perishing around him of sin and unbelief, and fruitful fields, and fair skies, a prosperous business, and even a happy home, cannot, and ought not, to blot the painful fact of prevailing moral evil from the good man's memory, nor a sense of personal responsibility from his conscience.

But the state of the Church often hinders his enjoyments, too. When he sees the Church with hardly love enough to keep it as a whole visibly together, with only zeal enough in many cases to keep its ground against the encroachments of the world, without being able to take possession of more territory for Christ; when many of its members in deep repose, though not in joy, seem as if they had already entered upon their final rest; when vigorous health seems almost the exception in the Church, and a kind of sickly life the rule, and death not rare—all this will cause pain to every real Christian, in the exact proportion that the brighter spots in the picture give him pleasure. Yes, the dawn of the millennium will bring much added rest and joy to every Christian, and the dawn of Heavenly glory yet more.

Secondly: But the rest promised here must grow into the rest of Heaven, because there is no second conversion takes place. Salvation once begun shall be carried on for evermore. Heaven only completes what justification begins.

The peace that follows believing on Jesus shall stand all life's sorrows, all time's changes, all death's terrors, all nature's convulsions, and all judgement's solemnities, and shall remain unbroken. " For the gifts and the calling of God are without repentance."

And now our duty is plain. "Come unto Me, all ye that labour and are heavy laden," says Christ, "and I will give you rest." "And the spirit and the bride say, come." Come from sin, the most degrading of all bondage, to freedom from sin, the freest of all liberty: for it is that wherewith Christ makes His people free. Here is a most blessed change, wrought upon the character and state of man! Where shall we find a comparison fit to rightly set forth this change? Shall it be in the degraded slave who, crushed in body and in spirit, groans under the iron rod of man's oppression when contrasted with the most delightful home of freedom and love which we have ever seen, or can even picture as possible?

Or shall we find the comparison that we seek in the undiscovered, but guilty murderer, who hears among his fellow-men an accusing voice which none else hear but he, and such as he, and who only remains among the haunts of men, because this unwelcome voice is loudest when he is alone? Who sees his victim as an unwelcome companion haunting him even at the unghostly hour of noon. Shall we find the parallel that we seek in the experience of such a man contrasted with the happy, laughing, innocence of childhood? No, they alike fail to set forth the full contrast between the experiences and the prospects of the natural and the spiritual man.

Earth has no other such fact as conversion to God. It presents no other such change as that. God has but one Son of equal nature; Christ our Saviour is God's only begotten Son. For man there is but one redemption provided, and only one state of probation; only one of two final abodes to be chosen; and that one to be fixed now as ours eternally. God is one; to whom shall we resemble Him? This is His own new creation in man; and where on earth shall we gather the materials to form its like?

We can only join the exulting strain of Scripture, and say: "Blessed is he whose transgression is forgiven, whose sin is covered. Blessed is the man unto whom the Lord imputeth not iniquity, and in whose spirit there is no guile." For he has entered into rest. His is "the peace of God which passeth all understanding."

VII.

THE GREAT BURDEN-BEARER.

THIRD SERMON.

"Come unto Me, all ye that labour and are heavy laden, and I will give you rest. Take my yoke upon you, and learn of me; for I am meek and lowly in heart: and ye shall find rest unto your souls. For my yoke is easy, and my burden is light."—MAT. XI., 28-30.

I HAVE already spoken of :

    I. The *state* of those who are here addressed by our Lord.
    II. The *invitation* which is given them by Christ.
    III. The *promise* which He makes to those who come to Him.

IV.—And now I would direct your attention to the *contrasted yokes* and burdens of which our text speaks.

The yoke of sin, Christ says, is laborious, and its burden is heavy. The yoke of Christ, which He calls "My yoke," He says "is easy," and the burden of Christ, which He calls "My burden," He says "is light."

And then the yoke of sin grows ever more and more grievous, and its burden grows heavier and heavier; while the yoke of Christ grows ever easier and easier, and His burden grows lighter and lighter.

And as the means by which the rest spoken of in the text is gained at first, is coming unto Jesus; so the means by which it grows up into the perfect and final rest of Heaven, is by willingly taking up Christ's yoke daily, and learning of Him. The rest that follows justification, comes from resting the soul on Jesus by faith. And the rest that springs up from a growing sanctification comes from evermore taking up the yoke of Jesus and learning of Him. And even the rest of Heaven, into which the believer enters, is Christ's own rest. So that this rest in its beginning, in its growth, and in its perfection is found in, and comes from, Jesus. He is "the author and the finisher" of that rest from the accusing guilt and reigning power of sin which the believer in Him ever enjoys.

We have already seen at length the nature of the one yoke and burden: that which man bears by nature. How different is Christ's yoke and burden! The burden of sin is heavy and grievous, while that of Christ is light and easy. But, perhaps, you ask, 'What is the meaning of Christ's yoke? What is the yoke?' I answer: The words "my yoke," as used by Jesus, may mean any one of two things. They may mean either the special yoke of service and suffering, that Christ as our Lord and Master imposes upon us. It is His, as given by Him. Or the words may mean the yoke that He, as our example and fellow-man bears along with us. For Christ as God imposes a yoke upon His servants. Yes, He is our Lord and Master; and He lays on us, as it is His right to do, our burdens.

But He Himself, as the sent of the Father, and as a man, bears a yoke as we do, the yoke of duty and service.

And all Christ's people are called upon to take up, and do take up along with Him, that yoke of duty, and learn of Him in the bearing of it, 'whose meat and drink it was to do God's will.' However, there is not all the difference between these two views of Christ's yoke that would at first sight appear. For the very yoke that Christ, as being Himself divine, imposes upon mankind, He, as being also human, bears along with us.

So that we shall, perhaps, most truly and fully apprehend the yoke of Christ if we understand that what He calls "my yoke" is not merely the yoke which He, as ruler, imposes on others; but that it is likewise the yoke which He Himself, as God's Son, apostle, and servant, bears.

And hence, taking up Christ's yoke is equal to taking up the cross, and bearing it after Christ. But the yoke of Christ does not involve the bare idea of subjection to authority. The Lord explains Himself by the words "learn of Me," instead of saying, submit to Me. Still both obeying God, and submitting to God, are involved in taking Christ's yoke upon us. For without this willing subjection to God we are not really learning of Christ. For to learn of Christ is not only to listen with the ear to His words, but also to drink into His spirit, and copy His actions. He cheerfully bowed His neck to the divine yoke. And truly to learn of Him means that we must go and do likewise, be what it may, that God lays on us.

But the words yoke and burden suggest the ideas of subjection and of labour. And we here learn that though the sinner may be, and is, set free from degrading subjection to sin and Satan, and a painful labouring in that evil service, yet he must still, as Christ's servant, bear a yoke and carry a burden.

As creatures, my hearers, we must bear a yoke. It may be the grevious yoke of sin that we bear, or it may be the easy yoke of Christ. But independent of service, and control we never can be. "Know ye not, that to whom ye present yourselves as servants unto obedience. His servants ye are whom ye obey, whether of sin unto death or of obedience unto righteousness? * * and being made free from sin, ye become servants of righteousness." Yes, all men serve righteousness or sin, God or Satan. None are without a master and a yoke. The yoke of Christ, as we shall see, is easy; still, "owing to the conflict with evil that is ever incident to our corrupt imperfect nature, even under grace, the rest which Christ gives is yet to be viewed as a yoke and a burden." There is something, with a measure of difficulty in it, to do and to bear still; but the inner rest in the soul, a peace "which passeth all understanding," bears the spirit up against all the conflict of the spiritual life.

It is remaining sin that makes religion a yoke at all. It was sin, not His own, but the sin of the world, that laid a yoke upon Christ.

Even the divine life appears to man in a measure onerous and oppressive, because there remain in him the workings of sin which formed so large a part of his old, and heavy burden.

But Christ's yoke and burden are only felt to be onerous by man to any extent so long, and so far, as he is encumbered by sin.

The nobler self of the renewed man, feels the spirit and life of Christ to be its very native air and vital element. And when the new nature shall be set quite free from the "bondage of corruption," and shall be translated to Heaven, then when there shall be no sin, then and there only no burden, and no yoke will remain, but freedom will be perfect and eternal.

But in entering into this fellowship of spirit and life with Christ, to which we are here invited, it is well to remember that, notwithstanding Christ's speaking of relief and rest, there is still something to be endured, still a yoke to be borne, and a burden to be carried. While there is, notwithstanding, and in the very bearing of them, something of inestimable value to be gained, rest—rest unto the soul. Notice then:

First, that there is something to be endured. "Take my yoke upon you." And again, "If any man would come after Me, let him deny himself, and take up his cross and follow me." In real religion there is ever something to do and suffer, as well as much to gain.

Observe the meaning of the terms which Christ uses. The yoke is an emblem of servitude, and servant is the Christian's relation and position to Christ, a voluntary and entire devotement of himself to Christ's work in the world. Servant to Christ, means an entire consecration to do Christ's will, to allow himself to be put to use in Christ's service, in any way that He, the Master, sees fit. And, as I have already said, Christ's yoke in our text does not mean, in my opinion, the yoke of Christ as a master strictly, or at least entirely, but also the yoke which Christ

Himself was then bearing as the Lord's servant for man's redemption, the yoke of a loyal obedience to God in all things.

And knowing, as Jesus Christ did, loving submission to God to be the only true bliss, and the only true freedom, He here invites those who have thrown off this yoke, and have taken upon themselves other yokes, heavy yokes, and grevious to be borne, as all men have done, to throw them all off, and to assume this in their place. This is a yoke in the bearing of which Christ Himself is our example, and fellow-labourer in the Kingdom of God.

The yoke is easy for us, mainly because we have an infinitely strong helper in bearing it. For Jesus has " borne " for us " the burden of the day and the scorching heat." He has performed all the services for us which lay beyond our own power. "His right hand, and His holy arm, hath wrought salvation" for us, and "gotten Him the victory" in our struggle. It now remains that we show our subjection to God by taking up along with Christ, and after Him, the yoke of willing obedience unto God; and God will accept our unworthy persons and services for the sake of Christ's all-worthy and perfect obedience, and give us rest in serving Him. The word translated burden is used in Scripture figuratively, to denote the burden of sin, and also to denote the Jewish ceremonial; and it denotes Christ's service by antithesis, as being in comparison with the Jewish ceremonial a light and easy service.

To "learn of me" means to learn in the sense of " be ye trained or discipled by me." For the force of this term "learn" is not exhausted by one formally teaching so much of any knowledge to anyone else, and by that other one formally acquiring that knowledge from the other. Really, to learn of one means much. To learn of Christ is to come under His personal tuition and influence, so as to be thoroughly indoctrinated by His views and spirit, to be entirely moulded by His character, and made anew.

But when Jesus Christ demands of His professed followers that they take up His yoke, and bear His burden, let it be remembered that His yoke and burden come in the place of far heavier yokes and burdens—in the place of yokes and burdens both heavy and numerous. For Christ asks no one to leave a better service for a worse, an easier service for a more difficult. The sinner is a great gainer in coming over to the service of Christ.

The yoke of Christ consists in doing, and in not doing. It consists in putting forth an activity for Christ which is contrary to the bent of the natural man, and in imposing a self-restraint, which is also contrary to the impulses of the natural man. What the actual yoke is which Christians have to bear, will be best seen by inquiring what the yoke was which Christ bore, not as the divine and sin-atoning Mediator, in which character He can be no example to us, but as a man, and thus under law to God. Christ's yoke in this sense may be summed up in an entire resignation to the divine will; a complete giving up of Himself to subserve the divine purposes without a single reserve. That is the yoke which God lays upon His family here below. And this yoke may once again be summed up in a life of self-denial to all that is wrong, and of self-renunciation for the promotion of all that is for God's glory and man's good. The Psalmist says, "The zeal of thine house hath eaten me up." And Christ's disciples remembered that this was written, and they applied it to their Master when in holy anger He drove the traffickers and their wares out of the temple of God.

And to Christ this yoke of duty was easy. Yes, the "yoke is easy," says Christ, and the "burden is light." Love makes it so to a Christian. For it is Christ's yoke, who bore for us, not only all that we bear along with Him, but an infinitely heavier yoke. Love makes all yokes easy. It is so in a family. Its natural and proper inter-communion of kind offices may be viewed as a disagreeable drudgery that is never done with; and the performance of family duties must be so viewed if love be absent or weak. But if love be present and strong, the services that we render to each other in the family afford abiding delight to both givers and receivers.

And so of all kinds of service that we do for each other. None of them is easy if love be awanting; while love can cheerfully render almost any service, and not feel it heavy. And divine love is the yoke that securely fastens the burden of Christ to the willing neck of the true disciple. I have already shown that love makes Christ's yoke easy. But that is not all. The ease of Christ's yoke is not imaginary. It is not mere sentiment. It is in itself easy. His service is a reasonable service. His commands are not grievous. Wisdom's " ways are ways of pleasantness, and all her paths are peace." As, for instance, the sum of God's law; that supreme love to God and man which is enjoined on us by Christ as the sum of the divine law! Well, the possession of that love, which is enjoined as duty, is yet found to be the life, and health, and joy of the human spirit, by all who cultivate it.

Again, that purity of heart, life, and action which is a part of Christ's yoke, is also a noble freedom from all debasement and pollution.

And so of the practical exercise of benevolence which is enjoined upon us by Jesus Christ. The injunction of benevolence as a duty, is really informing us how we may be happy ourselves, as well as how we may make human intercourse helpful to others.

And taking up the yoke of Christ as our religion is easy, compared with the practice of any other system of religious belief in the world.

Christianity is the simplest type of religion, requiring least of outward form, and resting most of any religion in the world, upon the spirit that we possess and manifest. And where it is most simple in its forms and observances, its inner life seems ever to thrive the best. Christianity is also an easy religion compared with any system of unbelief. For all such are systems of freezing, soul-killing negations.

Christ's yoke is an easy yoke, again, as it imposes restraint upon man at the point where restraint is most easy to be borne. For the Bible says: "Keep thy heart with all diligence, for out of it are the issues of life." And here the check upon what is wrong is not only most effective, but it is most easy to interpose.

And the yoke of Christ is easy—the easiest that can be put on—because every man, if he would not be an utter slave to evil, must put a restraint upon his own evil tendencies somewhere. And Christ's laws go to check them in the bud, or rather to hinder their springing up; and this early check is easy compared with checking them in any other stage of their growth.

As an illustration of this: The most depraved of men have often more severe struggles fighting unsuccessful battles with their sinful desires, appetites, and passions, than the most holy men have in fighting successful battles with the same evil things. Some of you may object to this, and say 'that the depraved man puts no restraint upon his evil desires.' But I say he must, and does. A man may put before him as his standard of conduct either the perfect law of Christ, or the imperfect average practice of the professing Church of Christ, or the practice of reputable society without religion, or the general practice of the avowedly ungodly, or even the riot of the libertine. No matter which standard of all each man adopts, that standard imposes its own restraint; and if an individual man go far beyond the laws of his circle, he loses caste. Even the dishonest, the intemperate, and the impure have their conventional laws and usages, which a member of the immoral fraternity dare not widely overstep if he would escape disgrace, and, it may be, expulsion.

Now, what I am asserting is that to put the restraint upon what is evil where Christ commands us to put it, upon the rising thought, upon the budding inclination to evil, is far easier than to put it on anywhere else in the chain of evil. While checking sin in the bud saves us from all its shame and misery, present and future. As an illustration: You will find single drunkards who make greater efforts to keep moderately sober, without accomplishing it, than all the practical abstainers from intoxicants in a whole town require to do. And so with a liar; so with a slanderer; so with all kinds of sinners. It is easy not to begin a sinful habit compared with the breaking it off when formed.

In contrast with the easy yoke of Christ, let me name some of the heavy yokes that men impose upon themselves, upon one another, and have imposed on them by sin, and Satan.

In one word, sin is that yoke which enslaves the world, and the devil is the hard task-master that fits a growingly heavy share of it upon every neck, unless the necks of those who have been emancipated by Christ, who alone sets men free from it. But the yoke of sin is complicated and varied in form. One of its forms is the yoke of evil thoughts indulged in until one is no fit company for himself, and is deluged by his own unholy and unhappy imaginations and memories. There is the yoke of evil, sinful habits, the yoke of unamiable dispositions, the yoke of unholy tempers, the yoke of God-dishonouring actions, the yokes of envy, pride, and hatred.

In a word, every unsubdued sin imposes a yoke upon the soul—lays on it a something harrowing and destructive of its peace. While Christ's yoke as a present service, altogether apart from a future world, and the contrasted reward or punishment that awaits severally those who fear God, and those who fear Him not, is far easier and more pleasant than the lightest yoke which sin imposes; and moreover Christ's yoke ever grows lighter, while every yoke of sin grows day by day more heavy.

Put in few words, Christ's yoke is, "Do thyself no harm," O man! Restrain thyself from sin, for in gratifying your sinful desires you commit self-destruction. And that needed, saving restraint should not seem to a wise man a grievous yoke. For, anomaly as it seems, self-denial to all that is wrong is on the whole, and in the long run, even for this world, an easier yoke than self-gratification.

And in our taking up Christ's yoke, and learning of Him, He puts before us something of immense importance to be gained, even rest to the soul.

We must observe and remember who the persons addressed are. They are those that suffer from the disquiet and unrest of sin. They are those "that labour and are heavy laden."

The rest of Christ begins with the forgiveness of sin, and it comes in its fulness by a personal resting of the soul upon Christ's atoning death, and whole work. That part of the rest of Christ which comes at once by faith I look on as specially referred to in the 28th verse; and having spoken of that already, I do not refer to it now, further than to remind you that this believing rest in Christ is the foundation of the growing rest which is more especially spoken of in verse 29th, and which arises from a personal likeness to Christ, and a living oneness with Him. Or, in other words, the one rest springs from justification before God, and the other springs from a growing sanctification in Christ Jesus.

And there is a very close connection between the two states. The connection, as we have said, of foundation and superstructure. We grasp Christ's atonement feebly as we wander away from following His steps. That atonement, it is true, is ever the same, and we may ever resort to it. For no personal merit is needed for our acceptance before God, and none avails.

But it is not any the less true that personal sin disturbs our rest upon the atonement of Christ, and darkens our confidence in it. It must be so. This painful but monitory effect of wrong-doing is one of our strongest protections from self-deception and ruin.

Every one in this assembly who has once trusted in Christ, and found rest in Him, shall, I believe, be finally saved as the result of a divine purpose. But no one here obtains rest to his soul from that divine decree apart from his present state, because no one knows anything about the purposes of God in regard to His own case, but as they are being realized. But God's people bear a certain moral image, and are stamped with a certain spiritual character, and the way in which everyone here who has rested on Christ, or thinks that he has, may prove this, or disprove it for himself, is by an habitual personal scrutiny of himself, and a careful testing of himself in God's sight by the presence, or absence, of the fruits of the Spirit.

What I now speak of is not anything to rest in towards God. But I speak of a satisfactory proof that we have rested on Christ, arising from finding that God has put His Spirit into our hearts, and made us, like Christ, "meek and lowly in heart."

You never can disjoin, therefore, the rest that springs from Christ's atonement, and that which springs from becoming possessed of Christ's spirit. It is true we distinguish, if not disjoin, the two in works on systematic theology, and properly so. So are man's mind and body treated as distinct in works on anatomy and surgery; and in works on mental and moral science. Yet mind and body never exist in this world apart. Neither do justification and sanctification.

Both states and experiences go to make a Christian, as much as both body and mind go to make a man. And it is as impossible to separate them in fact, and have a living Christian, as to separate soul and body in fact, and have a living man.

And this rest, as we saw in a former discourse, is what man needs. Yes, this rest for the soul is a universal want. For man, while a sinner, is out of harmony with God, and he is out of harmony with all the universe. He carries within him a heart ill at ease. He is haunted by a guilty conscience; and though he is ever seeking rest, he finds none that deserves the name. We find proof of this unrest in the many attempts which are everywhere made to remove it, and to find rest to the soul. We find proof, too, of man's unrest in the many and bloody sacrifices of heathendom.

We find like proof also among ourselves. We find the proof among the votaries of amusement on the one hand, who are anxiously seeking without themselves for what they cannot find within. And we also find proof that man needs rest for his soul among the votaries of the blind and uneducated religious impulses, on the other hand, who attempt in many man-appointed ways to please God, and to bribe Him to be at peace with them, while they have never come to Christ, and found rest in Him, which is God's way of being saved.

And then we must remember that but a very little of the actual unrest of the unconverted comes out. Men who continue in the ways of sin and worldliness, are ashamed to own that sin makes them unhappy, or so unhappy as it does. These men have no such experience meetings as our Methodist brethren hold. Men continue for years to be bosom companions in the ways of sin, and companions in disquiet and unrest, and yet never plainly confess to one another the existence of that disquiet and unrest, that 'vanity and vexation of spirit,' which they feel. And still they do have these feelings.

But from all this unrest Christ promises deliverance. He promises rest to the soul; and this being soul rest, reaches to the man proper.

Many people live for the body mainly, provide for, and nourish and cherish the body, mainly or solely; while not a few live mainly for the mind, which is a much higher object. But it is to be feared that fewer, than any of these, live for the soul, the spirit, the immortal man. But rest to the soul such as Christ promises, being for the immortal soul, must be, and is, an eternal, ever-enduring rest. For while the throne of God remains unshaken, and the walls of the New Jerusalem above remain unassailable and unassailed, so long the redeemed by Christ shall enjoy there, in that safe retreat, eternal rest and unending pleasure.

There is, in and through Christ, a present rest and peace, such as the world can neither give nor take away, in knowing and feeling that the Supreme Power in the universe is our friend, is with us, and not against us, and in being prepared willingly to yield ourselves up to His purposes and will. While there is, on the other hand, no rest to the man who has, and cherishes, favourite designs which he knows that God does not approve, but is ever counter-working, and will finally overturn. There is no rest to the man who is ever in dread lest the hand of Omnipotence should at any moment be raised to dash his favourite schemes all to pieces. And this is the position of all unbelieving men as the enemies of God.

VIII.

THE GREAT BURDEN-BEARER.

FOURTH SERMON.

"Come unto Me, all ye that labour and are heavy laden, and I will give you rest. Take my yoke upon you, and learn of me; for I am meek and lowly in heart: and ye shall find rest unto your souls. For my yoke is easy, and my burden is light."—Mat. XI., 28-30.

I WOULD now direct your attention :

V.—Fifthly, to the qualifications of Him who invites burdened sinners to Him, and promises them rest, for the fulfilment of what he thus undertakes.

It is matter of universal observation that man is easily taught by pictorial representations, while he is slow in learning rules and principles; that he cannot help being taught and influenced by examples, while he must determine to learn before he can readily master precepts.

We may find a field of observation where we can prove the truth of this assertion for ourselves, wherever we find humanity. We see it in the youngest child. We prescribe to the infant no formal tasks. He is not fit for them. We submit him to no formal examinations, and he could not pass them if we did. And yet it is a matter of universal observation and knowledge, how very much the infant learns from example only, before he understands the simplest precept.

The truth that "example is better than precept," is seen as we find the increased power that any principle obtains which is embodied in an earnest, able, and eloquent advocate. The truth, or the principle which he represents, though it may have been little known, or half forgotten before he took it up, obtains in him a resurrection to new life and power.

Look at the principle of "humanity to the prisoner," as it was embodied and represented in a Howard, and "the claims of the slave," as pleaded and put into prominence by a Wilberforce and a Buxton, and their many coadjutors in Great Britain, and later on by a Lloyd Garrison, a Harriet Beecher Stow, a Ward Beecher, and many such like in America. Remember the mighty, and beneficent, and permanent results of their labours; and learn what a few earnest men and women, inspired by a great principle, may do.

And forget not that, as a matter of fact, half the power of divine truth, to make its way in the world, lies in its becoming embodied in living men, and in being transferred from the Book of God into the life of man.

Here lies much of the Church's present weakness in influence upon the world. We have here in this perfect book, the whole truth needed to convert the world. But we need far more, and far better living examples of the truth. Men who desire not the knowledge of God's ways, can keep their Bibles shut, and often do, and then those Bibles are powerless for good. While shut and unread they utter no reproofs, they convey no warnings, they proclaim no promises, and they furnish no instructions.

But a living example of the transforming power of divine grace, you cannot lock up, or lay aside upon a shelf, and keep quiet as you may a book. A human character clearly seen to be of divine workmanship, created anew in Christ Jesus unto good works, with something truly Godlike about it, when found in a man among other men, you cannot shut up, and put away as you might put away an unwelcome book.

Hence, if we only had more earnest and living Christians to embody, and live out divine truth, it must mightily prevail. And to the extent that we do have them, they are powerful instruments for the propagation of the Redeemer's cause, and cannot fail to do good. So much so, that though the life of such men, as to its inspiration and power, depends entirely upon the Divine Book, and the Divine Spirit, though it is drawn from, and is sustained by them alone, yet, perhaps more truth is effectually taught to the unconverted, and more impression is made upon them by God's truth lived before them, than by God's truth read by them, or preached to them.

Hence, the dependence of the pulpit upon the pew, and the dependence of the Church upon the family. Here in the House of God we aim to beget, and endeavour to guide to saving issues, religious conviction. But you, my Christian brethren, may light up the torch, or extinguish it, by the character of your ordinary walk and conversation.

So mighty a power is there in a living, loving Christian example, that many a sinner who has not been convinced of sin, and allured to holiness by this perfect book, has yet been so by some imperfect Christian example. Nay, what Christ's perfect example in a written form, and read in the gospels, has not done, some faint and feeble, but true shadowing forth of it, in a living disciple has done, in turning many a sinner "from darkness to light, and from the power of Satan unto God." A Christian example is hence of vast importance. Divine truth lived, is one of the most potent instruments in operation for effecting the world's conversion to God.

But examples live in history, which is a record of deeds done. And when we cannot find all that we want, and need, in the living examples that we see around us, we may find many of the mighty dead of past times embalmed in history, not their bodies, but their thoughts and feelings, and experiences, and character, and spirit; and we may turn back to hold converse with them. It is often well for us to do so, if we do not carry admiration of the past too far; but ever remember, along with the aim to preserve all of the past that lives, or ought to be resuscitated, the poet's wise maxim : "Let the dead past bury its dead."

Here two opposing currents run strongly at the present time. One would carry us back in religion to some, it may be noble, but very imperfect past, and attempt to reproduce it in every respect, which is impossible and undesirable, even if it were possible.

The other current would hurry us forward at such a pace as to leave both the wisdom and the errors of the past alike behind us, which is both a folly and a crime. Let all of the wisdom and the truth of the past be made ours that we can. But if we would bear our proper share in the moulding of the present, we must first understand it, then adopt its forms of thought, and speak in its language. Let us be ourselves. A rigid imitation, in the region of religion, of any merely human models unfailingly dwarfs the proper development of the imitators.

But I turn you once again this morning to an example of the past that never grows old. And not I alone, but the exemplar Himself invites your attention to Himself. He is not a being of the past time however, and not of the present. He is the true contemporary of every generation. Before Abraham, and before angels He is, and was; and He ever lives. He is the first and the last, and the living one.

Who knows the power of noble examples? Who feels the force and the influence of exalted models? Let him accept Christ's own invitation, and make Him a study. How unspeakably important is it to have such a model as this to look upon! Doubtless, as we gaze upon this divine model, this imaged-forth God head, with devout awe, holy reverence, and admiring love, we shall be changed more and more into the same image, even as by the Spirit of the Lord.

You will observe that Jesus here invites us to fellowship with Himself. His teaching fixes on His own life and character as its great subject. Before entering upon the consideration of that fellowship with Christ, which is the remaining theme of our text, I would direct your special attention to the qualifications of Him who invites burdened sinners to Him, and promises them rest—His qualifications for the fulfilment of all that He here undertakes.

His qualifications as here given by Himself consist in His Almighty power, and in His divine gentleness. "All things have been delivered unto Me of my Father," says Jesus. And again he says, "And no one knoweth the Son, save the Father; neither doth any know the Father, save the Son, and he to whomsoever the Son willeth to reveal Him." Here the Son's power is set forth.

Among the "all things" that have been delivered unto Christ by the Father are all kinds of spiritual gifts to bestow upon men. "Thou hast ascended on high, thou hast led thy captivity captive; thou hast received gifts among men, yea, among the rebellious also, that the Lord God might dwell with them." And chief among these celestial gifts that Christ has received for men, we read that He, "the Son of Man, hath power on earth to forgive sins." Or, in other words, He has power to do what He in our text promises to do. He has power to lift off the heavy burden of human guilt and misery; he has power to break the grievous yoke of sin from off man's neck.

Nor let it be forgotten that this yoke of sin is a yoke under which 'the whole world has groaned and travailed in pain together until now.' And no man has been able to redeem his fellow-man from its power.

It must plainly appear then, that no one less mighty than He, to whom "all things have been delivered" by God, is equal to the task of being man's deliverer from sin. But Jesus is able to do this.

And again, Christ's ability to reveal the Father to men, qualifies him for the task which he has undertaken, of giving rest to the labouring and heavy laden sinner. For, as much of the sinner's burden consists in the unhappy effects of sin in itself, so does much of the burden also consist in this sad result of sin's presence: that it separates between the sinner and God, and hides God's face from the sinner. And therefore the Saviour that man needs, is one who can both remove the guilt of his many sins, and also unveil before him the true character of God, as just and holy, and yet a loving and merciful Father.

And Jesus Christ, in thus inviting a guilty world unto Himself, and promising to all "who labour and are heavy laden," but come to Him, "rest," puts Himself upon an equality with God the Father, who says: "Look unto Me, and be ye saved, all the ends of the earth: for I am God, and there is none else." Language this which is the same in substance, and in sweep with the invitation and promise of our text. They are divine utterances both.

But along with Christ's almighty power, the other great qualification that is possessed by Him for the accomplishment of what He here undertakes is His divine gentleness which is thus expressed: "For I am meek and lowly in heart." We read in the prophecies of Isaiah: "For thus saith this high and lofty One that inhabiteth eternity, whose name is Holy: I dwell in the high and holy place with him also that is of a contrite and humble spirit, to revive the spirit of the humble, and to revive the heart of the contrite ones." And here in our text the Lord Jesus

Christ, as the exemplar, leader, and prince of all meek and lowly ones and as Himself the perfect embodyment of this spirit, which is so attractive to the eyes of the High and Holy One, the spirit with which Jehovah promises to dwell, says to us all : " Come unto Me." " Come unto Me," for I only can teach you the proper spirit in which to draw nigh unto God. I only can bring you into His presence with acceptance. I am your example and model. " Take My yoke upon you, and learn of me; for I am meek and lowly in heart; and ye shall find rest unto your souls; for my yoke is easy and my burden is light."

This meek and lowly spirit best displayed itself in Christ's whole career. " He was oppressed, yet He humbled Himself and opened not His mouth ; as a lamb that is led to the slaughter, and as a sheep that before her shearers is dumb; yea, He opened not His mouth." He did " not strive nor cry." And when Christ's deepest cup of sorrow was presented to His lips, He said to His Heavenly Father, " Father, if thou be willing, remove this cup from Me; nevertheless, not My will, but Thine be done." It is this meek and lowly spirit, when found in man, in the renewed man, that makes the divine yoke easy and pleasant to him. Just as the possession of this spirit in perfection, made it ' Christ's meat and drink to do His Father's will, and to finish the work which was given Him to do.' This meek and lowly spirit, by whomsoever possessed, ever makes the divine yoke easy, and the burden that God lays on us light.

Nay, further observe, that the meekness, and lowliness of Christ when learnt, form in themselves the true rest of the soul, even though the burden of external disquietude may not be removed. Anger and pride, envy and hatred, discontent and self-will, create disquietude and turmoil in the human soul, which die out and give place to rest and peace as the meek and lowly spirit of Christ is learnt, and possessed.

VI.—Notice the *companionship* that is enjoyed by Christians in all their yokes, labours, and burdens. The yoke which I ask you to bear, says Christ, is "My yoke;" the burden that I call upon you to take up, is "My burden."

The easiness and lightness of the yoke and burden will thus more fully appear as we look at the delightful companionship which the Christian enjoys in bearing them.

He to whom all things have been delivered of the Father, He Himself bears along with us, the yoke which we must take up as Christians. He Himself takes hold of the yoke of sin, and removing it from our necks, He puts the easy yoke of duty in its place.

And Jesus Christ, taking hold with us of this, and of all the yokes and burdens of life, causes them all to appear easy, and to become easy.

The easiness of a yoke, and the lightness of a burden, are ever to be compared with the strength of him that bears them. And it is no longer our own strength alone which has to be counted, when we would estimate the weight of the Christian yoke, but it is Christ's strength, too. For we have His companionship and aid in bearing it. And "we can do all things in Christ that strengtheneth us."

It is "My yoke," and My burden, says Jesus Christ. They are Mine as well as yours, they are more Mine than yours. The words, "My yoke is easy" mean, My yoke is not exacting. The same word when used of persons is sometimes translated 'kind'

As of God Himself, "for He is 'kind' to the unthankful and evil." And the same word is used of the divine commands when we read: "and His commandments are not grievous."

Christ's yoke is easy, kindly, not burdensome, and His burden is light compared with the toilsome yokes, and the heavy burdens of sin. Christ's yoke is easy, and His burden is light in the same sense that it is an easy yoke and a light burden for the man who has long struggled with a deadly disease, that had almost sunk him into the grave, to use the health-restoring remedies of the physician. For Christ's yoke and burden just form a medicinal discipline and exercise, whereby the man who undergoes them, may attain to spiritual health, and may live for evermore. And to those who will keep this high end in view, this great design ever in mind, all the means that lead to and secure it must be counted easy.

When the prescribed remedies of the physician are day by day bringing renewed health to the late invalid, the most bitter pill will be looked upon as easy to take.

And so when a holy walk, and the service of Christ generally, bring growing rest and peace to the soul, the whole duty that Christ lays on us must be viewed as easy.

And again, the religion of Jesus Christ imposes on us an easy yoke and a light burden, if it be compared with any other religion in the world. Its outward observances are few and simple. Christ's commands are truly not grievous. He imposes no long and wearisome pilgrimages. He enjoins no bodily tortures as penance, or atonement for sin. He demands no human sacrifices, and He exacts no costly offerings. The man himself and all that He has are Christ's, it is true. For he is 'bought with a price,' even with 'the precious blood of Christ.' 'He is not his own.' But a man never rightly enjoys himself till he feels that he is not his own. He never has the proper use of what he possesses until he has learnt to count it not his own, but Christ's, and to act as a steward of all that he possesses, not as an owner.

But further, Christ's yoke is easy and His burden is light, because of the new spirit that He imparts to those who come to Him. For "the love of Christ constraineth" them. Their whole service of Christ is like the fourteen years' service of Jacob, to Laban, for Rachel, which "seemed unto him but a few days, for the love he had to her," and on account of the presence of her for whom the service was entered on and fulfilled. For the yoke of Christ is the yoke of love. And supposing that yoke to involve toils as exhausting both to the body and to the mind, as the service of sin does: and that is supposing much. Still these sacred toils are "works of faith, and labour of love." And hence there is all the contrast between them, that there is between the oftentimes over-wrought, but loved and honoured mother and wife, in voluntarily tending her own beloved children, and the compulsorily overtasked and whipped slave, in whose person every noble and elevated feeling and principle of humanity is oftentimes outraged and degraded.

Both labour equally, we shall suppose, and both excessively. But the one obeys the God-implanted and noble impulses of duty, and of love; and would not accept of freedom from her yoke, though you would add to this freedom a reward of gold and diamonds. While the other acts under the depressing pressure of fear, and the degrading influence of coercion, and often risks punishment, if not life, by attempting to run away. And so the one sings, and grows into noble wifehood, and motherhood amid her toils; and the other groans and becomes soured; though outwardly their toils are only equal.

And so with the exertions of the over-wrought, well-doer, and evil-doer, saint, and sinner. Let us suppose that their exertions are equal; yet in a higher sense they are most unequal. The Christian in the highest sense is free. He serves as a son with the Father. He bears the yoke of love. While the unforgiven sinner groans in spirit under the iron slavery of sin and Satan; and the iron enters into his soul.

But still further, Christ's yoke is easy in itself, and His burden is light in itself. There is, as we have seen, a new spirit possessed in bearing Christ's yoke. For it is the yoke of love. But that is not all the difference between Christ's yoke and burden, and the yoke and burden of sin. The yoke of sin would oftentimes be utterly intolerable did not the sinner love it too well, and roll its insnaring pleasures as a sweet morsel under his tongue. But the greatest slave of sin, he who loves it most, labours under it, and is heavy laden. While he who serves Christ has a yoke that is in itself easy, and a burden that is in itself light.

Christ's yoke is called a yoke, and is a yoke, and yet it is no yoke. St. Bernard finely says: "What can be lighter than a burden which takes our burdens away, and a yoke which bears up the bearer himself?" And such in truth are Christ's yoke and burden.

But in order that Christ's yoke and burden may become such an easy yoke and light burden, we must learn of Christ. For just as we do so, the yoke becomes easier, and the burden becomes lighter. The 'learning of Christ' which he commends to us, and the 'finding of rest' which He promises, go on together: both are continuous.

And the measure in which we learn of Christ, or become like Him, is the measure of His rest that we enjoy. To learn of Christ denotes that we come to Him, abide with Him, and ever look to Him. It is from His own teaching that we can best attain to any measure of His meekness and lowliness, and thus enjoy His rest. For His yoke is easy and pleasant, and His burden is light to the meek and lowly, because there is nothing in that yoke and burden to gall the yielding neck and the offered shoulder. There is nothing in Christ's yoke and burden to hurt, and much to refresh and cheer the humble spirit.

Christ's yoke and burden are especially easy, because of the companionship and assistance that we receive in bearing them. "This is the covenant that I will make with the House of Israel after those days," saith the Lord; "I will put my law in their inward parts, and in their heart will I write it; and I will be their God, and they shall be my people." "And I will sprinkle clean water upon you, and ye shall be clean: from all your filthiness and from all your idols will I cleanse you. A new heart also will I give you, and a new spirit will I put within you; and I will take away the stony heart out of your flesh, and I will give you a heart of flesh. And I will put my spirit within you, and cause you to walk in my statutes, and ye shall keep my judgements, and do them."

For observe that there is companionship both in what is to be endured, and in what is to be gained. If we inquire "how we are to bear the yoke?" the answer is: that it is Christ's yoke, and we must bear it after Him.

And if we inquire how the rest comes to us? the answer is: We have this rest just as we get Christ's spirit. He is 'meek and lowly,' and because He is so, those who 'learn of Him' somehow find such a rest springing up within them, as can be found nowhere else. How they find it we have seen. The rest grows out of the Christ-spirit, and hence we must get His meek and lowly spirit before we obtain this rest that is here promised.

Let us try to conceive, as justly as we can, what the elements of character are which Christ here claims for Himself, when He says: "I am meek and lowly in heart." He says, 'I am possessed of that meek and quiet spirit which, in the sight of God, is of great price.' The word low, or lowly, here means low in place, low in condition, as "the brother of low degree." And it is then applied to the mind, as here, and means lowly, modest, humble. And this is a spirit which, though it is pleasing to Christ, is most offensive to the world, and utterly alien from its spirit.

In nothing does the spirit of Christ and the spirit of the world contrast more widely than in the meekness of the one, and the arrogance of the other.

And because they do so contrast, the men of the world, while remaining such, cannot enter into the rest of Christ. God has 'hidden from the wise and understanding the things which He has revealed unto babes.'

As to God, human pride and passion often will not allow men to come unto God as humble suppliants for mercy, and thus obtain the rest of Christ to their souls. But he that comes to Christ and learns of Him, finds that Christ, though "being in the form of God," "He counted it not a prize to be on an equality with God;" "yet emptied Himself, taking the form of a servant * * and being found in fashion as a man," He took to Himself, and possessed that spirit of entire resignation to His Father's will, and reverence for His character, that when learned by any sinner puts him, and keeps, him in his proper position before God.

And so as to man. Very much unrest to us, and in us, springs from the character of our intercourse with our fellow-men in some way. Some real, or fancied injustice, or unkindness done to us, or some omission on the part of some one of what we think was due to us, chafes our self-love. Or the fact of our rights and interests in some way seeming to clash with the rights and interests of others, disturbs our peace of mind. Now, when we copy the meek and unselfish spirit of Christ, when we cease to try how much we can claim and exact from our fellow-men, and constantly try how much we can bear from them, and how much we can do for them, our selfish strife with them ceases, our struggle for unjust, or even for just ascendency, or a fuller recognition at the hands of our fellow-men, is broken off, and we sink into the rest of love and good will— the rest of Christ. Christ seems here to say that the types of character, after which we are ever prone to form ourselves, tend to mar, and to destroy our intercourse with both God and man, for time and for eternity.

And He here calls upon us to abandon all the false types of character after which we may have been trying to frame ourselves, and to make Him our type and exemplar, cultivating towards God and man, His own meek and lowly spirit, in which alone is real rest to the soul.

It is in this spirit that we must draw nigh to God, in order to find favour with Him. When we yield ourselves up to God, and accept His great salvation, our foolish, selfish struggle with Him ceases, and we find true, abiding rest. The want of this Heaven-taught spirit keeps us at a distance from Christ, and shuts us out from God. For when we come to Jesus humbly as sinners, we find access into God's presence with acceptance for Christ's sake.

The grand contest between God and the sinner at this point is, "How shall man be just with God?" 'You may be accepted and justified by Christ as your only way to My Throne.' These are God's terms. And to Him who comes to God as a sinner, and submits to Him, there is a blessed rest given: He is saved with an everlasting salvation. For there is "now no condemnation to them that are in Christ Jesus."

Christianity presents to our view, along with many things that are simple and plain, sublime mysteries and wondrous anomalies. Here is one of them, when Jesus speaks as He does in the text. For in it, He who is the Man of sorrows, promises to banish all our sorrows, not for time only, but also for eternity. He who is from some points of view the most heavily laden of mankind, promises to remove all our burdens, and does this to all who will trust Him, and cast their burdens upon Him. Yes, in this case, bearing a yoke lies in our way to being free and happy. Just as we bear that yoke, so do we find rest. "Never man so spake" as this Man speaks. "God, having of old time spoken unto the fathers in the prophets by divers portions and in divers manners, hath at the end of these days spoken unto us in His Son."

And He speaks to us thus still. "See that ye refuse not Him that speaketh. For if they escaped not when they refused Him that warned them on earth, much more shall not we escape, who turn away from Him that warneth from Heaven."

And what an instructor is Christ! What a maker and moulder of character! Those whom He teaches can teach others. Surely, too much has been said of the Apostles of our Lord, as the illiterate fishermen of Galilee. No doubt but they were in a sense unlettered, "unlearned, and ignorant men." But what ordinary educational advantages, what collegiate training at the feet of ancient scribe, or modern professor, let us ask, has in it so much power to evolve and stimulate the dormant intellect, to purify the depraved heart, to spiritualize the earthward affections, to ennoble the whole man, and thus to fit him for preaching the glorious gospel of the blessed God, holding forth and exalting the Lamb of God, and other such like Christian works, as two years of daily and hourly converse, with a mind so exalted, with a heart so pure, and a love to God and man so intense, as that of Christ, our Divine Redeemer!

The whole nature of the men must have been greatly ennobled by that intercourse. Christ's words, Christ's actions, Christ's spirit, His whole man, left an impression on them which one, speaking for all, thus describes: "And the word became flesh, and dwelt among us, and we beheld His glory." We ask what it was like? And the Apostle continues: " Glory as of the only begotten from the Father, full of grace and truth."

And these words leave us very much, as to objective portraiture, where we were. John is good at description, but the inner glory of Christ, rendering His very body a transparency for the indwelling-God to shine through, baffles even his spiritual insight and his utterance. John could not describe the glory of Christ; but he had seen much of it, and had felt its power. And so may we all do, with divinely opened and divinely anointed eyes. Let us covet and pursue this best of knowledge, that so the rest of sanctification, the seeing by faith, may, as we continue to look, become the rest of Heaven, the very vision of God.

IX.

LIVING UNION WITH CHRIST.

"Abide in me, and I in you. As the branch cannot bear fruit of itself, except it abide in the vine; so neither can ye, except ye abide in Me. I am the vine, ye are the branches: he that abideth in Me, and I in him, the same beareth much fruit; for apart from Me ye can do nothing. If a man abide not in Me, he is cast forth as a branch, and is withered; and they gather them, and cast them into the fire, and they are burned. If ye abide in Me, and My words abide in you, ask whatsoever ye will, and it shall be done unto you. Herein is My Father glorified, that ye bear much fruit; and so shall ye be My disciples."—John XV., 4-8.

THE union that exists between the Lord Jesus Christ and His own believing, regenerated people, is a very close, and a very endearing union. In proof of this, we find that in God's holy word all nature and all human life are ransacked and laid under contribution for fit emblems to set that blessed union forth.

Hence, Christ is spoken of as the head of "the Church which is His body." And to His whole people it is said: "Now are ye the body of Christ, and severally members thereof." There is a most entire oneness with Christ taught us here. And yet, though the body be one whole, there is inferiority in position, and honour, and there is subordination in the other members of the body to the head. And so is it of the Church, the body of Christ, to

Christ the Head. For as the head guides all the body, so does Christ guide the whole Church.

Again, Christ is spoken of as the husband of His Church, and she is spoken of as "the bride, the wife of the Lamb." There are the closest union and the warmest love between Christ and His Church, taught here in this relation in which "the twain become one flesh." For "he that is joined unto the Lord is one spirit." And Christ, who is 'our maker and our husband,' "also loved the Church, and gave Himself for it."

Again, Jesus Christ is spoken of as the Son of God, and our human brother, and thus appointed by God heir of all things for the whole redeemed family. And we all, as Christians, are the brethren of Christ, and, as children, fellow-heirs with Him of God. For "if children, then heirs; heirs of God, and joint heirs with Christ."

Again, Jesus is the friend who "loveth at all time," the "friend that sticketh closer than a brother." And He says to all His professed people: "Ye are my friends, if ye do the things which I command you."

And Jesus is 'the good shepherd that layeth down His life for the sheep,' and His disciples are 'the sheep of His pasture, who know Him and hear His voice.'

And so in our text the Lord Jesus adding another to the many terms used in Scripture to denote the close union that exists between Himself and His people, says to them: "I am the vine, ye are the branches." And every one of these figures is to be taken in its fullest meaning, and even then the figure comes far short of the great reality, to which it points. For Christ is the *true* vine, not a mere vine, not any vine. He says "I am the true vine, the real, the essential vine, of whom the vine of nature is but a shadow." Nor is the visible Church without Him, and apart from Him, any part of the vine. And so, again, He is the true manna, the real bread from Heaven. Thus He Himself speaks. He says: "I am the bread of life;" not that which fell in the wilderness. "I am the living bread which came down out of Heaven: if any man eat of this bread, he shall live for ever."

And *He* also, not Aaron, not Melchizedek, is the one true priest, "a great high priest who hath passed through the Heavens."

And He is the one real sacrifice for sin. It is His Blood that "cleanseth us from all sin." Not the blood of Abel: not the blood shed under the law. And so Jesus, in the first verse of this chapter, says: "I am the true vine, and my Father is the husbandman." These gracious love-strenghtening words were spoken by Jesus on the night in which he was betrayed. And not only so, but they were spoken very near in time to that event. They seem to have been spoken in the Garden of Gethsemane, or on the way thither. For Jesus had said, on rising from the last supper, as recorded at the close of the last chapter, "Arise, let us go hence."

And rising from the communion table with His disciples, they had walked forth together, and He had continued His instructions to them, as we find them recorded in this chapter. This figure of the living, growing vine, and its living, growing branches, as setting forth the relation of the living Christ, and His living members, may have been suggested to the mind of Jesus by the wine-cup which they had all so lately partaken of together; or, more likely still, the figure may have been suggested by the overhanging and surrounding vines, leading to and shading the Garden of Gethsemane. For, as you know, it was very often our Lord's method to teach spiritual and invisible realities by means of things that were near and visible. But whatever may have suggested the lesson of the vine, the lesson itself is plainly before us in our text, which is a truly South African text. In further attempting to open up these words by the aids of the Holy Spirit for our instruction and growth in grace, I shall direct your attention to:

I. The very close relationship which is spoken of in the text.
II. The duty of Christ's people in that relationship.
III. The glorious results of a real abiding union with Christ, and the terrible danger of a mere profession of religion without the reality.

I.—First, the very close relationship which is spoken of in the text, is that existing between Christ and Christians. And this spiritual relation is set forth by the relation of a vine and its branches. "I am the vine, ye are the branches," says Christ. He further says: "I am the true vine, and My Father is the husbandman." 'As I, not the material thing, am the true vine, so My Father is the husbandman; that is, My Father is the great vine proprietor, planter, and dresser, who has originated the relation between Me, the Christ, and you, My people.' 'For God sent Christ, His Son, into the world to save it,' while the Son willingly came on this, God's errand.

In Psalm 80th, from the 8th verse, Israel is represented by the same figure, substantially, as a single vine brought from Egypt, the ground having been prepared, which took deep root, and filled the land, covering the mountains, and sending out her branches unto the sea; and then it was burned with fire, and cut down.

And so in Isaiah, 5th chap., from the 1st verse, Israel is also represented as a vineyard in a very fruitful hill, prepared and hedged round, and planted with the choicest vine, which had yet brought forth " wild grapes." And in Jeremiah II., 21, God says of Israel: " Yet I had planted thee a noble vine, wholly a right seed : how then art thou turned into the degenerate plant of a strange vine unto me?" See also Ezekiel, 19th chap., 10th verse, where God says to the same people: " Thy mother was like a vine in thy blood, planted by the waters " And in our text, Christ Himself claims to be the living vine-stock, or parent-plant, into which every believer on Him has been engrafted, and of which each has become a living branch.

In seeking to unfold, so as to make real to you the analogy that there is between the relation of a vine-stock and its branches, and the relation of Christ and Christians, I remark :

First, that there is between a vine-stock and its branches the union, the connection of visible external support. Their connection is not a hidden thing. All the branches of the vine, or of any tree, are its visible offshoots. And the stock of the vine visibly and manifestly supports and upholds all its branches. It is plainly seen to do so by every onlooker. The beautiful spreading branches of the vine, or of any other tree that bear themselves aloft so gracefully, nodding gently to every passing breeze, or lean upon the artificial props along which vine branches are often trained, would all fall prostrate on the earth dead, decaying things, but for the external support which the tree gives them.

And in the same way every Christian is a visible offshoot from Christ; and all the Church is so. And as the vine-stock supports all its branches, so does Christ support all His people; and He is seen of all observers to do so. Their spiritual strength is visibly His strength imparted to them. As Christians, they all spring from Him at first, and they all hang upon Him for ever after. It is He alone who keeps them from falling. Without union with Christ, Christians would have no centre of union with each other, and no power of self-support.

And as of Christians individually, and collectively, so of the corporate system of Christianity. It, too, is an offshoot from Christ. For, but for Christ, Christianity, as an organization, and a power in the world, would never have been. And Christianity all hangs upon Christ still. That divine society, called the Church, which in its later form first sprung from Christ, and from His career on earth, still exists, has power, and spreads, because He manifestly supports and extends it.

But the union of visible external support is not the only union that exists between a vine and its branches, nor between Christ and His people.

For, secondly, there is a continual flowing of unseen

vitality proceeding from the vine-stock into its every living branch ; and this process both gives the branches their life, and maintains in them life, and greenness, and beauty, and fruitfulness.

Anyone, looking only from the outside, can see that a vine-stock supports its branches ; but anyone cannot see the internal processes by which the tree's own very life circulates and extends throughout all its branches.

Still that unseen process ever goes on as an essential part of the tree's inner economy. Now this diffusion of the tree's life through all its parts is far more than visible external support. The walls of this Church, or of any other building, as really uphold the roof as a tree supports its branches. So when two pieces of wood, or stone, are joined together to form a pillar, the lower piece supports, and visibly supports, the higher. But their mere mechanical, local relation to each other is not the living relation of a living tree and its branches. External support is all the union that exists in these cases. There is no common life passing from the walls of the house to the roof, and from the lower part of the pillar to the upper part. But there is such a communication and receiving of life ever going on between one part and another part of the same tree.

And this, Christ here teaches us is the kind of union that exists between Himself and believers on Him. Their life is hid with Christ in God. Their real life is drawn from Christ, and there is a continued flowing of His life into theirs. So that it is not so much they who live, as Christ who lives in them. He is the soul of their soul, and the life of their life. They live and believe on Him, and hence they shall never die.

Thirdly, but there is sameness of life between a tree and its branches, and between Christ and His people. There is not only a circulation and an interchange of life through the various parts of the tree, but there is sameness of life, there is sameness of nature, extending all through the tree from the deepest root to the topmost branch. So far as the tree is concerned, this point would hardly need separate mention, much less special emphasis.

But in relation to Christ and His people it is not so. He and we seem in many things so far apart, and so unlike, that this point of both having the one life calls for both mention and emphasis. For there is this sameness of life, there is this sameness of nature in Christ and in believers on Him.

The new life in us, is the same life as the life that is in Christ. This higher life is native, as found in Him; it is borrowed, as found in us. It is strong and perfect in Him; it is often weak and imperfect in us. And still it is the same life in kind, if not in degree. The supreme affections, and desires, and aims, and purposes of Christians, are the same as those of Christ in the sense of being borrowed from Him, and only becoming ours because they have been His first, and because we are in living union with Him.

For "Christ was always consciously in the presence of the Father, serving, praising," honouring, and pleasing Him. And such is the life, a life like His own, which He gives to them that come to Him, in order that they, too, may have it. This life, in and from Christ, is "a life of communion with God, of submission to His will, and of confidence in His love." "The intimacy" of the union between Christ and His people is as * * if one life, one blood poured through them all." But still further:

Fourthly, a vine-stock and its branches are connected together, in a real organic oneness, and so are Christ and His Church.

The vine-stock and its branches are not two separate organisms, two distinct plants; they form, when taken together, but one plant, but one vine, but one whole living thing. Not any part of the plant is complete in itself, without all the other parts. Branches alone do not form a tree or plant, nor does the stock alone form a tree, but the union of both parts, of all the parts forms the tree. So that there are—all through the tree—but the various parts of a common organization, and one and the same life.

And so there is in like manner a real union, a manifest oneness, between Christ and believers on Him. For just as all the members of a body form but one body, and as the vine-stock, including the root and all the branches, form but one vine, so of Christ and the Church—they are one. When He says to His disciples, "I am the vine, ye are the branches," He says in effect: 'Ye, my people, are not a complete body in yourselves; ye are only a part of Me.'

And as of Christ's people, so of Christ. In a very important sense Christ is not complete without His Church. Personally He is, but officially, mediatorially, as the head of humanity, He is not complete in Himself. The hidden life of the unseen Christ, which the world would not otherwise see, now that He is no longer upon the earth, unfolds itself in the spiritual life and beauty of His Church. It is He alone who in the fullest sense is "the righteous" one of the first psalm, " like a tree planted by the streams of water, that bringeth forth its fruit in its season, whose leaf also doth not wither; and whatsoever He doeth shall prosper." And every man who answers in any good measure to the great reality set forth by this fair figure does so because he is in Christ, and abiding in Him shares His fruitfulness.

And all this dependence of the branches upon the vine, and of Christians upon Christ, is apparent in the case of both. The union, the oneness of both the literal, and the spiritual tree can be seen. Nay, it is a oneness that cannot fail to be seen. And the other figures which are used in the word of God, to denote this same relation between Christ and His own redeemed, bring out the same grand central truth, of a real close union as existing between Christ, and His people.

For the Church and people of Christ are often represented in Scripture as the kingdom of Christ. And just as both the sovereign and his people united, form but one nation : so of Christ and His disciples—they, too, form but one nation, but one people. But you may ask me:

What does all this about Christ and His people truly mean without figure? What is the spiritual reality.

When St. Paul calls this mystery of Christ, and of the Church 'great,' we may well own that it leads us beyond our depth. But I answer, that from the practical side the text means two things.

First, that all who believe on Jesus are treated in law at once, according to His good deserts, and not according to their own evil deserts.

And, secondly, the text means, that all who believe on Jesus become really like Him in personal character, and disposition, and conduct. So that men 'marvel and take knowledge of them that they have been with Jesus,' and have caught His spirit and learnt His laws. And Christ's words, "I am the vine, ye are the branches," are true of all who are in Him, and they are true of none besides. For all others draw their true life from some quite different source. But "he that eateth My flesh," says Jesus, "and drinketh My blood, hath eternal life, and I will raise him up at the last day."

And out of this close and endearing union between Christ and his people springs another important union—their union with one another. Our text unfolds this union also, though it does so indirectly. For all the branches of a tree do not directly meet and touch each other—all are not directly joined to one another; but they all meet in a common centre, the trunk of the tree, and all join there in it, and become one.

And so is it with the inter-relationship of real Christians with each other. That is often not direct. The living members of Christ are often far separated from each other in many ways—as in time. For one is safe in Heaven long before the other comes upon the spiritual battlefield of earth. And they are often far separated in space, too. One lives in the torrid zone, another lives in one of the temperate zones, and another, still, lives in one of the frigid zones, and they have never met. Or they are far separated in rank and position. One is a nobleman, and the other is a peasant. They live very different outward lives; and they have never met on intimate and equal terms and unburdened to each other their common faith, and hope, and love, and life. And yet it is the Holy Spirit who by regeneration "fashioneth the hearts of them" all alike. Or some of the members of Christ may be so far separated in their speculative theological opinions, or in their ecclesiastical homes, as to consider each the other 'a heretic,' a dangerous man; so far as to keep wilfully aloof, and never to seek to know each other.

Or some personal misunderstanding, which probably ought not to have arisen, and certainly ought not to have been kept up between such persons, may have kept others, who were both Christ's, asunder for years, or for life.

But yet each true Christian is connected really and truly at the centre of his life with Jesus Christ, with whom each, and all other Christians are also really and truly connected. And that union with Christ is a strong, as well as a real bond with each other. This bond makes all Christians really one in spirit even on earth, whether they fully know it or not. For "all good men are exceedingly alike inside." And deeper than our many important differences of view and organization as Christians: "There is one body, and one spirit, * * one Lord, one faith, one baptism, one God and Father of all, who is over all, and through all, and in all." And these blessed bonds shall yet draw those who are in Christ all together in a visible, acknowledged union, and that for ever.

II.—Secondly, consider the duty of Christ's disciples in the relationship that is here unfolded. It is to "abide" in Christ. He says, "Abide in Me, and I in you." When the believer is engrafted into Christ, Christ becomes his only source of spiritual nourishment, and he must abide thus, keeping up the vital connection with Christ, living on Christ, living from Christ.

You observe that our Lord uses the figure of the vine, and its branches, as far as the figure will carry out His ideas. But He has always the reality of the relation with His people before His mind, and would make us have the same reality before our minds also.

And hence He says, "Abide in Me," thus departing from the figure, and speaking of the reality. For a branch can do nothing to make itself abide in the vine. Not can it do anything to sever itself from the vine. These words forsake the figure of the vine, and address the personal will and conscience of believing men. For we can strive to 'abide in Christ,' or we may exercise our free will in not striving to 'abide in Him.'

"Abide in Me," says Christ. There is no purely material figure there. But there is added to the figure, a personal duty held out before us in the plainest terms, and an appeal made to our freedom of will.

And the very words "abide in me," carry in them what the spiritual class of persons is to which they are addressed. "Abide in Me," says Jesus. Now, these words were manifestly addressed to those who were already in Christ, and they are addressed to such still.

To those who are not yet in Christ, His invitations are different. He addresses them in the words, "come unto Me," "believe on the Son of God." "Believe on the Lord Jesus Christ."

But not so is the order given in the text to abide in Christ. In these words, Jesus speaks to those who are already in Him.

First, and in order to see and set forth more clearly the duty of abiding in Christ, let us together look for a little at what it is to be in Christ. To be in Christ denotes both a certain state, and a certain character. The man who is in Christ is, as to state, a justified man, and he is, as to character, a sanctified man.

To return to the figure of our text, the believer on Jesus is cut off from the wild and worthless stock of nature, and by faith he is engrafted into Christ, the living vine. And just as we become united to Christ at first, and are found in Him by exercising faith on Him: so to abide in Christ, means ever to continue making Him the great object of our faith. Abiding in Christ, means a growing faith in His work, in His character, in His doing, and dying for us; but all as leading to a fuller faith in Himself. For He Himself is the glorious object of our faith.

And thus we abide in Christ by repeating, daily and hourly, the act of faith that first made Christ ours, until faith become with us, the unbroken habit of living a life of faith upon the Son of God.

Secondly, the expression "abide in Me" shows that the connection of the believer on Christ, with his Lord, is not an act, but a life-long connection. Christ is "the alpha and the omega" of the spiritual life in man. "He is the author and the perfecter of our faith." That which we at first receive from Christ by faith, is not a gift that never more needs to be repeated.

On the contrary, we must abide in Him by receiving daily supplies of grace, that so we may ever continue in a growing and fruit-bearing condition.

In order to abide in Christ, we must abide in the daily reception and use of that divine gift which first made Him, ours, and made us, His. For our connection as Christians with Christ is not an act, but a life.

Thirdly, our text plainly implies, that the believer on Jesus has means put within his power which he may use, and ought to use, for abiding in Christ. Two of the most important means of abiding in Christ, that we may use, are even mentioned and commended to us in verse 7th: and they are first having Christ's words abiding in us, leading to the right use of prayer to God and Christ. "If ye abide in Me, and My words abide in you, ask whatsoever ye will, and it shall be done unto you." What a lesson on the study of the Bible, and what a promise to prayer! Here we find that our abiding in Christ, and our having Christ's words abiding in us, are closely connected. For we abide in Christ best when His words abide in us most. The words, "Let the word of Christ dwell in you richly in all wisdom," are in the very spirit of our text.

And then the other important means of abiding in Christ that is mentioned is prayer. For both our abiding in Christ, and our having Christ's word abiding in us, are closely connected with our receiving answers to our prayers.

It is not any man and every man who may 'ask of God whatsoever he will, and find that it shall be done unto him.' But some people may do so. And it is the man who is abiding in Christ, and who has Christ's words abiding in him, who thus asks and gets, and he alone. For God gives the Holy Spirit to them that ask Him. And every such man who is thus taught from above asks "according to God," and asking so, gets what he asks. And the true Christian being thus under the guidance of the Holy Spirit, is sure to ask for things that are, in the main, agreeable to the will of God. "If ye abide in Me," says Christ, "and if My words abide in you," 'you will ask aright, and you will be answered.' So that prayer, too, is an important means of abiding in Christ. Prayer both private and social is so.

"Ask, and it shall be given you; seek, and ye shall find; knock, and it shall be opened unto you," is the promise. And social prayer has this blessed assurance from Christ: "Where two or three are gathered together in My name, there am I in the midst of them."

Christian fellowship also is a pleasing and helpful means to the same important end of abiding in Christ.

We have already seen, that abiding in Christ stands closely connected with success in prayer. Let us not forget this, but 'continue stedfast in prayer.'

Fourthly, and so does abiding in Christ stand closely connected with all spiritual good. It is with the believer on Christ, as it is with the vine-branch. It has no life or fruitfulness apart from the tree. And he has no life or fruitfulness apart from, or out of Christ.

A genial atmosphere, a fruitful soil, copious and refreshing showers, and fertilizing streams and rivers—all contribute greatly to the fruitfulness of the living branch that is in the living vine, and is drawing nourishment from its life. But atmosphere, and rain, and soil, and stream, produce no fruit from the broken withered branch, that lies on the ground separated from the vine. For the branches cannot get nourishment from the fruitful earth, nor from air and stream, but through the living vine.

And so is it with the soul of man, and Christ. Man's higher nature lives and grows by a living contact with Christ, not by the observance of ordinances and means of grace, out of, and apart from, Christ. The exercises of prayer and praise, the reading and preaching of God's holy word, Christian fellowship in the observance of the Lord's supper, and in much else, all these God-appointed things become real means of grace to him who is already in Christ, and is abiding in Christ. But even these divine institutions prove no vital spiritual blessings to the mere professor of religion, who, while he observes them, has no living union with Christ in them.

Hence, from the same religious services, the man who is in Christ retires, filled and refreshed with the goodness of God, and the man who is not in Christ, retires as empty of spiritual good as he came.

Hence, under the same preaching, and in the same Church fellowship, the one person grows strong in the Lord, and the other remains stationary, or goes back and becomes twice dead.

And Christ's abiding in us stands very closely connected with our abiding in Him. " Abide in Me," he says, " and I in you." There is thus a voluntary inter-communion between Christ and His people ; and there is here a clearly implied promise of Jesus, that if we do not forsake Him, but abide in Him, He will not forsake us, but abide in us. 'Abide you in Me, and I promise you that I will abide in you' is the force of Christ's loving words.

III.—Thirdly, we have in our text the glorious results of a real abiding union with Christ, and the terrible danger of a mere profession of religion without the reality.

Being in Christ, and abiding in Christ, are not mere names. " He that saith he abideth in Him ought himself also to walk even as He walked."

The glorious results of a living union between Christ and believers have in part appeared from the very nature of the union itself. We have seen that the believer obtains external visible support from Christ ; nay, he gets a new life from Christ, the same in kind with Christ's own life. And we have also seen that he becomes really one with Christ, as a vine and its branches are one. All this we have seen and dwelt upon.

But we have to notice further, now, that this union with Christ produces important results beyond the believer himself, results which are summed up in our text in the one attractive word, fruit! a thing which others pluck and enjoy. For you notice that our Lord selects a tree, or plant, that is not very valuable for its wood, but is very valuable for its rich, delicious, wholesome fruit. Jesus chooses a plant that its owner plants, and tends, and prunes, and nourishes, not for its worth as timber when once it has been cut down, but for its great value as a grape growing, fruit-bearing plant.

Now, it is so also with the believer in Jesus Christ. One of the most important purposes for which He, destined for transplantation into celestial soil, is left in the world for a time, is that he may bear fruit that shall be to God's glory and for man's good.

The design of God, the great husbandman of the moral world, in all His dealings with us Christians, is the same as the vine-dresser's design in planting and training his vines. Both seek fruit. God seeks 'the fruits of righteousness, which are to His own praise and glory.' And those who are in Christ, and those alone, yield such fruits. The sure result of union with Christ is always fruit, more or less abundant. And in some cases union with Christ produces much fruit. For even all the living branches of the living vine are not equally fruitful, and strong, nor alike fruitful and strong at all times.

But while all genuine fruit borne by us honours God, Christ affirms, in our text, that it is in those who bear much fruit that God is especially glorified.

But what is the fruit which is here spoken of? It must, of course, be like the vine and like the branches both. There is in this fruit something that is human, and much that is divine. We get in Galatians V., 22, a list of some of the fruits of union with Christ. For this is a vine "bearing twelve manner of fruits," and all are supernaturally good.

For "the fruit of the spirit is love, joy, peace, longsuffering, kindness, goodness, faithfulness, meekness, temperance." Enough of this kind of fruit would make the world to bloom as the Paradise of God. The fruit that is first named in the list is "love." 'For it is Christ's new commandment that His disciples should love one another.' 'And by this all men are to know them for His.' For "love is of God;" and love is mighty for good. Love has done much for humanity, and it can do much more. "Above all things put on love, which is the bond of perfectness."

Love, divine and human, 'shed abroad in human hearts,' and ruling human lives, is what the world most needs to heal its many wounds and woes, and give it health and joy. And the love of man to man, as well as the love of man to God, is a fruit of union with Christ.

Another 'fruit of the spirit,' or, what is the same thing, a fruit of 'abiding in Christ,' is "joy." "But if any man hath not the spirit of Christ, he is none of His." "For the joy of the Lord is our strength," as His people. 'The disciples of Jesus are always glad when they see their Lord.' And joy is a sure fruit of union with Christ.

And "peace," too, is another such fruit. "Peace I leave with you," said Jesus to His disciples; "My peace I give unto you." "Let the peace of God rule in your hearts." And this peace, which is a fruit of union with

Christ, is "the peace of God which passeth all understanding."

And so is "long suffering" a fruit of union with Christ. "And we exhort you, brethren," says Paul, * * "be long suffering toward all." And so we read: "Put on therefore, as God's elect, holy, and beloved, a heart of compassion, kindness, humilty, meekness, long suffering; forbearing one another, and forgiving each other, if any man have a complaint against any; even as the Lord forgave you, so also do ye." This grace, too, is learnt in the school of Christ.

And so is "gentleness." "Now I, Paul, myself intreat you by the meekness and gentleness of Christ." "For as many of you as were baptised into Christ did put on Christ."

Another fruit of this union with Christ is "goodness." Paul writes thus to the Romans, who were believers on Jesus: "And I myself also am persuaded of you, my brethren, that ye yourselves are full of goodness." But this goodness was not native to them or to any. It, too, was a fruit of union with Christ.

And so is "faith." "For we walk by faith, not by sight," says one speaking for all Christians. "Faith is counted for righteousness." "We are saved by faith."

We are exhorted to "put on the breast-plate and shield of faith and love." We are called on "to fight the good fight of the faith." For "without faith it is impossible to be well pleasing unto God." "And this is the victory that hath overcome the world, even our faith." 'And it is by faith that God cleanses our hearts.' And another fruit of this union with Christ is "meekness." And "blessed are the meek, for they shall inherit the earth."

Another fruit of union with Christ is "temperance." And the Christian, as a "man that striveth in the games," whose goal is glory, must be "temperate in all things."

And while all these, and many such like fruits, grow in greater or lesser abundance on all the living branches which are found in Christ, the living vine; you may as soon look for ripe grapes growing in the open air among the frosts and snows of Greenland, as you may look out of Christ, the true vine, for such excellent fruits of the Spirit as those upon which we have been looking. Let me again remind you of what our Lord here tells us, that God is not fully satisfied, or much glorified, with fruit in us without regard to its amount as well as its quality.

Our Heavenly Father seeks and expects much fruit. But there is oftentimes much wandering away from Christ among believers on Him, and hence there is but little fruit in them. It is by nearness to Jesus, it is by abiding in Him, that we are able to bring forth much fruit. From being in Christ comes fruit; and from abiding in Christ comes much fruit. For in proportion to the intimacy and the constancy of our union with Christ, will be our preparedness to bear much fruit, and so to glorify God, and to bless our fellow-men.

And, on the other hand, the text warns us against the terrible dangers of a mere profession of religion without the reality: or, in other words, against the danger of not abiding in Christ.

"For apart from Me," says Jesus, separated from Me, "ye can do nothing." "As the branch cannot bear fruit of itself, except it abide in the vine; so neither can ye, except ye abide in Me."

For as dependent as the branches of a vine are upon the parent stock for life, growth, and fruitfulness, so dependent are believers upon Christ for their life, growth, and fruitfulness.

I do not understand Christ to say in our text that a man may be a living branch in Him at one time, and then become withered, and be burned as a useless thing. The life that Christ gives is everlasting life.

But I take it that He speaks here as often, according to appearances. The withered and unfruitful branches which are spoken of in the text, are probably all professors of religion who are not its possessors; all who are in Christ by profession and appearance and outward connexion, but not in Him by a real living union. As, for example, the Jewish Church generally in the days of Christ, who were cut off from Him by their own act, but still were really cut off: for they were only withered branches, the Gentiles being grafted into Christ in their place. And all professing Christians who are not living members of Christ, are only withered branches of Him.

First we shall notice the description, that is here given of these withered branches, and then their doom. For the professor of Christianity who is not in Christ is withered and fruitless. I need not ask you if you ever saw such a withered professor of religion? For alas! alas! how many withered professors have we all seen; how many do we still see? And all from this cause that is named in the text, they are not in Christ, and abiding in Him; but they are separate from Christ, they are apart from Him. They are in the visible church, and they seem to be in Christ; but they begin to wither, and the withering process goes on, and that visible decay betrays, even to the eyes of men, that they are separate from Christ, and without the divine life of grace.

Observe some of the signs of one being only a withered professor of religion.

The visible signs of people being withered, fruitless professors of religion, generally begin with their devotions; and not in public prayer, but in the closet. The flame of devotion begins to become weak, and languid, and low in the closet. And then when the spiritual affections have become cold, such private devotions become irregular and infrequent, and by-and-bye they are often or quite neglected.

And then the conduct of devotion in the family becomes manifestly heartless and formal. And then public worship itself becomes a weariness, and attendance upon it irregular. And then the man's religious efforts become languid and relaxed. He gives up many or most of his former efforts to 'grow in grace,' and to save souls. Instead of doubling his diligence in the way and work of the Lord, as he sees the day of reckoning approaching, he halves his diligence, and then lessens it still more, and soon stands still.

And then in due time his own personal character manifestly suffers in all ways. His walk before God and man becomes less watchful, tender, and faultless than before. He does not keep the Sabbath holy, as he once did. He becomes more fond of worldly amusements, and less fond of religious services than once.

And in time all this often appears visible, even to the men of the world. As in the case of Judas Iscariot, who, though an Apostle of our Lord, came at the last to be known by all his contemporaries, and has been known since by all the ages, as only a withered, fruitless branch of Christ, the vine. But whether the real character of such a withered professor be seen and known by men or not, the fact is :

That such useless branches, such fruitless professors, are known unto God and reserved unto burning.

As men first cast away the withering, fruitless branches of fruit trees, and then gather them together and make firewood of them, and burn them : so does God cast forth and reject, and then gather for destruction, those whose religion is only a withered, empty, fruitless profession.

You remember that the word of God in the first Psalm says "the wicked are like the chaff which the wind driveth away," in the day of trial. They are light and worthless. And here in our text they are compared to worthless, withered branches of fruit trees, ready to be gathered together and burnt up as firewood.

These are figurative expressions, no doubt, but no unreal, empty figures come from the mouth of God, and of Christ; and the reality meant by them must be something inexpressibly awful. " Can thine heart endure, or can thine hands be strong, in the days that I shall deal with thee? I, the Lord, have spoken it, and will do it." Are there any here present who are consciously not in Christ? Any who have no personal experience of the soul-renewing truth of my text? Are there any here who are only withered branches of Christ, fruitless professors? or who do not even profess to be in Christ, and are not in Him? Why is this so? And of whom here is this terrible thing true? Let each one of us urge the question, "Is it I, Lord?" on Him who knows us as we are, and can let us see ourselves aright.

In conclusion, we learn that life is essential to religion, and so is also growth. All the branches of a fruit tree need not be of the same size, but for fruit, all must be living.

And we are specially taught how we may glorify God. It is by bearing much fruit.

The text urges self-examination on us all, lest any of us should be nothing to Christ. And this text explains many of our afflictions, trials, and sorrows. In and by them the great husbandman is 'cleansing every branch that beareth fruit, that it may bear more fruit.' He means no less good, and no less kind an issue by our afflictions than that. Let us therefore not shrink too readily from the uplifted pruning-shears that are wielded by the hand of love, with the design of obtaining from us, for our Lord's glory, more and better fruit.

X.

ETERNAL LIFE IN CHRIST.

"Verily, verily, I say unto you, he that believeth" [on Me] "hath eternal life."—JOHN VI., 47.

THE Bible contains no deeper truths regarding the relation of the Lord Jesus Christ to humanity than some of the utterances contained in this chapter; and all are from His own lips, 'into which grace was poured, lips that keep and disperse the knowledge of God.'

As an example, he says, in the words that follow our text and explain it, "I am the bread of life." 'I am the true manna which came down from Heaven.' And, again, "I am the resurrection and the life." And here in our text he says, in substance, 'I am not only the life, but the life-giver.'

The subject of this morning's discourse was given me as a magazine article by a friend now in glory—the Rev. Robert Spence, M.A., of Dundee—who named it "Eternal life the present possession of the believer in Jesus." And in turning the subject that he appointed me into a sermon, with bowed head I lovingly beckon my sorrowful, yet congratulatory, adieu to him who is gone. "Servant of God, well done." Thou hast gone before; we are all following, " but each in his own order." However, we who are in Christ all go to the fulness of life that is in God, and in glory. I speak ther. of life; for Jesus says, "Verily, verily, I say unto you, he that believeth" [on Me] " hath eternal life." So that eternal life is not only something to be hoped for, and waited and longed for, though in its perfection and fulness it is so. But this life in Christ is not all to come. It is both now, and it is to come. It begins here, but it ends never. It is something to be possessed, experienced, and enjoyed now, not fully, yet in part, and really.

I —The great theme that our text opens up on this occasion is life—life in the highest sense. What an overflowing fulness of meaning there is in that short word life! But what then is this highest form of life, which is called by Christ Himself eternal life? Nay, let us ask first of all: What is life? What is any form of life?

No one can tell by strict definition what life is. All life is a mystery, "hid in God," the great Author and Giver of life. Or, if science and philology will not own life to be a mystery, yet both theology and philosophy, looking deeper, readily own that life is a great mystery. Life overflows all the banks of scientific definition, and floods the universe everywhere as a great all-abounding mystery, whose solution is hid in God.

The Bible contains no deeper word, nor thing, than the word, and what it means, life. For all life brings us very near to Him who is the great central mystery of the universe—who is both the Living One and the life-giver, in whom "we live, move, and have our being."

It matters little to our present purpose what life is to scientific definition. Here it concerns us much more to know what, and how much, life is to sentiment, to the social affections, and to religion. If we cannot define, we can yet name some of the most characteristic elements and features of life; and we can see its forms of organization, and perceive its growth. We can see many of its workings, we can describe many of its outgoings, if we cannot see itself. We can describe living creatures as organized, capable of movement and of growth, and so forth. We can see the workings of life, if we cannot see life itself. The living move, and breathe, and act; the dead do not.

But more of definition and outside description of life I shall not at present attempt. But if you urge the question further, What is life? What is human life from the side of sentiment and the social affections? I shall attempt to describe, though not to define. For life represents ourselves. It is what is most truly ours, if not us. The living are of us, and with us; and the dead are not.

What, then, is life to us? I turn you to the shipwrecked voyager, the almost drowned, but saved man, who has been long exposed to death in the angry, raging sea, and has sternly struggled with this consciously impending death, been all but lost, and yet has at last been rescued and saved. That saved state is life. What joy and gratitude does the saved man feel! Ask him and his household, "What is life to you?" And with lively joy and gratitude, returning the glad looks of his wife and the hearty caresses of his children, he will say: "This that we now feel is life. Now we all live." How precious a thing, to those who love each other, is life spared and restored.

Or ask the bold professional gladiator of the deep, the long experienced sailor, amid the wild triumphant storm, "What life is?" Let it be when the greater his knowledge of the angry moods and dangerous ways of the mighty deep, in its dreadful majesty, the more clearly he sees how many chances there are against his deliverance at this time, and how few there are for it. But at last he is saved. God "maketh the storm a calm." "So He bringeth them unto their desired haven." And now the saved one can say: 'I yet live.' Yes, ask him what life is? And the lightest heart will give weighty answer. Spared life is sweet to such a man. He knows in this hour what life is. He says: 'This is it. I yet live, and life is sweeter than ever.'

Or ask our own Royal Family, with their former dread experience of death, and their lately added but joyful experience of restored life, what life is? and their answer will not be a light one. A single life may be much to a family. Ask the Queen, who is a widowed wife, and is also the mother of him who was sick; ask the sisters and brothers who, after weeks of intense and depressing anxiety, and more than one summons to see the loved one die—who yet, by God's mercy, lives—what this life of grief turned into joy, by having him spared and restored to them, was and is? And they will say spared life is a great joy.

Or ask many other families who have been in like

circumstances, and have been tried with like experiences, and who have watched over other imperilled lives of like private, though not of like public interest, and who have had loved ones restored from the gates of death ; ask such families, what life is to them ? and you will get like answers.

Or ask others of very unlike circumstances, because of the widely dissimilar issue of a like danger. For death has come into their home. Life has not been restored. Ask any such bereaved ones what life is, and what death is, and how full of meaning is their answer ? While those silent words of the heart, unbidden tears, will truly tell how precious and how cherished are the departed joys of this desolated home.

Or ask both the soldier himself and his family, either before he enters the perilous battle, or after he has narrowly escaped its terrible carnage, what his life in such circumstances is to them ? And the word life will stir their hearts to their inmost depths. For his life represents to the family continued union, and his death represents final separation for this world.

Or ask those themselves who have been long sick what life is ?—as the Prince of Wales on a late occasion— who, after having been dipped deeply into the river of death, even to the lips, feels himself sweetly, even if slowly, rising back into life again. Well, ask him what life is ? And if rightly exercised by God's dealings, his grateful emotion and interest in life will be too deep for utterance in words. Life must represent much to such a man. It may represent all that he knows and loves.

Yes, my hearers, life and death are great things to us mortals, even in this their lower sense.

At such times, and in such scenes as I have spoken of, we learn more fully than at ordinary times what life and death are to the human heart. And yet this earthly, dying life, to which we cling so fondly, is not the deepest and most precious life that we can live, even in itself and while it lasts ; and then it does not, to any one, remain long ; it soon passes away, and is no more.

We have now one foot on the ladder of ascent towards our theme ; but we must rise higher than this mortal life and its interests, in order to see and to reach the full height of our present subject—life in Christ. For mere existence is not life to us even now, much less is it the eternal life of which we are speaking. Life in man's case is more than being, life is well-being.

If from any cause the reason of the loved one who had been spared to us were hopelessly and finally taken away, we should hardly count that spared existence of his to be spared life. The love of the near and dear might survive even that terrible loss, and by the aid of memory and imagination love might live upon the past; but joyful fellowship would be past and gone. "The fellowship of kindred minds" survives not reason's dethronement.

But without the loss of reason, if from any cause, all joy to the persons themselves, and all sunshine, and all happiness, and all love were taken away from life, such a state of existence would be less than half life to them and to us.

Were even the vital powers to fail, were all strength of body and mind taken away, it would hardly either to the possessor, or to others, be life that would remain. For a human creature may vegetate, both body and mind rather than live. Body may live, and mind may die. A sound mind and a sound body together, are the normal and proper constituents of human life, even of the lower life. And he walks lame who wants either; and the measure of both kinds of soundness, both of body and mind, is the measure of life.

But life as applied to man graduates in meaning from animal life all up the scale of creation to angel life. Man touches at once both ends of creation's ladder, and all the steps between.

First, animal life is ours. That life we share with our humblest inferiors, with all the brute creation. It is ours as well as theirs.

But man is also an intellectual being and has an intellectual life above the animal. This kind of life we share with the whole intelligent creation, good and bad, of all orders, with angels both fallen and unfallen, and with God Himself. We, like them, think, feel, and understand. Intellectual life may be good or bad, and yet equally be life.

But rising another step, we touch the top of our subject. For what is still more important, and what we have specially to do with at present, is that man is a moral and spiritual being, and has, as the crowning glory of his nature, a moral and spiritual life, his deepest and most abiding life.

This is above mere mind. For the mind may live on, and yet the moral, spiritual soul may die daily.

It is this highest life which connects us more closely with God Himself, and His moral image, than aught beside, and with all holy beings. We share this life with God and all the holy, and with them only.

II.—And now, having spoken of life in general, and even named the kind of life which is spoken of in our text, I urge more closely the question: What is it? What is this highest kind of life? Not any longer what is life in general; but what is this life? And in what do its possessors differ from mere natural men?

Rising thus a step, we touch the top of our subject. Let us look at these points. Life—the spiritual life, of which our text speaks—is a certain spiritual state; it is a certain spiritual character, and relation to God.

And this life is composed of certain constituent elements which are known to us. It is a state of knowledge of God, and of the things of God. It is a state of faith, or spiritual perception and spiritual sympathy, which makes spiritual and invisible things real and near to us. It is a state of interest in things divine. It is a state of holiness; it is a state of love to God and man; it is a state of "joy in God through our Lord Jesus Christ;" it is a state of conscious peace with God. And the peace is the "peace of God that passeth all understanding." This peace does not come into the heart when worldly good flows upon us, nor is it taken away when that ebbs.

It is a life hid with Christ in God. This is the life that God made man for, and meant man for living. And our text tells us, that "he that believeth on Jesus" hath all these elements in his life now; and they are its best constituents.

It may throw further light on this spiritual, this higher life, if I attempt briefly to answer the question: What is spiritual death? For that is a state and an experience the very opposite of all this that I have tried to describe.

Spiritual death is the state of those who do not live this higher life. Spiritual death is ignorance of God, and of the things of God. Spiritual death is unbelief and distrust of God. It is blindness to spiritual and invisible realities, and want of interest in them. It is unholiness. It is want of love to God and man. It is want of joy in God, and want of peace with God. Such a moral and spiritual state the Bible calls death. He who is in this state is *dead* while he lives. He is "dead in trespasses and in sins." His intellect may be alive in all its vigour and brightness, and, what is lower, the passions and appetites may even be too much alive; but the higher elements, the truly God-like elements of man's spiritual nature, are in the unrenewed man, dead, or dying.

And the one state which the Bible calls life ends in final and glorious union and fellowship with God, who alone is good. While the other state leads to a growing separation and alienation from God and His love.

Now, that is not death in its darkest, grimmest features, which only makes strength and beauty to depart, and, bursting family ties, separates loved ones in space and from intercourse for a few years, but leaves us one in love, sympathy, and interest. That is not death.

But that is really death which, as the end of goodness, joy, and hope, separates us from God and from all good and happy beings now, and for evermore. That is death.

And that is not life in its truest, highest sense which only links us to flesh, and by the silken cords of the heart, to those we love on earth, for a few years. But that is life indeed which links us by bonds that last for ever, to God and to Christ in a real living union of thought and love, and that links us through God to all the good. That is life.

And not till we enter and know that future world as it is, can we fully estimate the worth of this highest life; and know what it is to gain, or to lose our true life.

III.—But as life rises to its source in a life-giver, I now come to show, as my text and context strongly affirm, that this noblest kind of life is connected in some very close way with faith in Jesus. Or, in other words, I seek to answer the question: How does faith in Jesus produce all these new and good elements of character that go to constitute the spiritual life? Or how is this life connected with faith in Jesus? For he that believeth on Jesus hath all these divinest elements of character in his life. They are, in truth, its best and largest constituents. This essential connection of faith and life is not only true, but it is the very Gospel of Christ: for " he that believeth not the Son shall not see life." While " he that believeth hath eternal life."

So you see that this highest, noblest kind of life—this true life of the soul—our Lord, who calls it eternal life, connects in the very closest way with faith in Himself.

'We live this life by the faith of the Son of God.' For he who believes on Jesus hath this life. Our text connects together faith and this life as closely as fountain and stream are connected, where the one originates, runs into, and becomes the other. Our text connects together faith and life as root and plant are connected, where the one gives and feeds, and the other gets and is fed; and yet they are organically and vitally one. They are parts of a whole. Our text connects together faith and life as body and soul are connected, where matter and spirit form but one wonderfully made man—for they are a unity. Our text connects together faith and life as fuel and fire, food and life are connected, where the grosser thing, changing its form, passes into and disappears in the more subtle essence. The one grows into the other.

So Christ, the fountain of life, fills the life of believing humanity with His own life, and yet ever remains full. Hear our Lord's own words on the nexus between faith and life: "Verily, verily, I say unto you, he that believeth [on Me] hath eternal life." This is a most solemn, strong, and clear utterance of the fact that the highest life in man is in and from Christ.

Nay, more, Jesus says: "I am the life and the life-giver. I give this higher life, as well as sustain it. Yea, and the bread which I will give is My flesh, for the life of the world."

Does this mean feeding upon Christ in the ordinance of the Lord's Supper only? and does this mean either a more palpable and fixed, or a more evanescent and flexible form of transubstantiation? Nay, hear the Master on the utterances of this chapter: "It is the spirit that quickeneth; the flesh profiteth nothing. The words that I have spoken unto you are spirit, and are life."

Whenever, and wherever faith on Jesus is in lively exercise, we draw life from Him.

And now let us inquire a little more closely: What is the relation of faith and life? Or, in other words, how does faith in Jesus produce all these higher elements of character? Is it so that he that believeth on Jesus hath this higher, this eternal life? Yes, this doctrine, that all spiritual blessings come to us by faith in Christ, is the very gospel.

But is the connection between faith and life, or faith and salvation, an arbitrary or ill-assorted union? Is it an appointment of God for which we can see no reason? No, it is not arbitrary. We can see good reasons for this life being linked to faith.

If you say, What is the reason? I answer: Look to what faith is, and to what it does. Faith, or trust, is all the world over, the key of the human soul, that opens it or shuts it to every personality outside itself. And the exercise of faith in Jesus is the taking of this key and turning the lock that opens the very citadel, the sacred arcanum of our nature, to the entrance of God Himself, to become our real King and Lord.

To this question, Why faith gives and sustains life? I answer again: Well, all life of which we know anything is fed by a provision outside of, and beyond, itself. This is a law of Nature that runs through all orders of beings and things. It is so with the plant, and with the animal, and with the human body; and it is so also with the intellect, the affections, and whole mind of man. It, too, is fed from without, with ideas, words, images, and things. The affections, too, have a life. They also demand objects on which to fix and feed. And so of the highest life, the spiritual nature, as here. It, too, is not a self-sustained life. It feeds on truth, on the highest truth, on moral and spiritual truth, and especially on Him who is the truth and the life. Jesus says: "I am the bread of life, the true manna that came down from Heaven." He says: 'I am the proper food of man's soul. What material bread is to the body, that I am in my person, teaching, and career to the soul of man. Men live by me; men die without me.'

Well, look at the facts which centre in the person and career of Jesus. See who He is, whence He came, and what He came for. He is from Eternity. He is before all things. He came from Heaven. He took on Him our nature. He lived among us. He taught us. He healed us. He died for us, to save us from our sins. He rose for us. He reigns for us.

I shall name for special emphasis two of the most essential facts of Christ's career—His incarnation and His atoning death.

Look also at the principles which are taught us by the facts of Christ's career, when the facts are rightly understood. These principles are specially God's justice, God's hatred of sin, God's love to man, God's mercy; or all, in one word, as giving birth and being to all the facts, God's love to man.

And look also at some of the inferences that naturally spring from both the principles and the facts of Christ's career.

I shall name only two such inferences expressed in Scripture words. "He that spared not His own Son, but delivered Him up for us all, how shall He not also with Him freely give us all things?" This is general. And also: "For if, while we were enemies, we were reconciled to God through the death of His Son, much more, being reconciled, shall we be saved by His life." This is special. Look at these most obvious inferences arising from these facts and utterances, inferences which may be summed up in one, and it is, that we need have no suspicion or fear for the future, after what God's love has already done for us.

Now, faith in Jesus Christ makes all these great things at once, and growingly, ours. And faith in Jesus means that these great facts, principles, and inferences, of which we have been speaking, are known and understood, and that their power is deeply felt and experienced by us.

For faith is the eye that sees these divine things in their beauty, and the hand that seizes, and holds them fast in their preciousness, and the mouth that receives and eats them up, and the inner organs that assimilate them, as the food by which our souls live.

And Christ affirms in our text that if these facts, principles, and inferences that take their rise in, and grow out of, and centre in Himself, the Christ, are received and realized, the men who do so must live, and do live, in this, the highest sense. All their highest nature now begins to live. 'These facts about Me,' says Jesus 'seen; these relationships to God,' says Jesus, 'realized, change all the present and all the future to a man. Old things pass away with him; behold all things become new.'

Yes, these facts about Christ change all the highest things of existence to the man who believes them. And they do this because they change the man himself. He was dead, now he lives. But how do they change him, and why? Where lies their mighty transforming power? In as much as they remove radical error from the man's mind about God and about himself. This is much. They change the heart, too, as well as the mind.

And no marvel if they do all this. There are no other facts known to us so fitted radically to change human character for the better as the facts of Christ's career. These true things of Christ change the believer's views of God and man too, and they change his heart to both. And they are well fitted to do so. They teach and make real to us, in the best possible manner, God's boundless love and goodness in view of man's evil; and they demonstrate man's need of salvation.

So that the sweetest, brightest, gladdest views, thoughts, and feelings in all the renewed man's soul are the views, thoughts, and affections that burst in upon him from God, as seen in and through Christ. This faith's view of God in Christ is the believer's new, better, truer, higher life, of which our Lord speaks in the text.

Now, if faith instrumentally do all these great things for the man who possesses it, I cannot but much doubt if the most common modern treatment of religious doubt, and of the religious doubter and unbeliever, by many leaders of theological thought among us, be quite on the lines of Christ, and of apostolic men. The doubting, the unbelieving, and to some extent the men of little faith, Christ blamed much, and sometimes sternly denounced, as the guilty authors of their own unbelief. While those who were great in simple, childlike faith, drew forth His warmest admiration. He highly praised and held them up as models to all men.

But many eminent theological doctors and able editors, writing on the Christian side, have been liberal enough largely to reverse Christ's verdict as to the comparative merits of faith and doubt. It has been a fashion for years past, for Christian writers with almost one accord, to carry "the honest doubter" aloft on their shoulders, and to accord him a public triumph in the name of Christianity!

Let it be granted that our fathers were very hard on this gentleman, harder far than the Master Himself, administering heavy theological blows, and even kicks, to him in great abundance, and, too roughly and roundly, denying his honesty altogether; and that for the treatment of him in some past times we owe him some generous amends. We have surely changed all that with a vengeance long ago. For the last quarter of a century, until lately, when a healthier tone has begun to prevail, has not the honest doubter been in many quarters a very special literary and theological pet, sick-nursed, spoon-fed, in all ways ministered to and much caressed of all compassionate-hearted Christian people?

Poets have sung him, divines have preached him, learned men have defended him, novelists have glorified him, all kinds of men in all kinds of books and periodicals have spoken well of him. Doctrine and miracle have been hustled into corners that their too prominent presence might not hurt his tender eyes. As "the offence of the cross" has not ceased, even the cross has been often veiled or shunted for his accommodation. He is so potent in influence that the sight and touch of him cure certain Christian writers, who in their utterances show but small reverence for churches, creeds, and even for the Book of God, and who suffer from a very general biliousness towards all such commonplace people, as believers in the divine and supernatural, of all their usual spleen, whenever they encounter him; and he renders both their words and spirit unwontedly sweet and gentle. Even the shadow of him passing by, will turn their cursing of others into blessing of him. But this imbecile treatment of him by the faculty has been seriously relaxing both to the honest doubter's health and honesty. He much needs a more bracing regimen. I can stand much praise bestowed upon distinguished virtue without envy: yet I am almost sick of the same kind of song always sung to the same hero by the same men, and in the name of Jesus, "the author and perfecter of our faith," too!

You much mistake my meaning, my hearers, if you think that I know nothing of the difficulties of belief, and am capable of speaking lightly of the really honest doubter. But I ask: Is it not more than time to cease from our foolish laudation of a state of mind that Christ gravely condemns as the great condemning sin, "the condemnation" of those to whom God's word and Son have come?

Is Christ's saying obsolete? "The light is come into the world, and men loved the darkness rather than the light."

It is Jesus Christ who says: "If any willeth to do God's will, he shall know of the teaching, whether it be of God." It speaks ill for the fitness of God's revelations of Himself for their purpose if ever, and especially in this nineteenth century, doubt be presumably a more honest state than faith. The words of Christ which I have just quoted, and many like words, reject such a presumption, and throw it strongly on the other side. Is the legitimate outcome of centuries of divine revelation and manifestation, that men ought to meet God and His utterances with doubt and suspicion? and that the more honest men are, they are the more likely to do so?

No, our pet, the honest doubter, is already sadly spoiled. Let our theological experts, for the patient's sake, change their diet and treatment. If they have not already nursed the honest doubter to death with their too many delicacies, and raised many dishonest doubters from his ashes, they soon will with such hurtful treatment. How can anyone expect 'the survival' of honest doubters when even in religious literature the temptation to the affectation, if not the hypocrisy of doubt, is often made stronger, even by good men, in their foolish angling to catch doubters, than ever the Church, by persecution and in other wrong ways, made the temptation to the hypocrisy of faith? Good as the motive was from which the gentle treatment of the doubter sprung, has not the process of a maudlin, coaxing of unbelief, to believe just a little, gone much too far for men who are " set for the defence of the gospel," and are conscious of a divine Master and a divine message, to commend and make known, " according to the commandment of the eternal God, unto all the nations, unto the obedience of faith ? "

Our final point of inquiry has relation to the duration of the life. I shall put it thus :

IV.—Well, but let it be granted that there is life for believers on Christ in Him and by Him, how is it our life, and how is it called eternal life? And how can a mortal man on earth here and now have eternal life? I answer: Look first at the essential truth of the text, that the life that springs up at conversion is, in its very nature and essence, immortal, everlasting life, fitted to last, and intended to last for ever. That is affirmed in the text in the word ' eternal.' And why should it not be everlasting?

Ordinary Scripture language does not lead us to expect second and third conversions, does it? A Christian is spoken of as born again; but we do not read, I think, of his being born again, and again.

And the immense stress laid in Scripture upon turning to God, believing the Gospel, and being born again, favours the view, as it seems to me—that like being born or dying, this change, call it by what name we may, is an event that stands alone in its magnitude and results.

And then it is affirmed that we have eternal life now whenever we believe on Jesus. We have not the fulness of this life now, we have not its fulness and perfection, but we have its germ, its infancy, even now. We have the same life which goes on to all eternity. The life of God in the soul of man is called eternal life, because of its essential elements. Such as faith, love, holiness, delight in God. These graces abide in the renewed man for evermore.

This life therefore is, and is called, eternal, because of its very nature. It is God's image restored in man. It is a life drawn from Christ. It is Christ's own life in us.

The life is eternal too, because of the immortality of the soul. Its destiny is immortality. Sin is soul disease and incipient death. It is a thing to be cast off. And all who believe in Jesus shall succeed in casting it off, shall return to their normal condition of spiritual health, and live on for ever. This life is eternal. For Christ affirms of every believer in Him, that he shall never die. The body may die, and will die, but not this life that comes from Christ. And thus it is that 'whosoever liveth and believeth in Jesus, though he were dead, yet shall he live.'

So that the life beyond death will not be a new life to the godly, but the completion and perfection of this life in Christ, that begins at regeneration.

And so there is no need for our walking in darkness and uncertainty about the future. For the Christian has

Christ formed in him, the hope of glory. And all the most essential elements of what shall be the perfect life of Heaven go to form, even now, the higher life of man upon the earth.

> " O, one, O only mansion,
>   O, paradise of joy,
> Where tears are ever banished,
>   And joys have no alloy !
>
> *   *   *   *
>
> O, land that see'st no sorrow !
>   O, state that know'st no strife !
> O, princely bowers ! O, land of flowers !
>   O, realm and home of life ! "

XI.

THE SUDDEN AND UNEXPECTED CALL.

A Sermon preached specially to the Young of the Congregation in the Congregational Church, Port Elizabeth, March 7th, 1875, on the sudden death, by drowning, of Emma Hughes and Alice Hallack. Republished by request.

PREFATORY NOTE.

About 5 o'clock on Saturday afternoon, February 27th, Emma, daughter of the late Rev. Isaac Hughes, of the London Missionary Society, and sister-in-law of the Rev. T. Durant Philip, B.A., of Hankey; and Alice, daughter of Mr. Russell Hallack, of this town, while bathing, along with others, in a tributary of the Gamtoos River at Hankey, got, in some way, beyond their depth, and, before help could reach them, were drowned. The preacher, on his return with the parents of Miss Hallack from the joint funeral—so uniquely sad and memorable—preached, from full notes, a sermon on the occasion, which, by request, he has done his best to reproduce: though every word that was then spoken may not be here, nor every word that is here have been spoken.

The seeming incongruity, in the sermon as printed, of greater prominence being given to the junior and less matured personality than to the senior and more matured character, was not an incongruity in the discourse as spoken to an audience, where the one girl was a stranger to almost all, and the other was one of us, brought up in our midst.

30*th March,* 1875.   J. C. M.

"Therefore be ye also ready; for in an hour that ye think not the Son of Man cometh."—MAT. XXIV., 44.

"THE coming of the Son of Man" is a phrase that has various references in Scripture: as to the incarnation, to the destruction of Jerusalem, to the final judgement, and also to *death*. I do not dwell now on these differing references of the phrase, nor on the connection of our text. It is enough for my present purpose, since we are to hold ourselves ready for all Christ's promised and anticipated comings, that my text urges on us the duty of preparation for Christ's coming.

He comes to us now, and He shall come to us in the future in many and various ways: and for all His comings we are to be ready. But I fix upon the one meaning that suits our present circumstances, and urge that on your notice now. The coming of Christ specially, and practically, as I believe, means to us—what it has been to His people in all the past—our own death. And of that coming of Christ I shall speak now. That is, the coming of Christ that most, or all, of us expect to see first, and that is the application of our text that I now make to myself and to you.

Christ is coming to us at death. Think then:

I.—Who comes? "The Son of Man" comes to us. Not a son of man simply—not one out of all the common millions of men—but '*the* Son of Man,' the Son of our humanity, in a special and peculiar sense, 'cometh' to us. This is a very solemn prospect, and yet a very soothing prospect, to all true Christians. The Son of Man Himself, who is also the Son of God, comes in person to lead, with His own protecting hand, His own loved ones into the unseen world of light, love, and glory.

Our text might have said that death cometh to us, which is true, and other Scriptures do say this. It might have said that sickness, decay, accident, and injury are coming to us, bringing death in their train, which is also true. But it does in truth say something far finer than any of these things, in telling us that our own Lord and Master Himself comes to us, and for us: for He says, "I Come again, and will receive you unto Myself." And He knows the way from this world into that: He Himself has trod it. And He, moved by His great love to desire the nearer presence of the loved ones, still prays with prevailing efficacy: "Father, I will that they also whom Thou hast given Me, be with Me where I am, that they may behold My glory which Thou hast given Me." And the Father, ever and anon, hears the Son's prayer for this, grants the desires of His heart, and, in fulfilment of His desires and prayers, is ever calling away some of the scattered ones of the redeemed family from earth home to glory.

But how disguised are Christ's appearances oftentimes, even to His own children! His love is measureless, and it is everlasting. It never changes; but its manifestations may take endless forms and hues. Even His most gracious approaches to render needed help often alarm and pain His children much. So was it when He came in a bodily shape to His distressed, tempest-tossed, alarmed disciples, walking on the stormy Sea of Galilee, and much alarmed them. They, when they first saw Him, "supposed that it was an apparition," and were more afraid of Him than they were of the yawning deep, and so cried out for fear. And so was it after His resurrection, when He appeared to Mary Magdalene, who, though she was weeping over His death, and searching for His body, did not know His living form, even when He addressed her, but for a time mistook her risen Lord for the gardener. And so not till the very close of their long, and blessed, and soul-cheering interview, did the two disciples, whom Jesus joined on their way to Emmaus, know Him for Jesus. It is often so still. Jesus comes to His people in many unexpected ways, and in many unwelcome forms, though He always comes really in love.

And so was it with His coming to her whom we, as a congregation, this evening specially mourn. She, dear departed one, could not at once have known her Lord's loving hand to be in the harsh cold touch of the hand of death, that was so suddenly, and roughly, laid on her tender frame to quench its vital functions. Nor could she at once have recognised her Lord's benign voice, in a sudden call to yield up her sweet, young life, that must have seemed to her so harsh and cruel. Amid her momentary surprise, and fear, and pain, and agony, could she have known assuredly that it was really Jesus Christ, her own beloved Lord, who had thus come for her to His own eternal glory? It may be not.

How strange a visit was this from the gentle Saviour to a lamb of His flock! And yet, as earth darkened and receded from her view, and "a light from Heaven, above the brightness of the sun," shone around, and within her from Christ's glorious person—she could not long mistake the "altogether lovely" for any one else. O most blessed, and consoling truth this! It is He Himself, the Son of Man, our own Lord and Master, who comes for us, and receives us into His own loving arms at death, if we are really His. This truth, fully believed, robs death of its worst terrors.

And how appalling and heart-breaking to survivors often would the outward circumstances and concomitants of death be, if we could not, even now, by faith break through the thick wall of dark and frowning facts, that is what sense can alone see; and see and feel behind that wall a loving Father's, and a loving Saviour's own hand, and hear His divine voice, saying: "It is I, be not afraid." Yes, it is Jesus Christ, though He is often much disguised, who always comes for His own at death. And *who* shall deny *Him*, or dictate to Him how He shall come, or when?

II.—To *whom* is Jesus coming? To us all. What the Son of Man says to one He says to all—Watch. Watch ye; watch each; watch all. For He comes to one now, and He comes to another again; but He comes to each, He comes to all soon. "What man is he that shall live, and not see death?" We are all enlisted for death, "and there is no discharge in that war." We are all warned. "Behold, we die; we perish; we all perish." To the old, and even to the middle-aged, the Son of Man is visibly coming near in the call of death. For He is adding even now one bodily frailty to another, and thus by them uttering, one voice of warning from the tomb after another voice.

But to the young the Son of Man is also coming by death. Oh! how plainly may He be seen and heard at many times and in many ways! and with what a stunning loudness does He now knock and call to us all, in the sad breavement to which I am now calling your willing attention, saying, "Be ye also ready!"

Surely, we can all, even the least attentive of us, distinctly hear the loud voice of God addressed directly to us, and see plainly the outstretched hand of God beckoning to us personally, in this sad breach which has been made among us. Yes, we can all, through this startling rift into the invisible, that has been so suddenly opened in the midst of us, see more clearly than usual the Son of Man coming to ourselves some early day; and so be more than ever ready when He knocks.

But while we may all see and hear Him coming to us all, yet to the young He most nearly of all comes in these deaths: to the young He most loudly of all calls in this event. For it is not two of us who, by our years, or our infirmities, have all been oftentimes warned; but it is two of the young and strong, unwarned by years or infirmities, who have so suddenly been taken from among us.

III.— *When* is Jesus coming to us, and for us? Does He come when we are ready, prepared, watching, waiting, and even longing to be gone? Not ordinarily. "In an hour that ye think not the Son of Man cometh." That is the rule. His coming is often sudden, unexpected, a great surprise to us. We know not any of us the hour, the day, nor the year, of our own death. We know only the fact that we must all die: and that we must all die soon. We know that "the numbered hour is on the wing that lays us with the dead."

And yet there is oftentimes nothing, as we look forward, that distinguishes, to our view, that coming hour, or those hours that are near it, from any other of all the hours that have come and gone, and are yet to come. Just as nothing said to Alice Hallack, or to us, when she was lately here, 'this is your last holiday, this is your last farewell to us, and this is your last embrace to those whom you are leaving at home; and you are hastening back to school to complete in a few weeks your last earthly task.' "There shall no sign be given to us." The year of our birth we know; but who of those celestials who are deeply read in the mysterious scrolls of the coming future will kindly impart to us that profoundly-kept secret—the year and the hour of our own death? Do the dear departed ones know *when* we are coming, and wait for us as the time approaches? Then why are they so silent all? We cry in our impatience at times,

"Oh that some courteous ghost would blab it out."

But as we reflect, and pray, and grow patient, we feel that perhaps this ignorance of when our Lord comes is best. But it adds much solemnity to life that we seldom know when we are speaking last words, or hearing last words; when we are doing last acts, or seeing last acts done! How often is "the coming of the Son of Man" at death a great surprise, both to the called and to survivors? How truly was it so with the summons of Alice Hallack and Emma Hughes, as well as with the call of some others who have been taken from us at various times, whom we still remember and miss.

This is the great *speciality* of both these deaths. No one here bids fairer for long life now than did she, when we saw her last, who lately went out from among us not to return. Nay, no one bids fairer for life than she did only eight days and three hours ago. Who of us is stronger, healthier, happier, more admired and beloved than she was; with more to live for, to hope for, and to enjoy than she had? She was happy and loved at home; and happy, beloved, and successful at school. She was gladly welcomed home for her holidays; and she was warmly welcomed back to her school duties both by teachers and pupils. Why should she, promising above many, die now?

Her time to die seemed not yet come. And all this was true of her friend and companion, who, equally talented and assiduous, in study was older and more matured in spiritual things, and exerted all her influence to quicken, mature, and develop Alice's religious affections. *Who* of us, looking round our immediate circle of relatives and friends, would have named her as the *probable* first to leave us who has been now the actual first to go?

The venerable Mrs. Robson, widow of that good missionary, the late Rev. Adam Robson, yet wears a mortal body that hangs as a heavy load on a spirit longing to be free from mortality, while Alice Hallack's and Emma Hughes' spirits have cast off the bodies without an hour's sickness or decay, that were year by year becoming fitter organs for their growing powers. Yes, to our puzzled surprise, this very aged, veteran missionary, and teacher of the young, who for half a century " hath been well reported of for good works, hath brought up children, hath used hospitality to strangers, hath washed the saints' feet, hath relieved the afflicted, hath diligently followed every good work," and is now twice widowed, and a great grandmother, yet lives on, though her work seems finished, and though she is waiting and longing to depart; and these budding maidens of thirteen and sixteen years, in whom so many loving hopes centred, are, in the space of a few minutes, dead and gone from earth, with no time to say farewell to any one. And so is it often as it was here: "For in an hour that ye think not the Son of Man cometh."

IV.—Let us reflect on *how* the Son of Man cometh. Not only in an hour that we think not, but also in such unlooked for ways oftentimes as we think not of. He comes sometimes, by long sickness and slow decay of the bodily powers, amid wearisome days and nights, while "waters of a full cup are wrung out by" the sufferers, so that in the morning they say: Would God it were even! and at even they say, would God it were morning!"

And yet amid the visible decay of the outward man, all see that they are going home to God, and find much spiritual profit in intercourse with their daily renewing inward man. Such a death-bed is eloquent for Christ, and such we might have chosen for those who have gone, if we had known that they must have died now, as to our view a fitter and more instructive death than the death which they died. But the *how* of our death is with God, as are the when and where of our death. Sometimes the Son of Man comes to one by sharp and rapid disease, and yet there is time for the sufferer, and all his, to be warned and prepared for the last change. And again the Son of Man comes to some of us riding upon the swift whirlwind of sudden calamity, as in this case, blasting in a moment our choicest plants and buds of promise, while but a minute before not a single premonition of the coming storm appeared in all the sky.

Our text and its context speaks to us of the Son of Man coming unexpectedly, and even stealthily; and the sorrow-laden event that, in God's all-wise providence, forms our second and newer text this evening, speaks impressively to the same effect. His coming as He did to those whom we are commemorating was indeed a sad and crushing surprise to us all; how much more to their nearest and dearest?

And if we ask *why* our Lord ever, and even often, comes to us so, the deepest, fullest, truest answer is, that God's "judgements are a great deep." "How unsearchable are His judgements, and His ways past tracing out." The answer is, that none can "by searching find out God," that none can "find out the Almighty unto perfection." Our fullest, truest answer is that we know not why our Lord comes so. We only know and feel sure that He is too wise to err, and too good to act unkindly; and we know that "all things work together for good" to them that love God. We only feel sure that we may safely trust Him, even when we cannot trace Him.

But there are plainer and simpler answers why our Lord comes in unexpected ways than His own unsearchableness, which, though they do not fathom the whole subject, yet explain much, and are very practical.

Why does our Lord come so? Well, one reason is because we will not be warned to prepare for death otherwise; because we mortals too often forget death; because we trifle with things divine; because we live at ease, although "the race that is set before us" in the gospel has now to be run : therefore does our Lord come so. To teach us with effect our mortality, our frailty, our weakness, our want of foresight, and our dependence on God in all things, such sad surprises are sometimes sent us. To make us all feel, even from the youngest to the oldest, that preparation for death is our immediate and urgent duty, our Lord comes so. And to make us all feel how weak our poor protection of those we love most is, and to lead us to commend each other to God's keeping, our Lord so comes.

If opportunity had been given for man to help, how many who could, would willingly, and at all risks, have rendered needed help to save two lives so promising and so precious to many? But during the few brief moments that such help would have availed to deliver from death, no eye that was linked to a hand that could help, saw the urgent danger.

And soon, alas! how very soon, no human help was of any avail then, or for ever after. For "there is no man that hath power over the spirit to retain the spirit; neither hath he power over the day of death." And that event brings such a change that no affection nor grief of ours can win back to earth those who, while here, ever sought our presence, and gladly consulted our every wish.

We might wonder, not that the good die, but that Jesus ever permits death to approach to His own children in its harsher and more alarming forms, did we not remember that from righteous Abel, who died a violent martyr-death, because Cain's works were evil and Abel's righteous, all down through martyr-prophets and righteous men to His own cruel and shameful death, and often since, it has seemed good in His sight to allow the godly, by rough roads and through much tribulation, to enter the Heavenly kingdom.

But then again: God comes not alone to rectify the wrong things that are in us, but also to perfect the right things; He comes not alone to correct our worldly-mindedness, but to make the Heavenly-minded more so. "For whom the Lord loveth He chasteneth, and scourgeth every son whom He receiveth." We thus "know in part, and we prophesy in part," *why* the Son of Man often comes at such times, and in such ways, as we think not of. For He often chooses in the furnace, and always refines in the furnace of affliction.

V.—Consider, in view of all such awakening visitations, our duty as it is brought before us in the text: "Therefore be ye also ready." But be ready for *what?* Be ready for our Lord's coming at any time, and in any way that He may choose to come. For He is verily coming to us. Let us make sure that He, whenever He comes, shall find us ready. But ready for what? For the solemn hour of our *death*. That event draws near to us also, as it has come to those who have gone. "Behold, we all die." Ready for what? For *judgement*: for this great assize follows after death. "It is appointed unto men once to die; but after this cometh judgement." Ready for what? Ready for that dread *eternity* that is ever so near, and yet stretches away before us like infinite space, without bound or limit: for on all those limitless fields of future time grow the boundless harvests of all that we sow here; and our earthly sowing may end, and the harvest of the future may begin, at any moment.

The duty urged upon us in the text further includes our being ready for all *life's work*, too. *That*, oftentimes we have not been in the past. Let us strive to be so now. Both text and fact are fitted to inspire this high resolve: "We must work the works of Him that sent us while it is day: the night cometh when no man can work." But you ask me: How can we be ready for all the future, since we know so little about it? I answer: By using the present aright. "Behold, now is the acceptable time; behold, now is the day of salvation." And how can we be ready for *death* especially? By living a life of faith on the Son of God. In other words, you ask me what is the true preparation for any and every future that can come to us? I say: A right relation to God the Father through Christ the Son. And that blessed state empties no young life of its joys. You ask me what shall we do that no future may find us unfit for it? I answer: "*Believe* on the Lord Jesus Christ." For salvation comes to mankind by faith in Jesus, and abiding union to God through Him. *Love* the Lord Jesus, and all things are yours—things present and things to come. Christ Himself is yours then and thus, and death is yours, and change and calamity are yours, as well as joy and success, and the world to come is yours. All are yours when Christ is yours. *Serve* the Lord now. This is your noblest mission, your highest happiness, and your best reward.

"Be ye *also* ready," says my text. I rejoice that I can use and emphasize the "also" in this present case. For we "sorrow not even as the rest which have no hope." No two pupils, say those at Hankey, who had excellent opportunities of judging, were more hopefully fit for a sudden call than those who now, as we believe, "sleep in Jesus." What has been described to me as their truly wonderful affection for each other, seems to have had in it the very highest love : 'first, that which is natural; then that which is spiritual.' Watch, my hearers, one and all ; be ye *also* ready. It is our Lord's own illustration, that because the good man of the house does not know what hour the thief will select to attempt to break into his house, therefore, for safety, he must watch all the night through. And it is the fundamental law of watching for the coming of Christ, to be always watching, because He, the Son of Man, often comes to us unexpectedly. Be ye always ready for your Lord's coming, is the spirit of our text.

VI.—If you ask me *why* I have chosen to speak to you on this most painful theme at this trying time ? My answer is, I have spoken to you thus, my dear young friends, because the *facts* of God's providence have spoken so loudly to you, and to us all. The sad event itself of these past days—death coming among us in a moment—has spoken plainly to all the living.

And still more pointedly has the *speciality* of this death spoken to us, and yet speaks. Death itself, under any form, is most monitory to mortals. Death to the living is the greatest of all preachers. Its voice, to the ear of wisdom, is most solemn, and most affecting. These twin-deaths of those, who were so closely united to each other in affection, who "were lovely and pleasant in their lives, and in their death were not divided"—are very *monitory* and affecting deaths in many ways.

They were so, in being so sudden, giving not a moment, it may be, for the unwarned ones to say each for herself: "God be merciful unto me a sinner"—"Lord Jesus receive my spirit." Ought any of us, in such a world as this, to risk our salvation on the improbable opportunity of a death-bed repentence? In suddenness this accident is very like some recent railway accidents and shipwrecks. I speak of these two deaths also, because they were so *unexpected*. No one concerned dreamt of danger. And the accident was, to our view as distant observers, possible only because no one specially concerned to prevent it dreamt of danger being near. I speak of these deaths, too, because they were so *unlikely*. The deceased were engaged in an ordinary recreation, at the ordinary place where they had often bathed, and they were not alone. Companions were with them, and help was not far off. Their cries, or the cries of their alarmed companions, were, I am told, heard by many, but were mistaken for the childrens' customary expressions of mirth and sport while bathing. How unlikely was help, if it should be needed, to fail, and death to linger under this bracing and coveted sport in yonder quiet retreat?

I speak to you of these deaths also, because they are so unexpressibly sad and grievous to their relations, guardians, friends, and to us all. Nothing sadder to survivors could have happened than the death of those dear girls, and death by such a mode, unless the deceased ones had been, in addition to their sad end, strangers to God. No language of mine can fully express the painful sadness of such events for this world, and of this very event, to all who are more closely associated with it especially. Many hearts that are dear to Christ have bled profusely over this calamity. Why have they been made to bleed? Not for His pleasure; but for our profit.

While almost all my words equally apply to the death of both the departed, I have spoken to you mainly of the death of the *one*, because we all *knew* her; most of us knew her well. We all have pleasing associations with her; some of one kind, and some of another, for she was one of ourselves. I speak of her, too, because we all *loved* her, which, as you who knew her best will bear me witness, was not a difficult thing to do. Once more, I speak of her now, because we all deeply *sorrow* for her untimely death, for the way she died, and for the time, and for the survivors of her own family. And I speak now at once, though with small preparation, because all our minds are full of the sorrowful event. I do not need to drag your minds unwillingly towards this subject. Sad as it is, I dare say that I could hardly draw them away from it to another, and I would fain use it while your minds are full of it for your good. And I speak because we may all still get a blessing *from* her who is gone, and a blessing *through* her: she "being dead yet speaketh." May not her lying asleep in death "awake to righteousness" some who are asleep in sin? God means it so.

And thus the actual, or possible *compensations* of such deaths are many. Is there any one here to whom such a sudden call would have been final ruin? Well, 'another' is 'taken,' and you are 'left' that you may seek Christ now. I speak to remind you of some of the blessed compensations which there are in this event to her, and to you, and to us all.

In the sense in which Christ says "whosoever liveth and believeth on Me shall never die," we may gladly say, in His own words on another occasion, "the damsel is not dead but sleepeth." She shall yet awake. "There is no death: what seems so is transition." 'For the godly to die is gain.' She, we believe, is now a conqueror over all evil, while we are yet in the battle. She has overcome the *last* enemy: that conflict yet awaits us all. She is now a leader of the Lord's host above, one who has overcome; we are but of His followers below. She, it may be, is a helper of us: we are but of the helped from on high. She is one of "a great cloud of witnesses:" we are only of the witnessed. She is "a forerunner, entered within the veil:" we at the best are only cleaving to the way that leads thither. She has got an early victory over all evil; we have not yet overcome. We are yet set over the "few things" of earth; she, already set over the "many things" above, has got a nobler sphere for all her perfected faculties than this earth could offer her. I have spoken of all this to you now because God has spoken to us all first. And I say to one and all who are here, "Prepare to meet thy God." Therefore "be ye also ready, for in an hour that ye think not the Son of Man cometh."

> "There is no flock, however watched and tended,
>   But one dead lamb is there!
> There is no fireside, howsoe'er defended,
>   But has one vacant chair!
>
> The air is full of farewells to the dying,
>   And mournings for the dead;
> The heart of Rachel, for her children crying,
>   Will not be comforted!
>
> Let us be patient! These severe afflictions
>   Not from the ground arise,
> But oftentimes celestial benedictions
>   Assume this dark disguise.
>
> We see but dimly through the mists and vapours;
>   Amid these earthly damps,
> What seem to us but sad, funereal tapers,
>   May be Heaven's distant lamps.
>
> There is no Death! What seems so is transition.
>   This life of mortal breath
> Is but a suburb of the life elysian,
>   Whose portal we call Death.
>
> She is not dead—the child of our affection—
>   But gone unto that school
> Where she no longer needs our poor protection,
>   And Christ Himself doth rule.
>
> In that great cloister's stillness and seclusion,
>   By guardian angels led,
> Safe from temptation, safe from sin's pollution,
>   She lives, whom we call dead.
>
> Day after day we think what she is doing
>   In those bright realms of air;
> Year after year her tender steps pursuing,
>   Behold her grown more fair.

Thus do we walk with her, and keep unbroken
    The bond which nature gives,
Thinking that our remembrance, though unspoken,
    May reach her where she lives.

Not as a child shall we again behold her;
    For when with raptures wild
In our embraces we again enfold her,
    She will not be a child;

But a fair maiden, in her Father's mansion,
    Clothed with celestial grace;
And beautiful with all the soul's expansion
    Shall we behold her face.

And though at times impetuous with emotion,
    And anguish long suppressed,
The swelling heart heaves, moaning like the ocean,
    That cannot be at rest,—

We will be patient, and assuage the feeling
    We may not wholly stay;
By silence sanctifying, not concealing,
    The grief that must have way."

XII.

A LOOKING BACKWARD THAT PREPARES FOR GOING FORWARD.

"I am the God of Beth-el, where thou anointedst a pillar, where thou vowedst a vow unto me: now arise, get thee out from this land, and return unto the land of thy nativity."—GENESIS XXXI., 13.

THESE words of God were addressed to Jacob in Paddan-aram. You remember what had been Jacob's errand thither. When God met him in that past time, he was fleeing for his life. For he, prompted and assisted by the too politic Rebekah, his mother, had deceived Isaac, his father, by personating Esau, his elder brother, and had thus taken away for himself, by craft and falsehood, the blessing that Isaac had intended for Esau. But it was the very blessing that God meant for Jacob, and would have made quite as sure to him without his lies and sinful, selfish craft.

Esau, who had never forgotten, and hardly forgiven the sharp bargain that Jacob had driven with him years before about the birth-right, was so wroth with him now on account of the greater wrong which Jacob had just done him, that in a fury of anger and hate, he fully made up his mind to kill Jacob, and thus to take an ample revenge at his own hand for all his wrongs.

But there was one barrier in the way of the angry revengeful Esau in accomplishing his evil purpose, which the better nature in him could not overleap, even when he was at his worst. He truly loved his father. He loved his father too well to vex him, so much as he knew it would do, to find one of his sons foully murdered, and the other the deliberate murderer. This filial love, and this only, held back Esau's hand from Jacob's blood. Not the fear of God. Not respect for law. Not pity for Jacob. Not love for his mother, for she lived also. And Esau well knew that the execution of his foul, fell purpose would pain his mother quite as much as it would pain his father. But he did not in this matter much regard her feelings. It was not in his plan to wait for her death. And why?

Parents, let us take the warning that is here given, and be righteously impartial in the treatment of our children. Esau's mother had shown an excessive partiality for Jacob, and had aided Jacob in injuring Esau; and even prompted the unwilling Jacob to steal away Esau's blessing.

And Esau, I fear, was not sorry that the prospect offered of soon making their mother also, to suffer in Jacob's punishment.

Esau was the unwise child of impulse and passion, a strange compound of anger and love, revenge and generosity.

And he was too impulsive, and at this time too angry, to keep his own dark secret for long. Such a secret must have weighed very heavily on such a mind. And sore burdened as he must have been, we find out that he uttered his evil intentions to someone, as an angry boast, it may be.

At any rate, the dark secret once uttered, was whispered about until the quick and watchful ear of Rebekah caught the ill rumour; and once warned, her sharp eye soon saw in Esau sufficient proof of its truth. And she, who was far from a helpless woman, acted promptly, and was glad to hurry her beloved favourite, Jacob, away from his home and hers, out of her sight and beyond her reach, in order that he might escape the infuriated Esau. It was to Rebekah a sad issue of all her seemingly successful scheming.

And though she flattered not only herself, but also Isaac and Jacob, with the fond hope that his absence would be short, she calls the expected time "a few days until thy brother's fury turn away;" yet Jacob's absence proved twenty long years, and she saw him no more in this world.

Both mother and son were severely punished for their sinful meddling to guide the unerring hand of providence. And in that severe punishment to them both—Jacob's enforced absence from home, and the separation for life by this means of mother and son, fondly attached as they were—they might well read, were meant to do so, and I hope they did read, their own sin in too much meddling to secure their own future. For God most manifestly 'made their own wickedness to correct them, and their back-slidings to reprove them, in order that they might know and see that it is an evil thing and a bitter that they had forsaken the Lord their God.'

Jacob goes from home at once; he goes without preparation, he goes alone, that he may the more surely go without Esau's knowledge. And on his way from home, and apparently the first night, Jacob slept in the open air, and dreamed.

You remember the place and the circumstances. " Jacob went out from Beer-sheba, and went toward Haran. And he lighted upon a certain place, and tarried there all night, because the sun was set." And though Jacob had been up to this time 'a plain,' or quiet 'man, dwelling in tents,' he has for this evening no shelter for his head. "And he took one of the stones of the place, and put it under his head, and lay down in that place to sleep. And he dreamed," no common earthly dream, the natural product of his anxious heart and sad circumstances. But he dreamed a supernatural dream that looked up as high as Heaven, and reached forward until all the families of the earth had been blessed in his seed.

It was then and there that Jacob saw that wonderful ladder set up on the earth which stretched away upward, and connected Heaven and earth, and on which he saw the angels of God ascending and descending, and above which the Lord stood and spake to him.

Mark the immediate, and the great effects of this eventful dream. For we read: "And Jacob awaked out of his sleep, and he said, surely the Lord is in this place, and I knew it not. And he was afraid, and said: How dreadful is this place! this is none other but the House of God, and this is the gate of Heaven. And Jacob rose up early in the morning, and took the stone that he had put under his head, and set it up for a pillar, and poured oil upon the top of it. And he called the name of that place

Beth-el," 'the House of God,' and vowed to God to be God's for all the time to come, and to love and serve Him only.

And so Jacob rose up, and went on his way with new thoughts, and new feelings, and new resolves—in truth, a new man, in much. But that was twenty years before the time when God spake to Jacob in the words of our text. And Jacob had known many changes during that long time. For next day after his memorable dream he rose up and went on from Beth-el, staff in hand: and God protected him, and guided him to his desired destination, the house of Laban, his mother's brother, in Paddan-aram. There he was well received, and lived usefully, and on the whole happily, for many years. He loved Rachel much, and was beloved in return. But he was himself cruelly deceived by Laban in the delicate and vitally important matter of his marriage, just as he had deceived his father and brother, and wounded them, in matters that were also very important. And as the result of this gross deception, Jacob was married unhappily to Leah, whom he loved but little; but he was also married happily to his own much-loved Rachel. He had a large family. And after many struggles with the greedy, selfish Laban for wages, and for general justice, he saw resting down upon the face of his father-in-law the settled look of anger and dissatisfaction growing into dislike.

So that this is a time of great darkness and trouble to Jacob. But in his need God visits him, speaks to him, and brings to him light, direction, and hope.

I take to do at present with only one part of God's important communications to Jacob—that part which is contained in the 13th verse: "I am the God of Beth-el, where thou anointedst a pillar, where thou vowedst a vow unto me: now arise, get thee out from this land, and return unto the land of thy nativity."

From which I remark:

I. That almost all men have, like Jacob, consciously met with God at some time of their life.

II. At such times, and in such meetings, such persons have done as Jacob did. They have prayed, and praised, and promised, and vowed to God.

III. God reminds us in this text that He remembers all such meetings with us, and He speaks in it to recall them to us, as to Jacob.

IV. As God reminded Jacob of the past, in order to stir him up to the performance of a present duty, so God in this text, and in many ways, is reminding us of the past, and still speaking to us, to command our immediate performance of present duty.

You will notice that this is the kind of sermon of which the hearers must bring the larger part with them.

The preacher on such a theme can hope to do no more than, under divine guidance, by stray touches to unlock the hearers' treasures of memory and of conscience.

Preaching some kinds of sermons may be compared to the one part of the process in which the monster steamship, the *Great Eastern*, was some years ago engaged, when she left the shores of Britain for America. Her first office, after taking on board the Atlantic cable, was to sail across the ocean gradually paying out the cable that she had on board as she went on. So, I say, in some sermons, our design is to give out on some topic, all that we have at hand that is best, or all that our hearers will take in. We are givers at such times.

But the *Great Eastern* had another, and also an important, work to do, to which the intention of other sermons may be compared. That other process which she also accomplished was fishing up from the bottom of the sea the lost cable of a former year. And this last is the kind of sermon that I seek to preach this evening, with a like design. The process that I attempt at present is not to tell you anything directly of my own religious experience, but to help you to grapple up, recover, and use, if I may, some of the lost, forgotten, submerged lines of your own experience, in the hope that the remembrance of some past may be the very thing that is most fitted to stir you up to present duty. I am a fisher to-night in the sea of your past experience.

I.—And the first plunge that I venture to take into the wide ocean of your experience is to affirm : That almost all men have consciously met with God at some time of their life. Nay, all of you, or almost all of you, I doubt not, have done so. Jacob did at Beth-el.

Jacob was not an earnestly godly man in his early days, if he was godly at all. Jacob was not manifestly a spiritually changed man when he left home at this time. If he was really a godly man then, his character was most faulty and ill-shaped. But he had on his way to Paddan-aram, as we have seen, a wonderful meeting with God, and a wonderful dream.

Yes, Jacob had real intercourse with God Himself on

that memorable night at Beth-el. That broad ladder, or rather terrace, that he saw stretching across the sky and joining Heaven and earth, connected Jacob, as he had never been before, with God and angels and Heaven: he heard and saw spiritual objects in his dream with a quickened interest, and he awoke a new man. And why not? "For God speaketh once, yea twice, though man regardeth it not. In a dream, in a vision of the night, when deep sleep falleth upon men, in slumberings upon the bed." And he speaks not always in vain. For we further read: "Then He openeth the ears of men, and sealeth their instruction, that He may withdraw man from his purpose, and hide pride from man."

I do not mean to say that Jacob was converted to God in his sleep. But I do mean that he may have had his first real soul-awakening meeting with God in sleep, and seems to have had. Jacob had, it would seem, his first soul-transforming view and thoughts of God in sleep by a dream.

And this meeting with God of Jacob when he was asleep, seems to have led to his conversion when he was awake. I believe that he had got from God in sleep a solution of the doubts, and difficulties, and burdens, and fears, and sorrows of the previous day, and of days past. So much for Jacob at present.

Now, almost all men, I believe, have, like Jacob, consciously met with God at some time or other of their lives, and been made to feel that He is, and that He is very near to us; and that He is the God with whom we have to do.

This awakened sense of God, may have been experienced by some of you when you first left a godly home, and went out into the world with its manifold temptations. This is a testing time. And to the young person who has enjoyed all the privileges of such a home without deciding for God, removal from home sometimes seems to say: 'Take your evil, godless way now without restraint, and reap its fruits, since you will prefer the way of sin to the way of God.'

But the real danger of the new position being realized, not seldom through God's mercy, leads the wisely alarmed soul to God.

So that many, like Jacob, have left a godly home unconverted to meet with God at, or soon after that time, and to be converted to Him.

Others of you may have had a first real meeting with God at the death-bed of some near and dear relative or friend, whether the friend has been godly or ungodly, and the lesson been, 'let me die such a death, or let me not.' When you lost your dearest earthly friend, and needed more than ever before an object to love, then God came near to you, and revealed Himself to you as the best of friends, and revealed Jesus as 'the brother born for adversity,' and so God won your heart for Himself.

Others of you may have really met with God first, in some great sorrow, or disappointment, or disaster, or bereavement. You then for the first time felt, in good earnest that you needed a comforter, a portion, and an inheritance more enduring than the world could give; and you sought and found that lasting joy and treasure in God Himself, the true portion of the human soul, the true home, shield, and reward of all His people.

Others here may have had such a real meeting with God after some great sin had been committed, and its bitter remorse felt. You then first felt the need of a saviour from sin. Before, you were wise in your own esteem. Till then you were the whole that did not need a physician. Then when you had plainly, it may be foully, fallen, you felt your hurt, you became conscious of your soul-sickness, and first betook yourself to the great physician.

Others here may have had such a conscious meeting with God when you were exposed to some great, visible danger. You then saw that you needed a deliverer from danger; and you sought and found in God the true deliverer from all dangers, seen and unseen, present and future.

And others of you may have truly met with God under some living, breathing, searching sermon, that singled you out, every word of which seemed spoken to you, and fitted for your case—just fitted for yourself alone, as much as if you only had been addressed. You then felt that God Himself, not the preacher only, was speaking to you in very deed.

And others of you, it may be, truly met with God by the means of some good, wise word, fitly spoken in private by some child of God. It is just as likely that the God-sent, God-owned word was spoken by some humble, obscure instrument of God's love, who had been watching in prayer for you, as by one who was eminent in the Church. The word was from God more than from man, and proved a word in season to your soul.

Some others of you, it may be, betook yourselves to earnest prayer; and while you prayed God heard, answered, and visited you. Almost 'before you called God answered, and while you were yet speaking He heard.'

God met others of you as you were devoutly reading and searching your Bibles; and He, God in Christ, showed Himself to be the treasure hid in the field, the pearl of great price, for which one may safely sell all that he has.

Another can trace the beginning of religious concern to nothing else than a train of thought, whence arising you cannot say, or you do not remember.

"I just began to think," was a young man's laconic account given to me, and more than once repeated in the same words, of the genesis of his religious thought and life, when I questioned him as to what had awaked his religious interest. And the answer was good. For some of you may not have got so far as to think much about God and the soul.

But it is little matter which of all these experiences was your first experience of religious concern; or if in some quite other way, less usual you obtained the experience which I have spoken of, if you really had it. That is the vital point. But the effect, if you have had such an experience, was to bring God near to you, and your heart near to God.

But I cannot grapple up from your past an experience that you never had. If you know no such experience of God being near to you as I have been speaking of, you will hardly understand what I mean by all that I have said.

But if you have met with God, and in His presence had the eternal world unveiled to you, had sin brought home to your conscience, death brought near, and judgement and eternity made most real, then you will understand quite well what I am now saying. You, too, will go back to some hour, or spot, or event, or exercise that brought God very near, and opened Heaven to you, which reproves your present state. But you must bring the personal experience for which I have been casting the net. I cannot give you that; I can only try to recall something of what has been, to arouse within you sacred memories that may have been slumbering, but are not yet dead.

II.—All who have had such meetings with God have at such times done in spirit as Jacob did.

Those of you who have had such meetings with God as Jacob had, and as I have been describing, have done in substance, if not in form, as Jacob did at Beth-el.

What things did Jacob do and say?

He "took the stone that he had put under his head, and set it up for a pillar, and poured oil upon the top of it. And he called the name of that place Beth-el." And he vowed a vow to God: To take Him, the Lord, for his God, to be His, and to love and serve Him.

His stone pillow he erected into a pillar as a monument of God's goodness in visiting him, and as a memorial of God's presence with him that night.

And Jacob anointed the pillar. For oil was much used in sacrifices, and in consecrations; and it had a deep religious meaning. The reality pointed at by the pouring of the holy oil in Scripture is the descent of the Holy

Spirit. And Jacob vowed to God. That is, he promised to be God's, not his own, and to serve God. And in particular he promised to make Luz, 'the place of meeting,' into Beth-el, 'the house of God.' Thus Jacob did three things.

He expressed a deep-felt sense of God's goodness to him. He next did God present service and worship.

And then he made solemn promise and entire surrender of himself, and his, unto God for the future.

And you, my hearers, if you have ever met with God, you also, I am sure, did likewise. You confessed something to God—your sins, your unworthiness. And you did something to God: you rendered Him a present worship and service. And you promised something to God for the future.

It is the practical atheism of not realizing who God is, and how near to us He is, that makes men irreligious. The sinner cannot realize God as living and near, and yet say and do nothing to please Him. Nay, the convinced sinner, when he really feels himself in God's presence, must worship Him. As soon as he believes that God is, he becomes in earnest in his intercourse with God. The man then feels it to be either a most dreadful or a most delightful thing to be in God's presence; but he is no longer indifferent to God.

When you, my friend, found yourself in this state, perhaps you turned to your Bible, your too much neglected Bible, and began to read and study it with new interest, as the work of a living author concerning you. You bowed the knee to God in prayer, though you had been prayerless before. Or if you had not been absolutely prayerless before, yet instead of the lifeless form which had satisfied you formerly, you now really poured out your heart before the Lord.

Instead of often neglecting the House of God as you did before, you now waited on public worship and the preaching of the gospel regularly. Or if you had been regular in your attendance before, you now heard the glad tidings of mercy with new interest; 'you received the word with joy.' You forsook also many evil things and ways of which you had been guilty before.

You shed tears of godly sorrow for sin. You were in deep earnest in seeking salvation.

And it may be that you, like Jacob, gave the place, and the time, and the experience a name. You called the place the House of God, and the time and the experience your conversion to God. You gave some solemn religious name to the experience of that time and place. You professed to accept of Christ as your Saviour, and to surrender yourself, soul, body, and spirit to His service. And you then and there raised some pillar, some memorial stone, and promised never to forget what had occurred. That was years ago, it may be.

And at such a time you doubtless, like Jacob, vowed to God; and whether you now remember your vow to God or not, it was doubtless recorded in Heaven.

You promised to renounce all sin, and to live a holy life. You promised to God that neither the prevailing theories, nor the ordinary practices of men, but His revealed will, as you read it in His word, should rule and regulate your life. Nay, only God and you know how much you promised, how far you went in 'opening your mouth to the Lord.'

But this I may safely affirm, that all of you who have really met with God, vowed some vow to Him. And He heard it, and hears it still as distinctly as when you were making it. We may change, but He changes not. We may forget our vows to Him, but He never does.

There are spots of earth where in the open air, and in solitude, or in the House of God, or in the closet in prayer, or in intercourse with some man of God, very solemn things were said and done between God and you, things like what passed between Jacob and God at Beth-el.

But we further learn from our text, that:

III.—God not only remembers all such meetings that we have had with Him, but He often reminds us, as He did Jacob, of them; and He does so with us, this day, in this text.

God says to us to-day as He did to Jacob in our text: 'Look back and remember the past.' Our text says to us now: 'God saw your memorial stone when you set it up, and He sees it now, for it still stands unchanged in His sight.' Yes, He ever sees all our memorial stones. He has seen your pillar of the past all the time that you have been walking away from it, and, it may be, forgetting it quite.

I do not know how it has been with you all. But we learn that Jacob too much forgot this solemn, sacred hour and place. He too much forgot both his own hallowed impressions, and his own sacred promises.

There were strange gods in Paddan-aram, and Jacob got so familiarized to them as to permit their presence in his own family. And he was not quite free from the charge of using doubtful arts to increase his substance. The process of 'diamond cut diamond' soon goes beyond honest cleverness, when an honest man honestly tries it against such a man as Laban.

It might be a hard question to answer: whether Jacob had gone backward or forward in spiritual things after the lapse of twenty years. And there can be no question at all, but that he should have made far more of twenty years given him to grow in grace than he had done.

And hence it was that though all God's spiritual promises to Jacob centred in Canaan, and his return there, God needed to remind him of it, and came to remind him of the past at Beth el, with the promises concerning Canaan which were linked to it, which he had too much forgotten. Jacob needed God's prompting by event and word to send him back to Canaan. He would not if Beth-el had been nearer his heart.

And so may you have forgotten the past, that you ought most to have remembered. Your goodness may have been "as a morning cloud, and as the dew that goeth early away." You may have been only a stony ground hearer, in whom the truth has taken no deep root. Or you may have proved a back-slider. Or you may have begun to be religious in your own strength, not in God's; and so you have soon halted, and declined. But now God this day in this text reminds you of the past. It was God who reminded Jacob of his past acts and words, of his too much forgotten past religious experiences and deliverances, saying, "I am the God of Beth-el, where thou anointedst a pillar, where thou vowedst a vow unto Me."

God says, 'You remember saying of Beth-el, "surely the Lord is in this place." I am the same God as I was then, when you felt Me to be so near, and so great, and My presence to be so solemn. I have been the same all the time since we met at Beth-el, and I am the same now. Are you the same to Me still? I remember all that passed just as it was; do you?'

It may be that God is saying to some of us: 'No, you have forgotten Me, and you have forgotten your own past experiences; and I am come to remind you that I am the Lord, and change not. I am come to carry you back, as I did Jacob, to the experiences of that night when you most vividly realized My presence and claims, and when you surrendered yourself to Me by solemn vows.'

And so God comes to remind each of you, my hearers, this evening, in this text, by my mouth, of some past in your experience.

God is telling you by my lips that He is as near to you now as you once saw Him to be, and as great, and as holy, and as good, and as rich in mercy, and as willing to save, and as terrible to the workers of iniquity. 'I am,' says Jehovah, 'the God of that past time as really as of this present time; and of this as of that. Go back to the hour when you left home, and met Me; or to that solemn death-bed where you met Me; or to that great sorrow; or to that great sin from which I lifted you; or to that searching sermon in which I spoke to you; or to that most affecting Bible reading where we met; or to that real outpouring of your heart in prayer which I heard. And know that all that you then saw Me, and felt Me to be, I am still.' "I am the God of Beth-el."

Thus God comes to us all this evening. And how much we all need to be reminded of the past—of the good that was in the past, as well as of the bad! And it is of the good in the past, not of the bad, that our text reminds us —of the best, not of the worst.

Are you sorry for much in your past, my friend? It is well. Godly sorrow is needed by us all in view of much in the past. And I would not, by a single iota undo the force of your penitent feeling for the faulty past. But I would recall your noblest and holiest past, and carry you back to it. What I would fain do now, is to add to penitence for the wrong past a deeper penitence on account of the wrong present.

With all that may be amiss in our past, and ought to be mourned over, are there no parts of that past which ought to make us much ashamed of this present?

Is there in our religious history no past that is better than the present, or at least relatively better? Better, taking the date into account?

A past that was more promising than the present? is a past that promised a better future than we have yet reached, and promised it soon?

Are you all satisfied with your own present, when you compare it with the best page in your past history? God means in the text: That Jacob's Beth-el experiences and doings shamed the experiences and doings of his later life. Is it so with you? Do any past experiences of yours shame your present experiences of things divine? And does any past course of action for God shame your present course of action?

IV.—Well, God still speaks to us in this text, and in many other ways, and commands us to arise to the performance of present duty; it may be of some specific duty.

God spoke so to Jacob. He said: " Now arise, get thee out from this land, and return unto the land of thy nativity." This was the present duty to which Jacob was imperatively called by God.

And the meaning of the divine command was this: 'I am the God of Beth-el, who met you there on your leaving home, who promised you guidance and protection on your journey, and afterwards; and I have fulfilled My part of the engagement thus far. You know something of what I have done for you. And now I am about to complete My promise of bringing you into your own Canaan. This is the promise that I made to you twenty years ago, when you were fleeing from Canaan, and saw no way of return. And now I say to you: Arise, get thee out of this land, and return to that. Do you still foresee danger from Esau? Yet confide in Me now, and obey Me by going back at once. My time for your return is come, and all the dark and painful events that tend to drive you from Paddan-aram, I intend as sails and oars urging you away from here, and wafting you thither—I intend them all as finger-posts, plainly pointing you away to the Canaan of my past promises.'

Well, so much for Jacob. But what is our duty, one and all, in this retrospect that I have been seeking to help us all to take? It must be to awake up and arise to the performance of some neglected duty, or duties, and to the better performance of all our duties. "Soul * * * take thine ease, eat, drink, be merry," are not God-given words. "Thou foolish one," is God's description of the man who so speaks. The words " soul, take thine ease," are not fit for saint or sinner. Not in this world of tremendous spiritual peril, where the soul must be saved or lost, where the good fight of faith must be fought and won, can souls wisely and safely take their ease. Nay, the words, 'Now arise, gird up the loins of your mind,' well describe the present duty of all here.

But to what shall we arise? you say. The duty may not be the same to us all. Doubtless it is not the same to us all. It may be to some of us, to seek the Lord, and thus to fulfil a promise made to Him years ago, but not yet performed. Is that not the special duty of some who are here?

But others, it may be, have gone further than to promise to serve God. One such says: 'I, like Jacob, did sacrifice to God. I sought the Lord, and thought that I had found Him. I thought that I both loved and served Him. But that is years ago. And I have practically forgotten my past agonised experiences and earnest promises both. They are almost strange to me now, when in my present comparative indifference I try to recall them. What a declension from God, and from godliness, I have been guilty of! I have back-slidden from God. I have been asleep in sin and wordliness.'

Well, I say in God's name, Arise now. It is not too late to be saved. God has spared you in the land of the living until now, and in the place of hope; and He yet waits to be gracious unto you. "Behold, now is the acceptable time; behold, now is the day of salvation."

The duty of others here may be to seek a deeper piety. You live to God, but you are not strong, earnest, and fervent. 'Arise: grow in grace.' But the immediate duty of others here may be different still. No matter what the special duty that God and your own past experience are laying on your conscience, my text speaks to you also. It says, 'Arise.'

What is your state of mind, one and all? The text is for you, whatever it be. Does anyone say: "Well, my state of mind is utter indifference to spiritual things." I answer: A very bad state indeed. But let me ask now: To what, and to whom are you utterly indifferent?

Do you say: To God, and to things divine?

Well, I answer: If it be so, you are, and must be much to blame for that indifference. If you are indifferent to God it must arise from ignorance of Him, ignorance of who He is, and of what He is, and of what He can do.

You cannot be indifferent to God, you dare not be indifferent to God, if you know Him, who He is, and what He can do, and how completely you are in His power, as an abiding realized knowledge. I might venture to challenge you to a daily and an earnest study of what the Bible says about God, and to assure you that if you will stand in such a light, your indifference will not long continue. You are not indifferent to your own happiness, and cannot be so. Nor can you be indifferent to God, in whose hands all your happiness is, if you know Him, and if you really believe that your well-being is entirely dependent upon Him, and on your standing in right relations to Him.

But that is not at all my state of mind, says another. My state of mind is despair, hopelessness, dark, dismal, leaden-eyed despair. But why should you despair, I ask? Where did you learn this godless mood of mind? God does not teach you that view of your relations to Himself. Look to the cross of Calvary. It teaches us quite another lessen than despair. Look there, and love, hope, and live. See Jesus the Saviour there. He is willingly doing, even to the death, His saving work on that painful, shameful cross. Saved men and women, the trophies of His mercy, are around the cross mourning His death. A suddenly saved man, who had lived an openly evil life, hangs by His side, rejoicing in a salvation both present and future.

Another says: 'None of all this meets my case. My state of mind is sorrow, shame, penitence.' That is well. There is room for all this, and there is need. "For godly sorrow worketh repentance, the repentance that needeth not to be repented of But the sorrow of the world worketh death." Sink not then into that last sad state. You have sorrowed after a godly sort, and God is now calling upon you to 'arise' from the good state of godly sorrow to the far better state of holy joy in Him.

For God is speaking to us now, not in cloud and thunder, and tempest, and earthquake, but in the still small voice of gospel mercy. "Come now, and let us reason together," saith the Lord: "though your sins be as scarlet, they shall be as white as snow; though they be red like crimson, they shall be as wool."

Does still another say: 'My state is different, my state of mind is humble gratitude for a present salvation.' That is well. Strive to grow greatly in gratitude to God. Yet be not satisfied with what you are and with where you are. Do not rest in present attainments, but advance. You may do far better in the divine life than you have yet done. God calls you to this. Let your motto be onward, and upward. Only take a humbling glance backward, as Jacob was called to do, in order to prepare you for a strenuous race forward in the footsteps of our great "Leader and Commander." "And the Lord said * * * speak unto the children of Israel that they go forward." And for the spiritual Israel this "word of the Lord endureth for ever.

XIII.

THE LAWS OF SPIRITUAL PROGRESS.

South African Congregational Union Sermon for 1869.

" Yet shall the righteous hold on his way: and he that hath clean hands shall wax stronger and stronger."—JOB XVII., 9.

BRETHREN beloved in the Lord, I have found it no easy task to select a subject of discourse for the present important occasion. But may I not hope that in the choice of a subject, at least, I have been in some degree successful, however I may succeed or fail in its treatment? For our text speaks of that which all men desire and value—it speaks of power, of strength. Who does not need, and who does not wish, to be strong? Yes, to wax stronger and stronger.

Weakness of all kinds is painful, inconvenient, and humiliating. So much indeed is power valued by us, that not a little of the world's hero-worship has been the ardent adoration of strength in some one of its three principal manifestations, of either physical, or intellectual, or moral might.

And all three have a glory, though not an equal glory. 'For there is one glory of the physical, and another glory of the intellectual, and another glory of the spiritual.'

But moral and spiritual power, in the average estimate of mankind, has as yet had far less glory attributed to it than any of the other forms of power; though, estimated truly, it deserves the most glory of all.

Intellectual power, by comparison with spiritual power, has had a large and, on the whole, a growing share of glory assigned to it. But looking at the whole history of the human race, we must, I think, admit that physical force has had the most extensive sway in the world, and the longest reign. Once men " seemed as men "—they " that lifted up axes upon a thicket of trees." This was the rough reign of physical strength—too often the modern public school boys' standard of being famous still—when a man took rank and precedence among his fellows according to the prowess of his arm. Then a man's greatest glory, in the eyes of other men, was the unequalled strength of his bodily frame.

Yet this is in truth the lowest manifestation of human power, the one in which " he is [most] like the beasts that perish;" and it could not always rank as the highest display of power, unless where men had become quite embruted.

Hence a time of mechanical invention, and of intellectual power, progress, and skill gradually drew on, when mind, penetrating the secrets of nature, and subjecting matter more cunningly to its potent sway, the few of wise heads and skilled hands became the acknowledged kings and chiefs of men, and came to guide the labours and rule the movements of the unskilled and unwise many. And then the rule of mere animal force gradually gave way before the uplifted sceptre of intellectual vigour. So that a man became more famed and looked up to for superior powers of mind than for superior powers of body.

And as human society, at any time or place, has become enlightened and refined, or has again receded into animalism and barbarism, so has either physical or intellectual strength been crowned and held the ascendant.

But, as I have said, these two kinds of power are not all the forces that man can wield. Our text speaks of another and a higher kind of power.

And that is our subject on the present occasion. Look then :

I. At the kind of strength and progress that is promised in the text to the righteous.

II. At who they are that obtain this strength, and make this progress. And

III. At some of the laws that regulate the growth of this kind of strength.

I.—Look first, I say, at the kind of strength and progress that is promised in the text to the righteous.

For our text does not speak of either purely bodily, or of purely mental power.

It brings before our attention a nobler kind of strength than even this last, though it is not unrelated to that.

Our text speaks of a strength whose greatest triumphs, in this world, are still future, as Christ's greatest triumphs in and over men are still future. When He, the true King of men, has been lifted up upon His throne of influence, the Cross, and lifted up in the life of the Church, and lifted up in the uttered gospel, until as thus lifted up He arrests the gaze of the wide world, and draws all men unto Himself, then shall this new reign of spiritual power be fully come.

It is a benign strength this that lies calmly resting on the sure promises and unchanging faithfulness of God, waiting, not in vain, for a fuller recognition and a nobler triumph in the world than it has ever yet had.

This kind of strength, of which I speak, is moral and spiritual might, is active, aggressive, victorious goodness.

The strength of our text is the strength of right in vanquishing wrong, the strength of moral goodness in overcoming moral evil, both in its possessor and around him. This is a gentle, subtle kind of strength, which is not seen to be strength, but is still counted weakness by the many. For they walk by sense, not by faith. And even the noblest triumphs of this spiritual strength are often undiscovered by the eye of sense. For "the natural man receiveth not the things of the Spirit of God, for they are foolishness unto him; and he cannot know them because they are spiritually judged."

This spiritual strength is also counted weakness by the world because its triumphs are not only like itself, spiritual, but they are often not immediate.

For although this spiritual power is destined ultimately to triumph over all baser kinds of power, it now seems, as it traverses its silent, unostentatous path to victory, to be oftentimes bent under the heavy foot of lawless might, and to be impotently suffering a hopeless defeat when subjected to the opposing grasp of physical and intellectual strength. For much of the history of the world as yet has been a record of the seeming triumphs of might, in its grosser forms, over right; or, in other words, of brute force, or mere mind force, over this gentler moral and spiritual might, called right, which is however, yet destined, under the promised reign of love in the world, to become the mightiest and most glorious of all earth's moving powers. For the time draws on when the good alone shall be seen and counted to be truly great.

But men who walk by sense, seeing not the things which are invisible, cannot wait God's time and way. They say: "Let Him make speed, let Him hasten His work, that we may see it; and let the counsel of the Holy One of Israel draw nigh and come, that we may know it!" They say: 'Let the right triumph now, if God be for it;' and if it does not triumph on the spot, before their eyes, they turn away to some other and visible helper rather than wait for God. Because the triumph of goodness on the earth is oftentimes not immediate, those who walk by sense despise that promised triumph, count goodness a weak and slow power, and cannot wait for its victories.

The world, too, both best discerns and most admires, not spiritual strength, but other kinds of might. Men will extol in their fellow-men acts of physical and intellectual power, who cannot see the greatness of truly heroic moral actions. The mass of men cannot be moved to admiration by marked displays of faith and patience, of love to God and man, of self-sacrifice for conscience sake, and of heroic self-control.

And yet to conquer sin and self is man's best and greatest triumph. Every man's noblest battlefield lies within, not without himself; lies within, not without his fellow-man. "He that is slow to anger is better than the mighty; and he that ruleth his spirit than he that taketh a city." But the world has most applauded, and yet applauds most, the world has best rewarded, and yet rewards best, the taking of cities. No doubt for years to come human society, even in Christendom, will continue to append its applause, its pensions, and its peerages to the taking of cities, and such warlike and statesman-like exploits; and, it may be, scornfully call the ruling of the spirit, and the aiming to gain a brother by love and forgiveness, meanness, or weakness, or want of courage.

Yea, so ingrained is the lower estimate of worth, that I am not at all sure that the man whose best victories are over himself and the evils of his own character, and over his fellow-man, only in 'not rendering evil for evil,' may not have to wait for his peerage even in the good days that are to come, not only for the millennium, but for Heaven.

And in harmony with this, the world's prevailing false ideal of greatness, the idol gods, and the human heroes that men have made or chosen for themselves, have for the most part been powerful, but not good. Look at the gods of the heathen which have ever been both ideal, objective creations of the human mind, embodying its own highest conceptions, and also true, though sometimes unconscious, reflections of the real moral quality of human character. And as you look at them you will see that they have been for the most part gods in power only, and in morals merely vile men. They have been super-human in power always, but human, and almost infra-human in character often. Showing that the highest degree of power, not the highest measure of goodness, is what fallen man naturally seeks most to attain himself, and to embody in his heroes.

Jupiter, the supreme divinity of both the Romans and the Greeks, was represented by his worshippers as incontrollable in power, but as stained with almost every human vice. Embodied power, physical and intellectual power, is the supreme god of heathenism. But it is power without goodness, purity, justice, truth, and mercy. And with most men among ourselves there is too much of this not yet extinct idolatry of mere power. Even the gifted Thomas Carlyle became too often, did he not, the apostle and prophet of this brutal god.

It is not moral and spiritual power, but grosser forms of power, that most people admire most. For instance, little admiration is excited in many minds by the fact that Jesus Christ, who was truly divine, and thus almighty in power, "when He was reviled, reviled not again," nor destroyed the revilers, but patiently suffered man's worst indignities, locking up the thunderbolts of His irresistible power behind the vivifying beams of His infinite goodness. Perhaps some of us little wonder at, and but little admire Christ's suffering patiently all that man could do against Him, and yet conquering man's force and enmity by the moral and spiritual strength that found their brightest expression in His voluntary sufferings on the Cross. This suffering attitude of Jesus seemed to His contemporaries, and still seems to the eye of the natural man, the weakest of all divine displays of power. Christ's contemporaries, seeing Him dying on the Cross, said, "He saved others; Himself He cannot save."

And yet this in truth is not only the highest kind of power, but it is the mightiest in moral result. For the Cross of Christ is the very 'power of God unto salvation.' It is the Cross that wins back to God all the hearts that are won on earth. Here in the Cross of Christ we see more of the peculiar power of 'God, who is love,' than anywhere else. It is not the arm of coercion that changes the sinner into the saint, but the sweetly drawing power of divine love. It is not the demand, 'you must yield to me,' imposed by the resistless authority of Omnipotence, so that we dare not refuse the mandate, that breaks down the stiff-neck of our rebellion against God. But it is the moral plea, 'you ought to yield to me,' urged on intellect, conscience, and heart, until we feel the claim to be so just, and right, and persuasive, and powerful, that we cannot, without self-loathing, refuse it, and do not any longer even wish to refuse.

Here lies the peculiar power of the gospel. It is the revelation of God's rich grace and love to the evil.

And in opposition to the coercive spirit of the world, it is this moral and spiritual strength, this power to 'overcome evil with good,' of which the Cross of Christ is the noblest display, that God holds out before us in His word, that 'lamp of our feet and light of our path,' as the strength that we should seek most to become possessed of, and to put forth.

God instructs us in the Bible, by precept and example, to seek as our best personal attainment, the possession of a goodness so strong, and pure, and lofty, that evil from within us, and from without us, shall flee away ashamed and vanquished before its overcoming and subduing power.

This strength needs to be all the more diligently cultivated by us because it is not natural to us. "For," in our fallen state, "we are carnal, and sold under sin." We are spiritually weak.

But yet this best kind of strength may be obtained. Do you ask, 'What is it, and what does it do?' I answer: It is the life of God in the soul of man, and it re-creates in God's image the soul that it enters, and its presence becomes in part visible.

The men in whom this life not only exists, but is abundant, by their very presence, both at rest and in action, exert a beneficent moral power and influence. These are the men from whose moral being a felt virtue goes forth that good men seek, and bad men shun. For there are men, every movement of whose mind creates currents of healthful, healing, spiritual influence, and such God-inspired men are strong.

While the minds of some others, who are not evil men, yet demand no room and displace no opposing evil forces. Such weak men, without any force of earnest spiritual convictions, take only the size of their bodies of room in the world. Such men are not strong. But the good are strong, and they naturally grow stronger.

Yes, our text holds out before us the encouraging promise that the really good man shall, by the inherent laws of goodness, go on his way, and become stronger and stronger in goodness, more and more successful in gaining victories over evil.

I do not mean that God, by exalting this moral power, teaches us not to admire, nor to cultivate any other kind of power; but I understand Him to say that our ambition for power should chiefly take this highest direction. All " power belongeth unto God." And God's good gifts of physical and intellectual strength are worth our admiration and cultivation also; but they are not worth the extravagant idolatry which men generally give them. For when they are severed from moral moving powers, these God-given gifts ever sink into the service of base and God-dishonouring purposes. And besides, they do not ever abide and grow, like this kind of power: for moral might alone has an intrinsic worth and an unfading glory.

Intellectual greatness we ought all profoundly to revere as one of God's best gifts to man; but we ought not to dishonour the Holy God, and His moral image in man by an unholy worship of intellect as disjoined from goodness. How much even in the service of religion is talent often exalted above grace? For how much that is amiss in a very clever man will his great talents atone in the average estimate that is formed of him!

This idolatry of talent has infected our language, so that even our 'speech bewrayeth us.'

Once it was a minister of the gospel's highest praise, flowing from an inspired pen in godly sincerity, that " he was a good man, and full of the Holy Ghost and of faith, and [that] much people was added unto the Lord " by His labours. Now, to call one " a good man " is small praise with many—a kind of praise that is often mingled with sneers and sarcasms. As if, in the opinion of the speaker, good men were not very likely to be strong and wise as well as good; or, in truth, likely to be fit for much. It is in such lips greater praise by far to call one a great man, or a clever man, or an eloquent man, than to call him a good man.

I speak against this dishonour of goodness in the interests of talent and of piety both. Why should they be put in opposition, or divorced from each other? Am I, in speaking so, pleading the cause of mental incompetency in the performance of God's glorious work of preaching the gospel, brethren? or in any department of God's work? So far from that, I deeply mourn the infrequency of great talent in the gospel ministry. I would to God, ministerial brethren, even though you and I, and all such like preachers, were to go quite out of sight in the rising splendour of consecrated talent and genius; still I would with all my heart that the Church's great men were very many instead of being so few. For there is much spiritual darkness to chase away: and the existence and the messages of such men, who are lights of the world, really form one of our Father's noblest answers to the cry of our benighted humanity for more light from on High. Yes, God's holy service more than deserves all the most capacious, brightest and best intellects in the world enthusiastically engaged in it. And it does possess a few such men of God, resplendent both in gifts and in graces. But well I know that many of earth's mightiest in all natural and acquired equipments are on the other side: that there are many good gifts of God of this intellectual kind, that could be worked into such jewels as Christ Himself would wear and rejoice in, that are wickedly or carelessly trodden under feet of the men who get them to polish and perfect for Him. But while we prize consecrated talent much, let us never forget what truly great men, who are also good men, are ever the first to acknowledge, that fitness for spiritual work, and success in it, depend far more upon spiritual than upon intellectual qualifications.

The gospel, when received in the love of it, raises man in every way, either directly or indirectly, but not in every way equally, for its great design is to raise him spiritually. And therefore spiritually enlightened men, 'endued with power from on High,' are needed, and are alone fitted to commend the gospel. "For as the man is, so is his strength."

Nor is the mere godless humanism that I condemn as a debasing of God's moral image in man, when put in the place of spiritual religion, the right road to attain the highest intellectual power. For that kind of "power belongeth unto God," as all kinds of power do. "If we speak of the strength of the mighty, lo, He is there!" And just as the Church looks away from God to man, and away from the morally God-like in man, to the naturally great, does she resemble the world in spirit, and become weak for spiritual purposes, like any merely human institution. For God ever, sooner or later, withdraws in such cases, and in just anger, the moral strength that the professing Church thus blindly undervalues, and often withdraws, even the talent that she has been too eagerly worshipping, reducing all our Church agencies to a weak mediocrity.

Nor is strength of character a thing of the intellect alone, but of the whole man, and especially of the moral nature. For without moral goodness, without faith, love, benevolence, justice, truth, and purity, a man with the noblest intellect which God ever made is not strong, nor fair. The most essential feature in a strong human character is the stamp of God's moral image, is personal goodness, is the righteousness of the text.

Let us seek, brethren, as our highest attainment, to be morally good, to be really Christ-like. This I am mainly anxious to help you, even if only by a passing word, to become. Without this we are not Christians at all; and the measure of this inward worth is the measure of our Christianity. May I not hope that all present who live to God are anxious for an increase of this best kind of strength which is here brought before us, and that some here are truly anxious to be strong in the Lord?

View our text, then, as a divine direction, and also as a positive promise of success, to every renewed soul that is trying to make progress in the divine life, and asks how, asks by what means he may become strong. Surely an answer to this inquiry, ' how to become strong in the Lord?' is much needed. For weakness is common. Babes in Christ are many in the Church, and men of God are few. Spiritual weakness is not a distant evil affecting those only who live near the poles, nor is it an antiquated evil from which only the antediluvians suffered. We all suffer from it here, and now: and we should all feel it more but for one of its symptoms—an accompanying spiritual topor which produces insensibility to divine things in general, and insensibility to our own spiritual state in particular. For only the spiritually living feel their weakness. Yea, more, spiritual weakness becomes most of all painful to him who most earnestly tries to do some spiritual task that well nigh overmasters him. He it is that most earnestly cries to the strong for strength.

An answer to the inquiry 'How to become strong?' is urgent again because many once promising professors of religion do not grow strong in the divine life, and hold on the way Heavenward, but grow weak and fall away from all that once gave hope concerning them. And we ought to fear for ourselves. 'For by faith we stand.'

Ours is the position, as Christians, of the shipwrecked mariner who has long supported himself in the water, and seen many of his companions, one after another, sink from his side and perish. And as he eagerly grasps any fit support that he can lay hold of, so, with a like eagerness and tenacity, ought we to grasp this divine promise of strength and progress, and all such like promises, and to see in them Heaven's life-boats come to save us from the devouring ocean of despair and death.

II.—But who are they that obtain the strength that is promised in the text? All do not. It is much to know that any poor, weak, imperfect men, like us, are able to stem the prevailing current of evil, and to hold on the way to glory. It is far more to know that we also may do so, and even to be taught how to do this great thing. And the direction of our text is simple and sure. The man who would be strong, and would hold on his way, must be in God's sense 'righteous, and keep his hands clean.'

But who are the righteous, and the clean of hands? And why are they so called? The great law of their life noticed in our text, is that they 'hold on their way, and become stronger.' So that it much concerns us to know who they are.

First, he who 'shall hold on his way' in the sense of the text is called 'the righteous.' The Hebrew word which is here used, and is translated 'righteous,' has a very extensive meaning, as upright, honest, virtuous, pious. And so does righteousness itself, the compound quality that makes the righteous man, also include much.

Remember that our obligations to God and man not only lie near together, but that at many points those obligations intersect and overlap each other, and that righteousness is a name which covers over and enters into the whole web of human duty. Righteousness towards God is the whole circle that includes righteousness towards man as an important part of it. So that while we may in so far be righteous to man, without being righteous to God, we cannot be righteous to God, without being righteous to man. For the whole includes the part. Hence we cannot be either just or righteous, in the Bible meaning of the words, if we are so only to man.

If you say to me, 'But none on earth are perfectly righteous to God and man, and how then can we, who are conscious of being sinners, take comfort from the promise of the text to the righteous?' I answer: That though by nature "there is none righteous, no, not one," yet through grace many are righteous. "It is God that justifieth; who is he that shall condemn?" It is God who throughout the whole Bible calls a whole class of men and women from Abel to Zacharias and Elizabeth righteous. A class that is not yet extinct even in this epoch, that has been so wickedly rich in false claimants, cooked accounts, defaulting directors and secretaries, sham bankruptcies, adulterated merchandize, bubble companies, divorce scandals, and all other kinds of gigantic frauds and immoralities.

For who shall dare to call those unrighteous whom God calls righteous? Surely no one.

The Bible name 'righteous' denotes a well-defined class of men, who are not now what they once were, but have been 'born again.' And the oft recurring name 'wicked' denotes that other class which includes in it all besides 'the righteous.' So that all the class which is spoken of in the text are, in regard to the wide circle of man's duty to God and man as a whole, 'righteous' compared with what they once were, and they are 'righteous' compared with what all unregenerated, unconverted men who neglect God, now are.

So that our text does not speak of any man in his natural unrenewed state: but it speaks of man when under a supernatural tuition of man the subject of divine grace. For of the renewed man alone does its blessed promise hold good. Or to put the meaning of the text in another form: Life comes before strength, and is more important still. Get life, and strength will follow. "For to him that is joined with all the living there is hope: for a living dog is better than a dead lion."

Our text, however, speaks not of how the righteous man became the righteous man that he is; but of what he is, and of what he is to be. Else did this text describe the man's transition from unrighteousness to righteousness, it would speak, like all other texts which speak on that subject, of man's sin, and of God's mercy, of penitence and pardon, of faith in God, and love to Him.

All this has been in the righteous man's past experience, and all this continues in the present, or else he would not be the righteous man at all. For there are not in the Bible from Genesis to Revelation two kinds of righteous men spoken of: nor two ways of making righteous men out of sinners.

'The Righteous' of Scripture are all begotten of one Father, God, and they are all sprinkled with the same precious blood of Christ, the Lamb slain, not only in fact at the beginning of our era, but slain in the divine purpose from the foundation of the world; and they are all renewed by the same Holy Spirit. They are both justified and sanctified. That is the kind of man that is here spoken of; for he is in the right way, he is in God's own way, and he only needs to 'hold on his way' in order to reach perfection. He has a measure of spiritual strength, and he only needs to grow stronger in order to be all that God would have him to be.

For righteous and wicked are standard designations

in the word of God, that always mean the same things, and divide mankind into two classes, the saved and the unsaved; believers, whose 'faith is counted to them for righteousness,' and unbelievers. But sin cannot go unpunished. There must be actual righteousness in us, or in our surety, and at length in us, through Him. For God does not justify the wicked; " he that committeth sin is of the devil "—" Whosoever abideth in Christ sinneth not." 'God cleanseth our hearts by faith.' Union with Christ is ever fruitful in righteousness · The righteous man of my text is he who believes in God's mercy, and whose 'faith is counted to him for righteousness.'

Now, the cheering assurance that we here get is that no such righteous man need faint, and fall down from want of strength to proceed on his righteous way; for the righteous man's way is just the way of righteousness, is the way of holiness; so that the promise of our text is that if the righteous man keep in the way that answers to his name, he shall never fail in his Heavenward journey, but shall go on his way to the very end, with ever-growing strength and alacrity. " Wherefore we faint not; but though our outward man is decaying, yet our inward man is renewed day by day." For the righteous man's way is the way everlasting; it never ends in darkness. The snares and pitfalls of life are encountered, not in this way, but by going out of this way.

Hear the way described, and described as it is: "And an highway shall be there, * * and it shall be called the way of holiness. The unclean shall not pass over it; * * the wayfaring men, yea, fools shall not err therein. No lion shall be there, nor shall any ravenous beast go up thereon; they shall not be found there. But the redeemed shall walk there; and the ransomed of the Lord shall return, and come with singing unto Zion, and everlasting joy shall be upon their heads; they shall obtain gladness and joy, and sorrow and sighing shall flee away." And the simplest description of the way is Christ's own: "I am the way." And the best direction how to find it is also His: "Follow Me."

The latter clause of our text still further reads: "And he that hath clean hands shall wax stronger and stronger." To be righteous and to have clean hands mean much the same thing. The former expression, "righteous," describes specially the inward side of character, and the latter expression, "clean hands," describes its outward side. The hands, as the instruments with which work of most kinds is principally performed, bear sure traces of our touching any impurity: and hence they very naturally represent the whole circle of our outward life and conduct, both words and actions. Clean hands denote a pure and fair character, the outgrowth and fruit of a pure and sanctified heart.

But "who can make his hands clean?" He whose hands are, in the Bible sense, really clean, has known the washing of regeneration, and the renewing of the Holy Ghost. God has fulfilled His promise to him: "And I will sprinkle clean water upon you and ye shall be clean."

R

And he who being thus purified does not willfully pollute himself with any impure action of mind or body, shall wax stronger and stronger. For every wrong action that a man does weakens him morally; while every right action gives him new power. In order then to spiritual strength a man must be on God's sure foundation, he must be righteous, and he must be in God's good and holy way; he must keep his hands clean. 'For if he do these things he shall never stumble.'

The strength of our text is power to will that which is right, and to perform one's will. The Christian who has true views and powerful convictions of duty, and who can execute efficiently what he sees to be duty, is strong. While he whose daily actions are out of harmony with his convictions of duty, is morally weak. And as he continues in that state, ever stifling and smothering his rising convicitons of duty, so does he become weaker and weaker.

Actions that move on differing lines from convictions defile the hands, and make the whole man weak. While actions that are pushed steadily up to a junction with convictions, put one on the straight road towards strength. He who is acting up to his light is keeping his hands clean, and ever grows stronger.

But the promise of the text is for the godly. The dead do not grow. Any growth of strength pre-supposes life to start with. But steady growth in spiritual strength pre-supposes much inward life and strength.

Strength shows itself. The strong can do much work easily and happily. While the weak can do but a little, and they soon become weary in well-doing. Spiritual strength is seen in how much a man can do, and suffer, and overcome in God's service, without sinking under his burdens and labours.

Well, my hearers, are we the righteous, and the clean of hands? Then, if we are so, the most blessed promise of the text is for us; and we shall grow stronger in this best kind of strength.

And that we may lay a firmer hold of the promised blessing,

III.—Consider some of the laws that regulate this growth of strength; or, in other words, let us ask: *How* it comes about that the righteous man holds on his way and grows stronger?

Who he is, and the fact that he does grow stronger, we have already seen. And now we seek for the reasons: now we look at the habits and principles that underlie the strength and progress of the righteous.

The reasons why the righteous grow stronger are both natural and supernatural, as we shall see.

Firstly, the righteous man holds on his way, and grows stronger and stronger by the operation of the great natural law that the *exercise* of our faculties strengthens them. This is a law of the mind as well as a law of the body; it is a law of the spiritual nature as well as of the intellectual nature.

And the religion of the Bible perfectly harmonizes with all divine law. It is a reasonable service which yet rises above reason. In the religion of God the natural and the supernatural, the human and the divine, beautifully blend and comingle. That due and proper exercise strengthens all our faculties bodily, mental, and spiritual, is a standing law of our nature. All our talents may be hid and wasted, or they may be traded with and increased. For strength of all kinds is closely connected with proper exercise. This kind is connected specially with exercising one's self unto godliness, and with working for God.

The severe repression of all ignoble aims and motives makes a man grow strong; and the grasping of great principles, and the nursing of noble aims, give him strength. Proper exercise, I say, strengthens all our spiritual faculties. As a man walks far in the ways of holiness, and as he walks fast he ever becomes able to walk farther and faster, because he has had his faculties strengthened by exercise. He who has often put implicit faith in God, and never found God to fail him, is abler to renew his hold of this divine helper in the hour of his present difficulty and trial than at first, or ever before. For faith, like all other graces, grows by fit exercise.

Mature piety is ordinarily the ripened product of years well spent. 'Spiritual days should speak, and multitude of spiritual years should teach wisdom.' It is true that years of formal religious profession will only bring growing formality, and that by the very law of use and wont of which I am speaking. For the indifference of the past has prepared the way for the greater indifference of the present. But I affirm, on the stable authority of my text, that years of vigorous exercise in faith, and prayer, and all kinds of Christian works of well-doing, and in patient waiting for God, will most surely bring growing strength. The great law of strength is that 'it is gradually acquired.' Fable and fact combine to teach us this lesson. For he was able at last, says the fable, to carry the ox who had early begun to carry the calf, and by continuing the practice every day grew in strength as fast as the growing animal grew in weight. The fable carries in it a great truth.

Since it is by the right exercise of strength already possessed that all the good men grow and wax strong in spirit, who ultimately become spiritual Samsons and John the Baptists. The mightiest and most prevailing wrestler with God who is now upon the earth, whoever he may be, no doubt began his life of prayer with a feeble and tremulous utterance of the personal cry, "God be merciful to me, a sinner." It was a contracted, purely personal prayer, and yet absorbed his whole soul. He thought of no more, and he could ask no more than mercy to himself, a sinner. But now the unselfish, expansive prayers of this same man grasp a world's sins, woes, and wants. He finds room in his prayers for all the interests of all men, the saved and the unsaved. And he has grown to this enlargement of heart by the exercise of prayer. His spiritual strength has not been the acquirement of a day, but the growth of years. So of the noblest champion for God and truth now alive, be he who he may. Once he could hardly venture to name and commend Jesus the Saviour to a bosom friend in the privacy of personal friendship. And now he could, at any personal risk, unshrinkingly commend the Redeemer of Men before the whole world. Prolonged effort to commend the Master, and thus to save some, cheered by tokens of divine approval, has made the once weak and timid one strong and bold.

The ultimate results of daily exercising one's self unto godliness are ever great. He who steadily and closely follows the light of God, which he has ever, sees it brighten. He who confesses and forsakes known sins gradually discovers in himself sins that were unknown to him before.

He who does not with his will omit any known duty soon has his views of duty both enlarged and elevated. He who can do but a little for Christ, when he does that little zealously and faithfully, soon becomes able to do more, and to do it better.

The holiest man on earth has grown holy, and doubtless is not now a young Christian. Youthful piety is very lovely and zealous. Nothing is so attractive and diffusive as this 'dew of youth' Oh, for more of this 'beauty of holiness' 'from the womb of the morning' visible among us.' But it is exercise in godliness that produces the strong manhood of piety. "A wise man is strong; yea, a man of knowledge increaseth might."

To be personal, are we, brethren, waxing stronger and stronger? If we are not, either we are not the righteous of whom my text speaks, or else we are not keeping our hands clean.

If we are real Christians, and yet are not growing stronger, there must be wilful stains in our hearts or upon our hands—some unforsaken, unforgiven sin that saps our spiritual strength, and bars our way to Heavenward progress.

Secondly, the righteous man who has clean hands holds on his way, and ever grows stronger through the ordinary operation of the great law of *habit*.

The righteous man of the text, as we have seen, is the renewed man. The text may be read to imply what is the fact: That the greatest difficulty is to get men to take the first step in religion. The first step is the greatest as well as the most difficult. It is a vital turning point. And none but God, by His Holy Spirit, can persuade the sinner to take that first step. But after that, all things are his. Get a man begun aright in religion, get a man of whom righteousness and cleaness of hands can be truly predicated, and new powers above nature have come into play. Such a man, even by the law of habit, with its new centre of gravity, whose uniform action is now upward and Heavenward, instead of downward and earthward, shall hold on his Godward way, and grow stronger in goodness.

He who has not only striven to enter in "by the narrow gate," but has already toiled far up "the straightened way that leadeth unto life," does not now find the way to Heaven so narrow or difficult as he once did. Habit helps him on. He now sighs far oftener that his companions in that way are so few, than that his own difficulties are so many.

Habit makes all things easier, and among others the most difficult Christian duties. For the law of habit comes into action in favour of duty as well as in favour of sin, in favour of holiness as well as against it. The law of habit is not, as some seem to speak, a minister of sin in the hands of Satan, to work his evil will with

We hear much solemn and alarming truth about the terrible power of the law of habit as leading us into sin, and as strengthening the hold of evil over us.

I do not say that we hear too much on this alarmingly solemn subject, but I am sure that we hear far too little on the other side, of the blessedly beneficent power of the law of habit.

Let none set this that I am now saying aside as being mere worldly wisdom taught in the name of religion. For while the power of habit is great, remember that the law of habit is God's law, and not the devil's, and its lessons, when taken all round, are most Christian.

Here is one practical direction in which they plainly point. Do you find some duty, that lies to your hand to do, very difficult and hard at present? Well, strive to do it, and to do it rightly, notwithstanding that it is so hard. And though no other power should come to your aid—and many others will work together with you, and in you—yet be sure of this, that the mighty power of habit will surely aid you, and aid you in a twofold manner. For while by its means you ever grow stronger, by the same means duty ever grows easier. So that your first struggle with a difficult duty, your first victory over a besetting sin, is the most difficult.

Have we all as Christians fully proved by experience how much the cultivation of holy habits may do in making duty become easy and pleasant to us?

Is the fixed and regular hour of prayer, sacredly kept, no aid to us in maintaining the true spirit of devotion, and no barrier put in the way of the subtle temptation to neglect prayer? Surely it is both.

And so, does not the law of habit help a regular attendance on public worship? The man who in health never raises the question, when the hour of prayer comes round, 'Shall I go to church to-day,' any more than he asks on other days, when well, 'Shall I go to business or to work to-day?' does not know the ever-recurring life-long battle with inertia and excuses, of the occasional church-goer, who has forged a law of habit against the duty, not for it.

And, in a word, does not the law of habit aid us in the performance of all oft-recurring duties? Yes, the law of habit, if we be the righteous, is acting for us, and not against us. Habits may become good habits.

I would that all good men understood this law better, and profited by it more.

Thirdly, the righteous man, and of clean hands, holds on his way and waxes stronger and stronger by the teachings of *experience*.

The nature of God's service in itself, and the godly man's past experiences of it, urge him strongly and steadily forward. "The fear of the Lord is the instruction of wisdom." And wisdom's "ways are ways of pleasantness, and all her paths are peace." They are oft untrodden, in large measure because they are but little known. But the farther that a man walks along those good ways, the less desire has he to return to the ways of folly and sin.

A holy moral necessity to go forward is more and more

firmly laid upon him who has entered on the ways of God, and has put them to the proof. He must go forward. He growingly feels that there is nothing in the world's ways, and in sin's ways, that is worth going back for.

He has found in the ways of God, by his own experience of them, the best of portions, the highest of joys, and the brightest of hopes. And his motto is onward and upward. His crown and kingdom are not behind him in Adam, but before him in Christ.

One, speaking for all growing Christians, says of himself: "One thing I do, forgetting the things which are behind, and stretching forward to the things which are before: I press on toward the goal, unto the prize of the high calling of God in Christ Jesus."

There is something so purifying and satisfying in the ways of God, that he who has truly known them cannot permanently return to the ways of sin. Almost as soon may a prince willingly become a beggar, or a seraph become a demon. Satisfaction with the path that he has entered on grows in a godly man at every step of advancement. So that he can say to other godly ones: "Rejoice in the Lord alway: again I will say, rejoice;" and to all men: "O taste and see that the Lord is good; blessed is the man that trusteth in Him."

And besides all this, one step of duty taken prepares for the next. Here are the names of some steps of this ascending spiritual ladder or terrace that leads from earth to the temple on high: 'Faith, virtue, knowledge, temperance, patience, godliness, love of the brethren, and love.' And from this last step of the terrace, love, not a little of Heaven's interior glories become visible to the single and purified eye. The interlinking of past progress with present progress is very close. One spiritual victory helps to another. The man who conquers one of his own evils is doubly armed to encounter and root out the next. For he knows how victory over evil is gained, and he has felt the pure joy that follows such victory.

And as it is of the war with inward, evil propensities so is it of the war with outward temptations. Experience of victory is one great element of strength for this war.

Do you point me to painful facts, and say: That it is seldom so with professed Christians; that often they do not seem to advance, often they do not seem to grow stronger. It may be so with many, and it may be so even with some of you. Painful experience as well as accurate observation may dictate your objection. No matter, our text is true, and the explanation of the sad facts is simple. If it be so, have we been righteous and kept our hands clean? Have we really tried to progress in goodness? Surely not.

If we have halted or gone back, may we not all discover when our growth in spiritual strength stopped, and from what cause? I am sure we shall not inquire earnestly, as a matter of life and death, why we do not advance in divine things without discovering the true reason. "If any man willeth to do God's will, he shall know" that will. But do we all fully mean what we say in our prayers for spiritual progress?

And do we act out our prayers to the full? Ye who

stand still in religion, or go back, instead of holding on your way, surely you are not righteous, or your hands are not clean. You are regarding iniquity in your heart; you are clinging secretly or openly to known sin.

Fourthly, but the righteous man, and of clean hands, holds on his way, and grows stronger and stronger because *religion is a life* of which Christ is the source. Regeneration is the beginning of this life. The man is first of all born again. And then comes his spiritual infancy. He is yet but a babe in Christ, and must grow.

And he who does not grow stronger in the divine life may well doubt if ever he has 'died unto sin, and become alive unto righteousness.' For as really as it is the nature of an infant to grow, so really is it the nature of a child of God to grow in grace. A child of God must grow.

> " Rivers to the ocean run,
>   Nor stay in their course;
> Fire ascending seeks the sun:
>   Both speed them to their source.
>
> So, a soul that's born of God
>   Pants to view His glorious face;
> Upwards tends to His abode,
>   To rest in His embrace."

But this life is immortal, eternal, everlasting life. And "he that believeth on the Son hath [that] eternal life." "And whosoever liveth and believeth on Him shall never die." He whose "goodness is as a morning cloud, and as the dew that goeth early away," has not this life. Surely that is not the divine life which dies out of man's soul as mortal life does out of his body; nor is that fire from Heaven that dies from off the altar of his heart, as an earthly affection may die.

But all life is much affected by food, climate, and exercise, and so is this higher life. Divine truth is the fit food of this life. And hence we must, if we would grow in grace, "as new born babes, long for the spiritual milk which is without guile, that we may grow thereby unto salvation." We must avoid a too spare diet, and we must not partake of this Heavenly manna too seldom.

The climate of earth, too, is unfavourable to the highest spiritual health, but it is varied. Let us not choose its worst places, but its best. Earth has Beth-els, Peniels, Olivets, and Bethanies, its places 'where God dwells,' where 'prayer is wont to be made,' and where 'they that fear the Lord speak one with another'—it has home retreats in which there are confined sick ones whom Jesus loves and visits. Earth has also Sodoms, Babylons, Chorazins, and Jerusalems, places where 'there is no fear of God before men's eyes,' and where 'the wickedness of the inhabitants is great.' Let us choose well.

The prayer meeting and the theatre are both open for our entrance, and so are both the House of God, where His word is preached, and the spirit shop, where that is sold which makes reason reel and passion burn.

Even on earth we may choose our haunts, and find them spiritually wide apart. We may spend our evenings in the ball-room and at the card-table, or we may spend them in reading our Bibles, and such books as lead to the Bible, and in speaking one to another of the best things such words as God Himself shall hear and record.

But, fifthly and lastly, the great reason why the righteous man, and of clean hands, holds on his way and grows stronger and stronger, is that his God and Father *holds him up* and strengthens him. And He is the living God.

According to the divine constitution of this spiritual kingdom, "whosoever hath," as the result of improving whatever God gives him, " to him shall be given, and he shall have abundance;" and the greater the man's improvement of God's older gifts, the greater God's newer gifts become.

And thus the good man grows. For he 'may boldly say, the Lord is my helper.' This warrior ever grows stronger for battle because the great Captain of our salvation 'teaches His hands to war, and His fingers to fight.'

All through life God makes good the promise when the way proves rough: "Thy shoes shall be iron and brass; and as thy days, so shall thy strength be."

Thus when others stumble and fall, the righteous man rises and stands upright, because God strengthens and upholds him.

But for this mighty hand even the righteous man could not hold on his way against the opposition of the world, the devil, and the flesh. For his strength is derived. It comes from God. Hence it is great, and it never fails. For he trusts in God, and by faith he walks with God. His outer life is moulded into beauty and usefulness after Christ's all perfect life, and his inner life is hid with Christ in God. 'He walks by faith, not by sight.'

His hands are not only clean before men, but He has 'washed His hands in innocency' before God.

He 'works out his own salvation with fear and trembling; for it is God which worketh in him both to will and to work for His good pleasure.'

Our text does not stand alone in its gospel of God-given strength. Listen to the words that follow: "Who shall ascend into the hill of the Lord? And who shall stand in His holy place?

He that hath clean hands, and a pure heart; who hath not lifted up his soul into vanity, and hath not sworn deceitfully. He shall receive a blessing from the Lord, and righteousness from the God of his salvation."

Yes, the measure of our hold upon God's strength is the measure of our own strength. Well may the righteous man wax stronger and stronger when he is so helped.

"He shall be like a tree planted by the streams of water, that bringeth forth its fruit in its season, whose leaf also doth not wither; and whatsoever he doeth shall prosper. The wicked are not so."

Yes the two, the good man and the fruitful tree, are very like each other in many things. Both are fertile, and the fertility of both is seen. But the source of that fertility in both is deeply hidden in the well-watered earth, and in God.

And so of their beauty, strength, and fruitfulness. All spring from unseen roots, grasping invisible nourishment. The godly man's invisible life of faith in God feeds his visible life of works. As his inner life lays hold on God, so does his outer life expand in beauty, strength, and fruitfulness.

Hence it is that the righteous, though in himself weak and dead as other men are, "shall flourish like the palm tree: He shall grow like a cedar in Lebanon."

Who then need fall down in the Christian journey, overcome by weakness, when the strength of the Divine arm is pledged for his support, if he will only lean upon that invisible stay?

Who can fail to grow stronger when he is ever being strengthened and renewed by God in the inner man?

A godly man is only weak when he feels strong in himself, and does not go out of himself for strength from God.

If he but feel his own weakness, and his need of divine help, he has any amount of strength at his command that he will draw upon the Almighty God for. 'For God's strength is made perfect in his weakness:' and he who has that strength in sufficient measure 'can do all things in Christ that strengtheneth him.'

But the unbelieving and unrighteous heart does not cling to God in love and confidence. Such a heart cannot make God's faithful promises its own; only the believing heart can do so. The lips that have not a believing heart to prompt their utterances, will not so ask of God that they shall receive. "I will not let thee go except thou bless Me," is the language of faith as well as of importunity.

And so clean hands and such alone can lay a firm hold upon God, and lovingly constrain Him in His visits to leave a blessing behind Him. Polluted hands have no such power. While the stronger that our hold of God is, the stronger we are. It is, then, an essential condition of growing strength that we cleave fast unto God. For there is much in this world that is fitted to impair spiritual strength. Our way is often difficult. It is a pilgrimage. It is a race. It is a struggle with inveterate enemies. Many are against us. There are sources of weakness within and without us. But despite of all opposers, we, who live in Christ, and in whom Christ lives, shall grow strong if we rightly exercise ourselves in the ways of God; if we make His service the daily habit of our life; if we faithfully follow the God-given teachings of our own experience; if we earnestly cultivate and nourish religion as the true life of our soul; and if, above all, we rise to a living union and an abiding communion with God. And thus we see that spiritual strength is the joint result of God's best gifts and of man's best endeavours. " Fear not, thou worm Jacob, and ye men of Israel : I will help thee," saith the Lord, " and thy redeemer is the Holy One of Israel."

The man who seeks and finds this helper must hold on his way, and grow stronger. 'For the Lord is his God, and underneath and around him are the everlasting arms.'

" Why sayest thou, O Jacob, and speakest, O Israel, my way is hid from the Lord, and my judgement is passed away from my God? Hast thou not known? hast thou not heard? the everlasting God, the Lord, the creator of the ends of the earth, fainteth not, neither is weary; there is no searching of His understanding. He giveth power to the faint; and to him that hath no might he increaseth strength. Even the youths shall faint and be weary, and the young men shall utterly fall; but they that wait upon the Lord shall renew their strength; they shall mount up with wings as eagles; they shall run and not be weary; they shall walk and not faint."

Wait, then, upon the Lord in His word and in prayer, and be strong. For it is in the Bible that we learn to know God, whom to know is life and strength.

The beneficial influence of the Bible on the formation of character is incalculable. Its holy precepts, its noble examples, its lofty principles, its inspiring motives, its ennobling prospects, its glorious rewards, its terrible punishments, its realized power from on high, act on human character, brought truly under their benign influence, as light and air, sunshine and shower, act on springing seed and on growing grain.

The whole atmosphere of Scripture is strongly provocative of robust spiritual health. Here we may daily kneel with ever growing admiration before the Lord Jesus Christ, that only perfect model of all worth, who combines in Himself all divine and all human beauty.

This Godward attitude continued in makes weak men to become strong, and strong men to become stronger and stronger.

But in order to fully benefit by this Book divine, we much need a profound humility towards God, who speaks in it, and a large-hearted receptivity of all divine light and influence.

If you would be strong, brother, " wait on the Lord : * * and let thine heart take courage ; yea, wait thou on the Lord," and be strong.

XIV.

DIVINE TREASURE IN EARTHEN VESSELS.

"But we have this treasure in earthen vessels, that the exceeding greatness of the power may be of God, and not from ourselves."— 2 Cor., IV., 7.

OUR text is very like its human author. It is a very Pauline utterance. It is very full of both human tenderness and pathos, and also of a fervent desire for the glory of God. It touches human frailty, and lays hold of it, only to link it to divine power.

What the apostle Paul evidently means by "this treasure" is the gospel of Jesus Christ—is the message of God's love to man—is, in one word, Christianity. Paul also calls it "our gospel."

And this gospel is to its possessor, as you know, Christian brethren, an enriching treasure beyond all price. And Paul as evidently means by the "earthen vessels" that hold this precious treasure, himself and his fellow-apostles, and the preachers of the gospel as a whole. He means by this phrase the whole human ministry of the gospel who were then on the earth.

And if they were such as Paul here describes them to be, so are we all who are still in any way engaged in the same great work.

You observe that the apostle strongly contrasts the two things—the "treasure," which is so precious, and the "vessels," which are so frail and weak.

And this wide contrast which is here noted as existing between the earthen vessels that contain the gospel treasure and the treasure itself, which is contained in them, is a fine, instructive thought, most true and most affecting. It is a thought that is full of practical importance, and of tender teaching, for both ministers of the gospel and their people. For we here learn that the ministers of the gospel are only earthen vessels, and that yet though they are so, the truth of God as ministered by them is none the less precious, and it is none the less life-giving on that account.

The gospel is God's own gift to man. And God, in giving His treasures to men, may put them into whatever kind of vessels He pleases; but they are His treasures all the same, and are to be valued by us accordingly.

This thought of our text, affirming the all-sided frailty of the ministers of the gospel, may teach us all many lessons worth learning. But it specially teaches, I think, the gospel ministry a godly humility, and it teaches the people of their charge a true and wise sympathy with their ministers.

And the text clearly teaches us all, ministers and people alike, to look in all our Church relations first, last, and supremely to God, if we would have the gospel in them and by them to become 'the power of God unto our salvation.'

But those of you who may have been led by the words of the text, and by these words of mine in explanation of it, to expect this morning a sermon all about ministers, and on the not quite unknown subject to most congregations of ministerial frailties, will not on this occasion realize your expectations. For that is not my subject. I intend at this time to take a far wider view of the main affirmation of the text than the apostle Paul's present application of the leading idea to the gospel ministry: although I do not exclude that more specific application of the apostolic idea, but fully embrace it in my wider survey, and even emphasize its special lessons on the subject of the ministry.

But still I intend to apply the text in this sermon, not to the gospel ministry only, but to the whole of the gospel instrumentalities by which God usually reveals Himself to man. I want to show you that all God's instrumentalities, and all the varied agencies by which He reveals Himself to us in the gospel, are, in the sense of the text, but "earthen vessels," and yet that all of them contain "divine treasures" for our enrichment.

So that my present subject is this : 'That the instruments and the agents by which God sends us the gospel are all of them, as well as the preachers of the gospel, but frail earthen vessels in contrast with the divine treasure which they contain. And yet it is God Himself who puts the divine treasure into them all.'

But let me warn you that I do not attempt to embrace in my present survey all the instrumentalities by which God is revealing Himself to us, though, as I have said, my text might be shown to hold true of them all. Nay, I purposely exclude from our view at this time God's revelation of Himself in His works in external nature, because they reveal God the Creator, but they do not reveal God the Redeemer. But I shall on this occasion name five of the principal instruments by which God is ever revealing Himself to man as the God of Salvation. And I shall try to show you that they are all apt illustrations of the one truth of our text, that God is wont to send to us mankind, as our text says that He does, Heavenly treasures in earthen vessels.

On reflection you will see this to be true :
I. Of *Man* himself.
II. Of the *Ministry* of the Gospel.
III. Of the *Church* of Christ.
IV. Of the *Bible*. And
V. Of *Christ* Himself.

All these are divine agencies and instrumentalities that God is ever using for the preservation, and the circulation, and the inculcation of His own gospel. And I shall try to show you that in all of them we have these two things —divine treasure, and earthen vessel—brought into close contact, and into striking contrast. We have in all of them a divine treasure contained in an earthen vessel. And I shall strive to show the reason why such a treasure is put into such vessels; that in all cases we have these two things thus brought into contact, and into contrast, by God's own deliberate design; and that God has done this, at first glance, strange thing, for the purpose of making the divineness of that which is revealed more manifiest to us than it would have been, if it had been sent to us by a different, and more perfect instrumentality.

For, as the arrival of night permits the stars, which are hidden from our view by day, to become visible, and as dark settings often best show off brilliant things, so do earthen vessels become, on the whole, the fittest holders and conveyers of divine treasures to mankind.

Now for the practical application of this divine law and usage of wrapping up sacred and divine things in humble earthly exteriors. The proper lesson is: That if this humble earthen element be a true characteristic of all the instruments that God employs for our spiritual good, then when we see such a contrast re-appearing in any particular case between the human messenger and the divine message, we should, instead of stumbling at the earthen vessel as disproving the divinity of the message which is being brought to us, rather stand prepared to expect God's hand to be there, sending us in this way some fresh utterance of His truth. For—

I.—We have in *man* himself, as a son of God, and God's chief work on earth—when he is in any way used as an instrument for teaching God's truth—just such a combination of earthen vessel and precious treasure as our text describes. Yes, we have in man a combination of earth and diamond, of pottery and precious stones, of earthly and Heavenly things. For both the very great and the very little meet and mingle in man.

It has been boldly said that "man is compounded of dust and Deity." Man, as we see, is largely an animal, and yet he may become largely an angel, even on earth. Man has in himself both a material body and an immaterial soul. He is both mortal and immortal. Man is a creature of here and now, and he also belongs to all the ages to come. Man has relations with the humblest of earthly things, and also with the loftiest of Heavenly things.

Man is in himself both an animal—only the crown of the animal creation—and he is also a son of God, made in the image of God, and an heir of coming glory.

As to part of us, 'we die daily.' We are perishing, and passing away. 'Our outward man is decaying.' 'Behold, we are all dying.' But as to part of us, we 'live for ever.'

Yes; and if we live and believe on Jesus we cannot die. But for the present we but dimly see the divine and deathless in man, for it is half hidden under a humble material, mortal form.

And because the spiritual in man is so largely concealed, and because many people are so spiritually blind, some who wear the human form are earthly enough, and animal enough to deny the divine in man, and to claim to be all of the earth, earthly. An idea which is as base-born as it is false.

Does it not seem to all of us, brethren, a most ignoble kind of humility for any of us, men to deny our nobler self? For we are the sons of God, who 'is a spirit;' we are made in His image. We are not mere material things. Our true 'life is hid with Christ in God.'

You thus see that my first point—in which I trust you all fully go with me—is that man has in his own nature both an earthen vessel and a divine treasure; and yet that

God uses man, the earthen vessel, as well as immortal man, His son, to be the messenger of His divine truth, to be the ordinary teacher of his fellow-man in the very highest things. For all our human relations, though imperfect, are emblems of Heavenly things. These relations are all from God, and, true to their divine origin, they all speak for God, and are all meant and fitted to lead to God.

II.—But what our text directly affirms is that we have in the gospel *ministry* such a combination and contrast in vessel and treasure, as we have already seen is to be found in the whole family of man as the representatives of God on the earth.

Yes, as it is with man himself, so is it with the gospel ministry which we exercise among you—this, the highest human ministry of which we know anything. The gospel, which is the message of our Father, God's own love and grace, and is an inestimable treasure to man, is yet ministered instrumentally to man by man.

The twofold idea which is mainly conveyed to our minds by the words "earthen vessels" is first frailty, weakness, and then imperfection, the being of slight worth. And both the things, frailty and imperfection, are most true of the human ministry of the gospel.

We sorrowfully own that the apostolic expression in our text, "earthen vessels," is profoundly true of Christian ministers. In all ways we are but earthen vessels, as you no doubt very well know.

I name the gospel ministry in this connection separately from the Church as a whole, because the apostle does so in our text. But I would have you to remember that, in strict truth, the ministers of the gospel are only a part of the Church itself. They hold a special office in the Church, but they are not an order apart from, and outside of, the Church. And Paul, no doubt, names the gospel ministry separately here because the work of the ministry is his great theme in our text, and context; and also because he desires, in treating of it, to emphasize the importance of its teaching and preaching functions.

For the apostle speaks of the ministry as having, in a special sense, had a dispensation of the gospel committed to it; as having, in a special sense, had the precious treasure of the gospel put into it.

And the phrase "earthen vessels" closely applies to the ministry of the gospel in many ways. For instance, Paul says: 'We are troubled, perplexed, persecuted, cast down, with death working in us.' How very human is all this!

The phrase "earthen vessels" applies to the views of divine truth, which are taken by the ministers of the gospel as a whole. How slight and partial are those views often, how one-sided, how incorrect, how contradictory often.

All who are the professed preachers of the one gospel of Christ do not manifestly speak the same thing, as all real preachers of Christ ought in spirit to do. And though all preachers of the gospel are by their sacred profession the ministers of the truth, yet herein the earthen vessel prominently appears in that in all of them some error, and in many of them much error, often mingles with, and corrupts 'the truth as it is in Jesus,' which by their sacred profession, their life is given up to teaching.

Alas! 'how far is the gospel of Christ from being made in fact, all the world over, by the lips of its living teachers, the clear, glorious one message of God's great love to man, that it really is in truth! And then the gospel ministry is sometimes perverted into a human priesthood, of which no man finds any trace in the New Testament, either by precept or example.

And then again, all the ministers of the gospel are but "earthen vessels" as to personal character. How faulty in many respects are most of us! How faulty in some respects are we all?

And then as to ability our text holds true. How ordinary in this respect is the gospel ministry! Great men are almost always rare, in the gospel ministry as everywhere else. Burning and shining lights in the gospel ministry, are they not all too rare among us?

And then as to want of adaptation, our text is often painfully true. How easy, and how common is it for us to miss the minds and the hearts of the very people who are before us, though we may have that in our own minds and hearts which, really transferred as a living thing to theirs, would do them large and lasting good! Not all those who are godly, and able and earnest ministers of Christ, have always the right word, in its right season to speak to those before them who need it most.

And in truth it is easy to find, not only manufactured faults, but real faults in every preacher of the gospel whom you know and hear. For all of us are but "earthen vessels." The preacher and pastor who is the minister eagerly coveted of all the churches, the much looked for and longed for man, who should be both negatively faultless, and possess in over-flowing measure all positive excellencies of body and mind, conscience and heart, is yet an ideal, not a fact—one sought for, but not yet found. We have not seen him, and we shall nowhere find him on earth. While an American college professor is reported to have warned certain American churches that the now perfected preachers, who, he thinks, are alone quite equal to what some of the churches would desire to have, as Paul, Peter, Apollos, and John, who now belong to the church celestial, will not, he is sure, accept the inducements that churches in America hold out to preachers and return to earth.

And thus both there and here we have only "earthen vessels" for preachers; though it seems to me that here in South Africa, as well as in America, something more perfect, and something more ethereal than " earthen vessels " is very generally desired by many persons in all our churches. But facts are facts. The perfect men are eagerly sought for, but they are not found. And the preacher being himself faulty, so do his personal faults necessarily run more or less into all his presentations of divine truth. More than a fair share of gifts and graces combined in one man is not an attainment so common in the gospel ministry as it ought to be.

Nor is eminent grace much more common among ministers than eminent talent. And then the strong in spirit may be frail in body. The best of men grow old, too. 'The outward man decays.' All die. And the most useful often die soon. By the time that a man has got a real hold of something to teach that is worth teaching, it not seldom happens that he is getting too old to teach it with effect. Sometimes eminent men find no fit successors, so that their work languishes. And yet the gospel deserves the best of advocacy.

Now, an agency with all this of human frailty, "compassed with infirmity," may seem to us but a poor instrumentality for the performance of so divinely great a work as preaching the glorious gospel of the blessed God. And yet this selection of frail, imperfect men, not of holy angels, nor of 'the spirits of just men made perfect'—for the stated preachers of the gospel is of God, not of man— and it is, our text assures us, no mistake.

This human instrumentality, Paul affirms, is not, as some seem to say, a regrettable weakness in the divine plan of saving men that needs to be apologised for. Nay, God's purpose in the selection of this instrumentality for the promulgation of His gospel is a high and wise purpose. For it is God's design thereby to strongly emphasize the wide contrast that there is between the divine things and the human things that are in the gospel. That by men's seeing how very human the human vessel that carries the divine treasure is, God Himself may be the more glorified in all its success. Elsewhere the divine lesson is put thus: "Therefore let no man glory in men; but he that glorieth, let him glory in the Lord." For though the truth of God is necessarily more or less coloured and flavoured by the human medium—by the earthen vessels through which it comes to men—yet it is the saving truth of God still.

The human infirmity of the gospel ministry does not destroy the divine efficacy of the truth which we proclaim. So that one of the greatest and most successful of preachers said: "Most gladly therefore will I rather glory in my weaknesses, that the strength of Christ may rest upon me." And so ought we who preach the gospel now, to glory in all that exalts the message itself, and exalts Him who sends it. For the gospel as preached by weak men is still seen to be the power of God unto salvation. For "we preach Christ crucified."

But do not, I pray you, read into these pathetic, noble words of Paul, nor read into my honest, if poor, words on the imperfections of ministers, any plea for bad men as preachers of the gospel, or even for the bad preaching of good men. I believe in neither. Neither "cometh from above." But the apostle means to affirm, I take it, that if we wisely look at what the gospel ministry as a whole really is, so human, so frail, so imperfect, and at what the gospel of Christ, as preached by that ministry actually is, and does, manifestly a most divine thing with most divine issues, we shall have overwhelming evidence brought home to our hearts of the divinity of the gospel message itself. He says: That rightly viewed, the evidence of the divinity of the gospel will be more overpowering, in view of the actual instrumentality that has been selected for its dissemination, than it would have been if the instrumentality which God has employed for this purpose had been a more perfect, and a more faultless agency. "O the depth of the riches, both of the wisdom and knowledge of God! How unsearchable are His judgements, and His ways past tracing out!"

Why is any man converted to God by another man's preaching? That grand result is really of God in every case, and not of man. "Come, Holy Spirit, come." And yet there are men wise in winning souls. But Christ Himself is the real treasure that the vessels carry. He is the pearl of great price. "For we preach not ourselves, but Christ Jesus as Lord, and ourselves as your servants for Jesus' sake."

III.—Further, I ask you to consider, that not only the whole Christian ministry, but—though this that I am now going to say to you may be a truth less fully known to some of you, and its presentation less welcomed than a confession of the infirmities of ministers—that the *whole Church* of Christ contains just such a combination of the human and the divine, of the weak and the strong, of the worthless and the precious, as our text describes. Yes, this description is more or less true of any church, and it is true of the whole Church of Christ.

As Christians we are put in trust with the gospel of Christ. It is ours to spread abroad as widely as we can. But the divine "treasure" being entrusted to us, is put into "earthen vessels." It is "our gospel" as we have it in our hearts and on our lips, and in our commission as the servants of Christ.

Surely the contrast between the human vessel and the divine treasure, between the earthly casket and the Heavenly jewel, is great. For the glorious gospel of the blessed God is a treasure of inestimable and enduring worth. The gospel is a treasure in God's estimation. The gospel is a God-given treasure. The gospel is in its own nature a treasure. The gospel is above all a treasure to the man who really receives it in its power and love. But the gospel, like food or medicine, must be taken into us in order to do us its greatest possible good. While in and by the gospel he who receives it into his heart is made rich for evermore. For it means to him who so uses it, the pardon of sin now, and "glory, honour, and immortality" in the world to come.

And the Churches of Christ, though they are imperfect and divided, still both contain and convey to men the precious treasure of God's saving truth. Moreover, the living Church never dies out of the world; nor does the living ministry of the gospel die out: though opinions may and do differ as to how the life of both the Church and the Ministry is created, sustained, and perpetuated.

I cannot see how any particular kind of Church order, or any kind of external, historic succession from the apostles, but only the power of the Holy Spirit and the presence of the truth of Christ, quickening dead souls into a divine life, can possibly perpetuate a living Church and a living Ministry. The apostles have no successors. But in an important sense not only the ministers, but all the living members of all sections of Christ's Church, are successors or followers of the apostles, just as far as they hold the doctrine of the apostles, and walk in their footsteps.

For although the claim of any exclusive apostolic succession made in a polemic sense as something belonging

T

to one section of the Church, but not to another, without any apostolic powers of words or works in those who make it, beyond their brethren, is, so far as I can see, but an unsupported fiction, a hollow figment without either soul or body—a phantom product of the priestly brain, used sometimes as a scare-crow in order to frighten away from the exercise of their God-given ministry the rejectors of Priests and of priestly theories in the New Testament Church—an intended effect which it mostly does not have, I am glad to hope. Still the doctrine of an apostolic succession, that some hold and teach, is only an important truth caricatured into an exclusive and polemic form. It is a wedge put in where a bond ought to be.

But the truth of a succession of men full of apostolic truth and life, we ought all to hold and to teach and to turn into fact in our own persons in its scriptural simplicity. We do hold that there is in Christ's Church a living succession of God-made and God-called ministers, which has not ceased, and will not cease, unless the living Church ceases. For men cannot make ministers of Christ. God only can fit them and call them. But this good gift of Christ to His churches, the gift of "this ministry," is surely not a mechanical succession of so-called ministers of all spiritual kinds and qualities, good, bad, and indifferent, whose unseen powers and unreal authority are alleged to have been transmitted, no one knows how, by the touch of some men's hands, and through one or two self-selected Church organisations only.

That erection has no divine seal upon it: it stands neither on Scripture, nor on fact, but is in the face of both. The ministerial and Church succession that, based on Holy Scripture, we ought to hold and teach, is a God-made spiritual succession of living souls born from above, born of the Holy Spirit, out of which a ministry is called of God. And to that one universal Church, which is a holy priesthood, men and women alike, and to that ministry which, though a special office and variously organised, is only part of the priesthood of all believers on Jesus, the gospel, the treasure of the text, is entrusted for a world-wide dissemination. We "believe in the Holy Catholic Church." And while we own that the whole Church of Christ, at the best, is but an earthen vessel for holding and transmitting such a divine treasure, yet at the worst she is God's own instrument for this purpose. No other, and no better, instrument for saving souls exists than 'the Church, which is Christ's body.'

And yet our Church systems, too, as well as the persons composing the various churches, are only earthen vessels for holding and conveying the divine treasure of the gospel. There is more or less of divine truth and of divine method embodied in all our Church systems, for healing virtue goes out of them all. And we should adopt and hold to what seems to us the most divine in Church order and government, as well as in doctrine. But manifestly there is also more or less of the flaws and diversities of the earthen vessel in all those systems as they are found in actual working among us. And yet souls are saved by them all; men are spiritually bettered by them all. God puts of His treasure into them all.

And to Him alone be all the glory of all the good that they do.

IV.—But I want to show you that we have even in the *Bible* itself such a combination of vessel and treasure as our text describes.

The Bible, I believe to have less of the human, and more of the divine in it than either the Ministry or the Church. And yet it has both elements.

I look on the Bible as being a fuller, truer, and purer embodiment of divine treasures than either the Ministry or the Church, even at their best. Yet the Bible, in some aspects of it, is but an earthen vessel when you look at it as receiving, holding, and transmitting such a divine treasure as the saving knowledge of God.

For the language of the Bible is but human language. Hence it is burdened with all the customary limitations and imperfections of human language.

And though we and all mankind owe the Hebrew Church and people an immense debt of gratitude for their extreme care, extending through long ages, in faithfully preserving and transmitting to us, with so great accuracy, the Old Testament Scriptures; yet as those sacred writings came from many human hands, and have been transmitted from age to age by many human means, and have been preserved by such means without miracle, so the use of that human medium for conveying the divine revelation has always involved the possibility of mistakes creeping into the sacred Scriptures.

And it is not pretended that no minor differences, which may mean minor errors, have crept into the Old Testament.

And the same thing is true of the New Testament, allowing for differences of age in the documents, and for some other differences mostly in favour of the New Testament, such as the documents, all at once, falling into the hands of persons of many nations, instead of being long kept, as the Old Testament was, in the hands of persons of only one.

And, again, the writers of the Bible, though they were inspired men, God-moved men, were but men, and imperfect. The Bible's heroes, too, were very human, and oftentimes very imperfect. And its biographies being models of honesty, speak of the men who are described just as they were. The records are thus all the better fitted for our instruction, because they are so true. But all the more sure are they to present to us but imperfect characters, as they do.

And yet various objections have been made to the Bible, and to the gospel, and to the men whom Scripture sets before us for imitation—and such are still made by some—that really amount to no more, when we summarise them and extract their essence, than this very thing which our text frankly admits: " But we have this treasure in earthen vessels."

First, there is the objection of sense, which is in substance this: 'We can see most clearly the human in the Bible. Hence we resolutely deny that it is divine. Why, the men who wrote it—all, or almost all, Jews—wrote such Hebrew and Greek as the other Jews of their day did! How can you call these documents, which are manifestly things of time, and of human production, the

Book of God? Is not each of its many books clearly the book of some man, and full of his personality?

And, again, there is the objection of practical unbelief. For many readers of the Bible, in the spirit of verbal, critical comment, linger in and around the human and the fallible elements in Scripture; and they never rise so high upon its mountain tops, nor go so deeply into its innermost recesses, as to see the divinest things that are there. For "the meek will God guide in judgement; and the meek will He teach His way."

But if—because of this confession which I now make, that our actual Bible is one of the earthen vessels of the text, and, as being human as well as divine, may contain some elements of human imperfection—any man, or any ecclesiastical body, given to calling the Protestant view of the Bible bibliolatry, shall proceed in triumphant spirit and tones to say, 'we thought so,' and to offer us, as a better, surer, and more perfect guide, an infallible Church, or an infallible Pope, our sufficient answer to such a mentor is at hand.

We say to the offerer of a more infallible guide than the Bible: 'Stop, friend; not so fast. The question of light is always one of proportion, more or less. And there may be earthen vessels, and there may be still more earthen vessels; and there may be vessels which are most of all earthen; and such have infallible churches ever been. We see in them painfully much of earthen vessel, and painfully little of divine treasure. We do see, as has been said, what may be specks in the glorious, God-given sun of the Bible, but yet it gives us ample light.

And, on the other hand, we are quite sure that we can clearly see in the sun of any so-called infallible Church, not only a few specks and obscurities, but we see this sun raying forth much mist, darkness, and delusion. Yes, we see an almost total eclipse of light where human infallibility shines the most. So that with an intelligent preference that leaves no room for hesitancy, we eagerly choose the Bible, and not the Church, or the Pope, for our supreme spiritual guide.'

And, once again, there are the objections to the Bible of avowed theoretic scepticism. Many sceptics say practically, if not in words: 'We have this so-called treasure in only earthen vessels; therefore we reject it, and we deny its being a divine treasure at all. It cannot be a divine treasure, for the vessel that holds it has flaws and leaks, which we can see.' They say: 'How can men like ourselves, whose faults and imperfections we can see, whose fathers and mothers we know as ordinary Jews, how can they above others know God's mind for themselves; and how can they, for all time to come, speak it to others?' They say: 'We can distinctly hear men speaking to us in the Bible, but we much doubt if God does really speak to us there.'

Now, our text answers all this. It says in effect to us all, and to all objectors: 'Listen, and hear what the Bible says; look and see what the Bible reveals; and you will see that the Bible is not only a divine revelation, but that it is all the more manifestly divine because it is also so manifestly human.'

Yes, brethren, we know the human authors of the

Bible; and all the more do we know it to have been simply impossible for them to have produced it of themselves. We know the common, hard, and arid Hebrew soil in which this unique, unequalled plant of renown, the Bible, grew; and we know that the soil could not have grown this marvellous product unless a supernatural vigour and energy had been imparted to it by God. The commonness of the soil but heightens the uncommonness of the product.

And we also know that this mixing up of the divine and the human in the Bible does not stand alone. We know that this is God's ordinary way of giving us the divinest things. We have seen that God is wont to put His Heavenly treasures into earthen vessels.

And yet Christ Himself affirms, in the parable of Dives and Lazarus, that no means could be better fitted to win us back to God than the ordinary means that God uses with us. He even says that 'if we hear not Moses and the prophets, the preacher and the Bible, neither will we be persuaded, though one rose from the dead.'

So that God not only sends us the right treasure, Christ says, but he sends us the right treasure in the right way. He sends us the right treasure by the right means So that we are inexcusable if we reject either the treasure or the vessel. "How shall we escape if we neglect so great salvation," brought so nigh to us?

And why should we be so foolish as to cavil at, or stumble over, the imperfections of the gospel ministry, and of the churches of Christ, or at those things in the Bible that are either 'hard to be understood,' or that seem more human than divine, if it be part of God's fixed, avowed plan to give us all His best gifts by just such imperfect means and instruments? It is rather ours to hear God by whomsoever He speaks. Yes, by whatsoever voice He speaks, 'to hear Him, and fear, and live for ever.'

V.—But I venture, with reverence, on a more delicate and yet a stronger statement still; and I now say finally that this combination of frailty and worth is in some measure true, even of *Christ*, our blessed Lord Himself, who is the sum of divine revelation—"He who was manifested in the flesh." For Christ was a real man, possessed with the sinless frailties of humanity. Yes, as to Christ's human origin, and His human nature, you see even in Him the earthen vessel of the text. We see Him to be not ordinary, but "wonderful," as "God manifested in the flesh." For we do not naturally expect to see God Himself in a man!

And hence the ancient Jew and the modern Unitarian both say in substance: 'The human in Christ is so clear, so manifest, so abundantly proved, that we must deny the divine being there.' 'Jesus Christ is manifestly a man, and therefore we affirm that He is not God.'

But we, in accordance with the spirit of our text, answer: Yes, Christ is a man, but it does not follow that He is not divine. For it is in harmony with God's whole plan of revealing Himself to us that we find—the very largest and richest display of divine treasure which God has anywhere made—put into the person of the man Christ Jesus, and thus in Him put into the earthen vessel of our humanity. For the man Christ Jesus is also the "effulgence of God's glory and the very image of His substance."

So that the measureless treasure of God-head itself was, in the person of Christ, put into the earthen vessel of our humanity. And thus Christ Himself is the noblest, fullest proof and example of the truth of our text.

And once again Christ answers to the earthen vessel of our text, as to His family circumstances, which were very lowly. And hence the Jews of His day said of Him: "Is this not Jesus, the Son of Joseph, whose father and mother we know?" Christ might have become a man, and yet have been outwardly in place and rank "the foremost man in all the world." No Jew expected the promised Messiah of the nation, the son of David, to come in such humble guise as Jesus came.

And the same thing is seen as to Christ's nationality. He sprung from a conquered and a despised people during a time of deep humiliation.

This same thing, the earthen vessel, is also seen in Christ's early disciples. They were mostly "unlearned and ignorant men."

This same principle is seen, too, as to Christ's chosen instruments of service, and His agents as a whole. For they, in apostolic days, were not the most likely men in the eye of sense to overturn the prevailing religious beliefs of the world. And yet Christ sent His followers forth to do this great thing, and meant them to do it, and they had a wonderful success. And many of the successes of Christianity of to-day are hardly less wonderful than those of its early days.

And our text is true also as to Christ's methods of operation in extending His Kingdom. Christ, when on earth, put all His trust in truth, love, and righteousness, and He put no trust in worldly greatness, or policy, or force.

And so was it as to Christ's manifestations of power. Christ trusted entirely for the coming of His Kingdom to moral and spiritual forces, which most people do not yet understand to be power at all, but often take for weakness. In truth, the church as a whole has never well understood that legitimate church power is only light, love, and conviction. And Christ's weapons for the conquest of the world still are, just truth and love, goodness and kindness. And hence the conquests which Christ has already won, as they cannot be traced to any merely human influence and power, make Christ's spiritual power and divinity to shine forth all the more brightly.

Still, some may say of this use of earthen vessels, and they do say in substance: 'But is it the fairest thing, or, at any rate, is it the kindest thing for God to send us what is so precious, and what it concerns us all so much to receive, in any but the most attractive and the most winning ways, accompanied with the most notable and the most luminous evidence?' 'Why,' they say, 'should Christianity ever seem to hide in obscure places, as if it were not beautiful, and were not from above?' They say: 'Why has God not put what is the best of treasures, the blessed gospel, into the finest and most attractive of vessels, in order that men may the more easily know the precious treasure for what it is?'

And, again, some ask: 'Can certain means by which God reveals Himself to man be, as the text seems to say, at once, in the view of men, the most unlikely means for the end, and yet in reality the best means for saving man?

Now, the right answer to both these questions, and to many such, it seems to me, is the same, and it is this:

Yes, God in all His revelations of Himself to us shows Himself to be the wisest and the kindest of Fathers. And thus God's means, and God's agents, are always the very best that are to be had for God's designs, though they are often not the best to the eye of sense. And they are the best in this case. For Christ's spiritual kingdom of truth and love is not best promoted by the kind of outward attractions that rather tend to dim and obscure the truth, than to make it shine forth in its own pure and holy light. For such extraneous attractions, super-added to Christianity, tend to draw the wrong kind of people, and they tend to draw men to the wrong kind of thing. The allurements of sense and sight cannot build up a kingdom of faith and truth. Mere sensuous and worldly attractions do not draw truth-seekers to the truth. Yet that is what God seeks to do. Nay, such things tend rather to draw mere sight-seers to the empty pomps of earth. And that explains in part why God chooses to put the gospel treasure into earthen, not into golden, vessels.

Even a new system of philosophy, or an important discovery in science, that one should wish to be taken purely on its own merits, and not adopted as a prevailing fashion, under the cover of great names, had better, for such a true estimate of its real worth, take its origin in a cottage than in a court.

And for like high reasons Christ did not seek for His spiritual kingdom of truth and love, at its origin, a single worldly alliance. Nor has *He* done so yet, though His professed followers have often foolishly thought that by seeking such alliances they were doing Him service, and have many times sold the truth in order to buy them.

And you observe that the apostle Paul's idea, as expressed in our text, is not simply that we should not reject divine messages, even although they may be closely associated with imperfect human instrumentality. Paul's great point is much more than that. For he means that in this way God manifests in the gospel "the exceeding greatness of His power" more fully and more luminously than it could be manifested in any other way. And he assumes that we, as Christians, are meant to see this to be so, and the more gladly to embrace the gospel as it is ministered to us, ever coming to see more and more of the divine in and through the human, and gladly seeking to spread the truth for the truth's own sake.

God in this close union of the divine and human in Christ comes very near to us, and graciously adapts Himself to the needs and interests of our higher nature. Do not, then, let any of us foolishly reject Him, or His loving messages, on account of this His gracious condescension. Be sure of this, that God's instruments best suit God's purposes. It was to express how near to us in heart God is, that the sinless and divine founder of our religion died the shameful death of a malefactor. And Jesus shone, and yet shines, in the divinest glory of His love, on and from that cross of pain and ignominy.

And so the agents of the gospel must harmonize with its spirit. It were possible so to present, but it would be misrepresenting, the truth of God as to attract to the system of Christianity those who are not really of the truth. If all the finest talent in the world were enlisted on Christ's side, and all the greatest learning, and all the deepest wisdom, and all the most moving eloquence, and all the world's social influence and fashion, and all its rank, honour, and wealth were on Christ's side, would not all lesser lights seek to be so, too? Would it be a spiritual wonder if then, would it be a miraculous and divine thing if then, the common voice were to say, 'We, too, are all Christ's.' Nay, for the very same men, who call themselves Christ's for such reasons would have rejected Jesus of Nazareth, and cried, "Crucify Him," with those who did so.

We know well what the persons and things are which draw the men of the world. We have had Christian kingdoms in abundance of that outward kind, that all can see and 'know, after the flesh.' We have had men who were the renowned champions of the Church engaging in literal, bloody war on its behalf, who have yet remained in their sins, untamed, unsaved, and unsanctified.

But how, if that kind of Church power and Church action be put forward as the true Christian ideal, can the Church shine forth in "the beauties of holiness" as a fair and luminous body, elected out of the world to represent her Lord, and to draw it to Him? She cannot.

None of these attractive human things, which I have named, are to be rejected as helpers of the truth, if they are only its real servants and subordinates. But such things as talent, learning, rank, and wealth—in and of themselves—are of the world, and "the world will love its own." Yet "if any man love the world, the love of the Father is not in him."

But to be on the side of these much-coveted, honourable, potent human powers, and to be on the side of Christ, the rejected and crucified of men, are surely not the same things.

Christ, however, by permitting matters to be as they are —when the agents of the gospel are mostly very ordinary people in position and personal qualities—means that those who are really of the truth, and love the truth, should know Him himself, and should hear His own voice, and should come to Him whether He be heard speaking to us from lofty, or from lowly places. He means that the very frailty of the human should let the divine shine through it upon us all the more brightly and clearly.

'Hence God often chooses the weak things of the world, and the things that are despised' by the men who walk by sense, as his favourite instruments for doing great things for His Church, and Kingdom. God not intending thereby to keep any away from the truth of the gospel, by making it artificially unattractive, or difficult of reception to those who are really seeking the truth.

I admit that persons have been known to do and say most forbidding things in the name of Christ, and even churches have done so, but not by the Master's orders, and only in long past times, let us charitably hope! But God does as He does in making this kind of selection of the instruments of His gospel, in order to test and to sift the characters of men, and to make and keep His Kingdom a kingdom of truth seekers, and of truth lovers, and to draw to Himself the genuine and the true.

Hence Jesus says: "To this end have I been born, and to this end am I come into the world, that I should bear witness unto the truth. Everyone that is of the truth heareth My voice."

And we can see therefore that for God's saving purposes the "earthen vessels" that He employs for spreading abroad His gospel are the right kind of vessels. For all God's revelations say plainly, 'Let God be exalted, Let the pride of man be abased.' It is the Master Himself who says: "Verily, I say unto you, except ye turn and become as little children, ye shall in no wise enter into the Kingdom of Heaven." Truth is "when unadorned adorned the most."

Let us all beware, then, lest any of us be driven away from the gospel by the admittedly human things in it, which God in His condescension has only put there in order to draw us to the gospel, and which He means to be His interpreters to us, who are ourselves human, of its highest beauties and deepest mysteries. For divine treasures in earthen vessels! the mingling together of lofty and of lowly things, is Christianity all over.

My closing word is to ask you all to remember, as a key to open many divine treasures, that our text not only finds its crowning illustration in Christ Himself, in whom divinest treasure is contained in an earthen vessel, but the text finds this, its crowning illustration, in that most humbling transaction of Christ's career—His crucifixion!

When God's beloved Son, in whom His soul is well pleased, was crucified, not crowned, and thus triumphed; when He thus became the "grain of wheat" that by 'falling into the earth and dying has borne much fruit,' and thus became the world's Redeemer: then it was that the great idea of our text, that 'God is wont to put rich jewels into humble caskets,' found its greatest, grandest illustration.

XV.

THE PERFECT BOND.

"And above all these things put on love, which is the bond of perfectness."—COLOSSIANS III., 14.

FOUR points, my brethren, claim our earnest attention in this beautiful text; but they are all parts of a great whole; they all form a commendation of love. They are:

I. The thing, or grace, which is here spoken of.

II. Its use as here described.

III. Its quality or worth.

IV. Our personal duty in regard to it.

Almost all the words of the text are emphatic and important—as 'love,' 'bond,' 'perfectness,' 'put on,' and 'above all.'

I.—First, I shall speak to you of love itself, the grace that is spoken of and commended to us in our text.

You will not have failed to notice that our text has lost much in euphony, and gained much in correct sense, in the revised version. For this New Testament love ought not to be confounded, as it often has been, with charity, in the sense of alms-giving. For one may not only give much alms without himself having this highest kind of love, but he "may bestow all his goods to feed the poor," and yet he may not have this love. Although this love includes in it, of course, the important duty of alms-giving in proper place and measure. But alms-giving is no more this complete love or charity itself than South Africa is the whole world, or than Port Elizabeth is the whole of South Africa.

And yet South Africa is in the world, and is a considerable part of it; and Port Elizabeth is in South Africa, and is an important town there. So is alms-giving a true, and an important part of love, or charity; but yet it is very far from being the whole of that great and all-embracing grace.

For the love spoken of in our text is Christian love. It is the love to God, and then the love to man, that is the fruit of faith in Jesus Christ.

Look at some of the most essential elements of this Christian love: for love is the sum of all the Christian graces. It is above all the other graces, and it is eternal. "Now abideth faith, hope, love, these three; and the greatest of these is love."

This divinest kind of love is like all other kinds of love in its practical aims. For it seeks, as all love does, the good of its object; and it is like all other love, too, in its results. For it gives joy, as all love does; it gives joy to both the loving and to the loved. But this love is unlike all other love in its quality, and in its extent. For it is finer and more comprehensive than any other love.

For while all love seeks the good of its object, only Christian love is able to seek the highest good of the loved.

And while all love gives pleasure, this only gives lofty and unmixed pleasure. Its aims, too, are the very highest.

The great aim of this love with the converted, is to make them more and more like to Jesus; while its great aim with the unconverted is to bring them to Jesus.

Its results also, both on the loving and on the loved, are purity and happiness. Love, like mercy, "is twice blessed: it blesseth him that gives and him that takes."

As an example of the benign power of this highest love, look at parental love, without the presence of this diviner element; look at parental love also with this higher love present. Without this love, even parental love, with all its strength and self-sacrifice, is, if not quite blind, yet very low-aimed and shortsighted. While the strengthened vision of parental love with this love in it stretches away into the invisible and the eternal.

So is it of friendship, and of any other bond of the spirit that binds man to man, when you look at them with this bond super-added, in contrast with the same bonds when they are without this perfecting bond.

For Christian love strengthens, ennobles, and perpetuates all proper bonds that unite man to man; while its absence weakens and destroys them all.

For this bond, which is commended in our text, is the best thing in even the best of relationships. We have seen that love and joy have much to do with each other. For we have seen that it is of the nature of love to give joy.

Yes, the joy that was set before Christ in the work of human redemption was largely the joy of gratified love.

And the want of fervent love in our religion explains in many cases its want of fervent joy. And so does the presence of much love in our religion explain the presence of much joy.

The love commended in our text is not so much ignorance of faults, and blindness to the faults of brethren, as it is an eye opened by the God of love to see and to value their excellencies and beauties of character, and their potencies of further good.

The presence of the loving, warm heart, that we ordinarily find in the young child, explains much of childhood's joy.

A man with a child's heart as to freshness, but enlarged, combined with a man's head—a head always up to date—is the very highest type of a man. For there is something better possible to a man than even having a child's heart, and that is having in addition his heart renewed by God's spirit; and thus a heart which combines in it the mellow ripeness begotten of godly sorrow for sin, devout piety and patience, along with the spontaneous warmth of youthful feelings. It is then and there in such a man that this love has its perfect work. And thus it is that, in a very fine and true sense, the warm-hearted man never grows old.

It is this Heaven-born love which makes the true Christian to flourish and grow ever fresh and green even in old age, when others fade. Now, this divinely implanted love is what my text speaks of, and commends. For the grace, or thing which is spoken of in the text is love, which is the greatest of all the graces. And thus what is here said about love demands our best attention, and our deepest interest. And to the descriptive utterance of our text about love, we now turn and look:

II.—Secondly, at the use which is here ascribed to love, the grace which is here spoken of. True, the use of love is not single. For this divine gem, love, is a unity, a beauty, and a joy. Nay, the uses of love are both manifold and varied. We cannot remember nor recount all the uses of love. And I do not attempt to name and to recount on the present occasion even some of its many uses. For our text speaks of just one use of love, and I also speak at present only of that. Love, our text says, is a bond, or band—it is what binds together.

But what does this mean? What is a bond, and what is this bond, and why is love, by an inspired pen, here called a bond? Yes, why?

Because a bond is something that always attaches certain persons or things; it always unites certain objects to each other, and it also hinders, or keeps the objects that are so bound together away from certain other objects; and so does this bond, it does all these things. It is both a connecting bond, and a disconnecting bond. But you rightly ask me, 'what then does this bond unite?' I answer: It unites together first of all the personal qualities of him who wears it.

Love unites grace to grace, and virtue to virtue, in the man himself who wears this sacred bond. It adorns and crowns his own character. But love is also a collective bond. It unites man to man. It also unites redeemed men to holy angels. And it further unites saved men to

God, to God in Christ. But love first unites men to Christ, who is the way to God. Love is thus a long and a strong bond.

It is a bond that reaches all the way down from Heaven to earth, and it encircles all the earth, and then it reaches all the way up to Heaven again. So that love unites God's high throne to man's extremest misery. Yes, in so far as it operates, it unites in one the whole moral universe. Love is thus a strong bond.

It is so strong a bond as to draw sinful men up to the Holy God. And all who have been drawn up from sin and Satan to God and goodness, have been drawn up by this strong bond of love.

But a bond, as I have said, is also meant to restrain from something. And this bond is meant to restrain as well as to unite. This bond, as it is put on, restrains its wearer from all hurtfulness to others, and from all wrong-doing.

In truth, the wide universe would be one great, mutually destructive battlefield, without the action throughout it of this powerfully-restraining, healing bond of love.

Even Heaven was a battlefield once. For love lost its proper power over some of the inhabitants of Heaven, and war arose and raged there, till all the unloving among the angels were cast out of Heaven.

Now, this God-given bond, which is spoken of in our text, is meant to restrain its wearers from all hurtfulness and from all wrong-doing; and it does so just in so far as it exists and acts with its proper power.

Hence love is called the fulfilling of the law. Not as being in fact, and of itself, all that the law of God demands of us, for God and for our neighbour, but as being the germ and principle of all, and also the inspiring motive of all acceptable obedience to God. For no one will designedly hurt the object whom he tenderly loves.

Love is properly called a bond, too, because it is so very strong. See the proof of this, the great strength of love, in that the All-wise God entrusts to it so much that is precious. Remember that God has specially entrusted to the protecting power of love all the very young, and all the very old, and all the weak, and all the sick.

This bond is God's real provision for the helpless, new-born infant, as it first sees the light of this world. Yes, this is God's best provision for the babe then, and for many years after. And this bond, love, is God's best provision, too, for the aged, when they become too feeble to care for themselves.

And this bond is also the real protection and safeguard of woman from the greater strength of man. Her best protection as girl, maiden, and mother is being loved and delighted in, and hence not being wronged and injured, but cherished and protected. For the true man not only loves and reverences his own, but womanhood itself, and woman as such. And as in nature, so in grace.

This bond, love, is God's real provision for babes in Christ, who must be nursed, and for all the weak, and sick, and ignorant in the Church. Yes, love is God's provision for all perishing sinners. And this bond will bear much, and does on the whole bear well the great strain that is put upon it by both God and man.

But what is this love of which our text speaks so highly? Well, it is a most divine thing. For "God is love." And love is always the deepest, and the best, and the most characteristic quality in the best of beings.

And the better the being, the purer a thing is his love. Love is a God-begotten, and God-nourished life. And it is the highest life of which any being is capable.

But for our present practical purpose I shall say, in plain and simple words, that 'love in its most general and most simple sense is good-will in active exercise.' Hence love is an excellent bond in the family, in the Church, and in general society. And it is also, as we have partly seen, a strong bond. See further proof of this fact in what love can do, and in what it can suffer and give up for those who are its objects.

'Well,' says some hearer, 'love seems one of the best of bonds, but I do not like to be in bonds; I like to be free. I dislike bonds.' Well, I am with you so far. Freedom is a good and noble thing, my friend.

We Independents were born of freedom, we were cradled in freedom, we love freedom, and I trust will part with our freedom for no price; but know and remember this, that all creature freedom is comparative. True freedom consists in yielding ourselves up willingly to all proper bonds, and in firmly rejecting all improper bonds. There is no absolute freedom possible to a creature. One main difference between freedom and slavery, lies in the kind of bonds to which one yields.

All creature-freedom is of necessity limited. Do not shrink from bonds as such. For God, our maker and ruler, puts bonds upon us all.

Restraints laid upon us by God's appointment meet us early, and meet us everywhere. And our highest possible freedom consists in an intelligent and willing submission to all divinely fashioned and divinely affixed bonds—to the bonds that have been formed for our bodies and for our minds by Him who made us. Law, divine and human law, is one such bond, and love, divine and human love, is one. Yes, love is the strongest and the best of all bonds. All bonds do not hurt their wearers. Some bonds are very sweet and pleasant. The bond of divine law, and even of human law, is so to the dutiful. More sweet and pleasant still is the bond of divine and human love. For this love is the highest life of the human soul. And of this most divine thing our text speaks, to describe it and to commend its quality.

III.—Thirdly, consider, then, the quality or worth of the thing which is here spoken of—the bond of the text. For our text passes upon love high praise, an almost extravagant eulogy.

Love, the writer affirms, is not only a good, but a perfect bond. Love "is the bond of perfectness," or the perfect bond. Why is it so? Why does love get, and of course deserve, such a lofty eulogium from an inspired penman? Yes, why? Love, I answer, deserves to be called the bond of perfectness on many grounds. But it deserves this praise principally on account of its great strength; on account of the ease with which it is worn;

on account of what it unites; on account of its attractive look; on account of its endless duration; and, lastly, because it is a self-imposed bond. Love is the bond of perfectness on all these grounds, and on other grounds.

Let us look briefly at each proof which I have named of love being the bond of perfectness.

First, love is the bond of perfectness, if you look at its great strength. See love at its best, and it takes the place of all other bonds, and supersedes them all. There is no place in God's universe so free as Heaven.

There are no other bonds in Heaven but the bond of love, because there this bond is so strong. Heaven is so free because in Heaven love is so perfect.

And even in those relationships into which other bonds than love enter, such as the bonds of law, justice, private interest, and public opinion, as in the relation of marriage, of Church-fellowship, and in the relations of parent and child, of king and subject, ruler and ruled—yet in all it is not the bond of law, but the bond of love that is the stronger, that is the highest or perfect bond.

As an example of this: The law of the land will not allow a man to treat even his own wife, or his own child just as he pleases. And yet when this bond of love is as strong in the family and in the Church as it ought to be, or half as strong, the other and coarser bonds of law, of interest, and coercion are unheard of, and unneeded.

In such relations as I have named, only where the bond of love is awanting, or is abnormally weak, are these other bonds either needed or employed. Who ever heard of the dutiful and loving wife, or child, resorting to the arm of law against the like dutiful and loving husband or father?

Secondly, love is the bond of perfectness if we also look at the perfect ease with which it is worn. Some bonds are very heavy, painful, and galling to the wearer, but not so is this bond of love. It gives strength to the wearer, and lightens all his burdens. Love is a bond so easy and pleasant, that all true hearts long for it, and rejoice under it. Love is indeed the bond of perfectness, for it is a bond so strong that it will not easily break, and yet it is so divinely soft and gentle that it does not hurt the most delicately moulded wearer, but does much to heal the hurts of all other and rougher bonds.

Thirdly, love is also seen to be the bond of perfectness if you look at what it unites, and at those whom it unites. For love unites, not purses as in business, though that lower bond is not wrong in its own place; love unites, not bodies as in slavery, joint imprisonment, marriages without love and all other forced, painful and revolting unions of mere personal proximity; love unites, not fortunes and residences as in unloving marriages of mere interest and convenience; but this bond, like all noblest bonds, unites together hearts. Yes, as the higher forms of love only act with real power upon the morally pure and good, so this bond of Christian love unites most closely the best of beings by what is best in them. This love unites most firmly the best of beings by their noblest and purest affections.

Hence this holy love is the true and perfect bond

of the moral universe. It is an all-embracing bond, stretching far into the unseen, and the invisible.

There are many blessed unions formed in the world, but there are none so holy, there are none so spiritual, there are none so disinterested as those into which the Church of Christ introduces us; and in the Church, as every where else, the perfect bond of all bonds is the bond of love.

Fourthly, love is the bond of perfectness if you look at its more than earthly beauty. "By this shall all men know that ye are my disciples if ye have love one to another."

Whether you look to the individual, or to the family, or to the Church, or to the community, this is the perfect bond of perfect beauty, which gives the crowning touch of Heavenly grace to all manifestations of human character. It is no wonder that He, in whose 'sanctuary are strength and beauty,' calls upon us to put on this beautiful bond.

Fifthly, love is the bond of perfectness if you consider its endless duration. For love "abideth." "Love never faileth." It is an everlasting bond. And this bond not only forms a lasting union in itself, but it is this bond alone which makes other unions, as the family and the Church, of which it becomes one of the bonds, everlasting also.

Let us in this world of death and decay more and more put on love, the bond of perfectness, which 'never faileth.'

Sixthly, love is the bond of perfectness, as it includes in itself, and binds up in one, all the other graces and virtues of the Christian character. 'Eloquent speech, prophetic insight, large knowledge, strong faith, abundant alms-giving, and martyr-zeal, profit him nothing who has not love.' While 'long-suffering, kindness, humility, unselfishness, gentleness, and love of truth' are the sure accompaniments and fruits of this divine love.

Seventhly, love is the bond of perfectness, as it is always a self-imposed bond. Love is such a bond as must be self-imposed, or it cannot be at all. In many respects the self-imposed bonds are ever the best of bonds. Unions that are in and of themselves God-given, God-imposed unions, and thus truly blessed, are only seen at their best when their God-imposed bonds also include, as self-imposed bonds, the ties of love and duty.

Take as examples of unions, which are only perfected by the presence of this bond in its power, the unions of marriage, of family relations generally, of Church fellowship, and of religious friendship. In all of these unions with their manifold and strong bonds, Christian love is yet the crowning bond, "the bond of perfectness."

And now, men and brethren, what shall we do in this matter of love?

IV.—Fourthly, as an answer to this question, in the last place consider how we shall use this bond, or our duty in relation to this bond.

The duty here urged on our attention in relation to the bond of love, is to put it on. "Put on love." This is not only the command of Paul in the text, but it is the urgent command of Christ by His own lips, as recorded in John's gospel, that we love one another. And in our text this is a command addressed to every Christian. For we must each one put on this bond upon ourselves.

We must do this thing, each for himself and for herself. I cannot put this bond upon you, and you cannot put it upon me. And yet there is, I am sure, a very common mistake made as to the person on whom this bond ought to be put. A mistake that has been rather common wherever I have lived and laboured. Hence I warn you of it. And we can see how the mistake arises. We more readily notice anything wrong with what another has on, than with what we have on ourselves. At any rate, I have not seldom known good, well-meaning people, very busy, trying to put on this bond of love upon other people, before they had very visibly put it on upon themselves, and, of course, always unsuccessfully. And I have generally observed that they felt much heat and bitterness of spirit at their non-success.

In particular, I once well knew a good old minister who made the want of love to the brethren in the modern Church an oft-recurring speciality in his teaching and preaching, which sad defect he usually fiercely condemned with much biting bitterness and an overflowing, righteous anger! This once called forth—when he was enlarging on the subject in private in the usual manner—from a friend who had not found his own love promoted by his friend's favourite mode of 'following after love,' some such remark as this: 'Do you know, Mr. ——, that I like your utterances on Christian love best, and profit by them most when you speak in love, and do not become hard, bitter, and angry in commending it.' His short, sharp answer was, 'I suppose so.'

Let us all be sure of this, that half the effort spent to

put on the bond of love upon ourselves, that we often spend to put it upon others, will do twice the good both to the Church and to the world, and will produce double the imitation.

Really fair things, when visibly worn, are always copied. You can do most to improve your neighbour's dress, either of body or of spirit, by dressing well yourself. For, as a rule, no amount of fault-finding, or meddling with what your neighbour puts on, will benefit him equally with your putting on and wearing the right thing yourself.

Let each of us put the perfect bond of love on upon ourselves, then, first. Let us have this bond in possession first, and then let us show it. Let us first put on this divine love as individual Christians, to unite all our personal graces into an harmonious union, as one would put on a finishing part of dress, which should both complete their equipment, and bind together in one all the other parts of their apparel.

Let us, too, put on this beautiful bond as a Church, and as churches; for without this there is no real union among us, and union is strength. It is the bond of love which, above all other things, binds, unites, firmly ties together all the members of the whole Church of Christ. And this also is the true bond that ought to exist between pastor and people, and between all the individual members of the same Church.

It is of great importance to know that good as union is, love and union are not the same things; for love is greater than union; but yet they stand in a very close connection. The relation of love to union is such a relation as the relation of soul to body. Union is only the body, while love is the soul. And just as the soul animates the body, so does love, the soul of union, when present, animate a visibly united body of men. This is true of any union. Hence, though union is good, the love that gives life to it is better.

And yet love for manifestation, health, and influence must embody itself in unions. This is not the right kind of world for disembodied spirits. For here on earth souls need bodies to act through. Some religious communions, it seems to me, make too much of union, the body. Some of us Congregationalists, in our zeal for the inward oneness of life and sympathy, the soul of all real unions, sometimes, I fear, too much neglect the outward union, the body, do we not? Let us care well for both. We must also put on the bond of love to men as men, and not simply love our own. But this loving of man as man is not the world's way, but only Christ's way of looking at our fellow-men; that is with a true loving and living interest.

We must specially put on the bond of love towards Christian men as such.

We must then have a supreme love to God Himself, and seek fit expression for it.

But we must put on this perfect bond of love to God and man in the inverse order which I have named. That is, we must have a supreme love to God first; and then we must have a great and growing love to all those who bear God's image; and then we shall be growingly able, like God, to embrace in our love mankind, even the undeserving. This divine love, in its glorious perfection and attractiveness, has as yet been only a visitant among us, and not an abiding resident upon the earth.

Divine love came down to our world perfectly embodied in the person of Jesus Christ So that the exhortation of another Scripture, "But put ye on the Lord Jesus Christ." is only the more concrete form of this exhortation of Scripture contained in our text: "Put on love, which is the bond of perfectness."

We also learn from our text where this bond of love should be worn—namely, uppermost, manifestly as an outer robe, to be seen of all men. "And above all these things," or over all these things—above all the excellent graces that have been named before, 'compassion, kindness, humility, meekness, long-suffering, forbearance, forgiveness'—'above all these things,' says our text, 'put on love'

Yes. let us, brethren, put on love as our upper garment, as our outer robe, as our celestial livery, plainly marking us out to all eyes that can see spiritual things as belonging to the household of the God of Love.

This prominent place, which is here assigned to the grace of love in the adornment of the Christian character, denotes its perfect beauty in God's eyes. And love, which is the bond of perfectness, is indeed fair.

But do not, on account of the outwardness of the figure of putting on love as a piece of dress, or adornment, miss the inwardness of the reality. For we must put on love outwardly, as one puts on from within the glow of health, or as a flower puts on its beauty, or a bird renews its plumage, with the inwardness of life and reality, as part of us, as well as with the outwardness of visibility.

This divine love, when it is prominently present in redeemed humanity, gives the crowning, finishing touch to the Christian character. It is so of the individual, and it is so of the community. When Christian love, this most divine form of a most divine thing, comes to be worn manifestly and prominently by the whole Church of Christ as the natural expression of what she is, even those who too often keep their Bibles shut will then, almost despite of themselves, be forced to see and read in the disciples of Jesus a living, walking, embodied gospel, and the world will thus be led to the feet of Christ, the loving Saviour.

Let me name, as worthy examples of this beautiful grace of love, David and Jonathan as noble examples of love on its human side, of love in friendship; and Jacob and Joseph as beautiful examples of love in the family, the love of parent and child.

See, as a noble example of love in its higher form, that which is commended in the text—St. Paul's love to Christ. This love to Christ is the great central bond in the Church, as love to the father and mother of the family forms the central bond in the home.

See also in this greatest apostle and finest missionary of Jesus Christ a splendid illustration and example of an imperishable, unconquerable love to man as man, and to good men as bearing the image of Christ.

Above all, see the God-man, Christ Jesus, as the perfect example and illustration of this grace of graces. See Christ's supreme and all-embracing love to God manifested in all ways, and failing in none. See His great love to a perishing world expressed in word and deed, even to the death, and you will then best understand what this love commended in our text is, and how it acts when rightly exercised. You may see in Christ, our Lord, " love, which is the bond of perfectness," in its utmost possible beauty and perfection. Yes, let us all see, admire, copy, and be transformed into His image.

THE END.

www.ingramcontent.com/pod-product-compliance
Lightning Source LLC
Chambersburg PA
CBHW021203230426
43667CB00006B/531